FAYKE
NEWES

The Media vs The Mighty
From Henry VIII to Donald Trump

Derek J. Taylor

To Terry Lloyd of ITN
Miguel Gil and Myles Tierney of APTN
and all those who've lost their lives while
bringing us the news.

By the same author:

A Horse in the Bathroom
Magna Carta in 20 Places
Who do the English Think They Are?

Cover Illustration © Adrian Teale

First published 2018

The History Press
The Mill, Brimscombe Port
Stroud, Gloucestershire, GL5 2QG
www.thehistorypress.co.uk

© Derek J. Taylor, 2018

The right of Derek J. Taylor to be identified as the Author
of this work has been asserted in accordance with the
Copyright, Designs and Patents Act 1988.

British Library Cataloguing in Publication Data.
A catalogue record for this book is available from the British Library.

ISBN 978 0 7509 8778 3

Typesetting and origination by The History Press
Printed and bound in Great Britain by TJ International Ltd

CONTENTS

1 The Tudors. *Traitors and Heretics* 5

2 Civil War and Oliver Cromwell. *The Poisoner of the People* 25

3 John Wilkes. *The Terror of all Bad Ministers* 42

4 The American Revolution. *Forge of Sedition* 60

5 The Political Cartoon. *Poking Fun* 80

6 Nineteenth-Century Radicals. *Guerrilla Journalism* 99

7 The Crimean War. *That Miserable Scribbler* 117

8 The American Civil War. *Wild Ravings* 134

9 Suffragettes. *The Truth for a Penny* 150

10 The First World War. *A Few Writing Chappies* 171

11 The Press Barons. *Mad, Bad and Dangerous* 189

12 The Second World War. *Bloody Marvellous!* 209

13 TV News. *The Idiot's Lantern* 227

14 The Soviet Union. *Scruffy, Dog-Eared and Undaunted* 244

15 Vietnam. *Bang-Bang and Body Bags* 256

16 Watergate. *Deep Throat and Dirty Tricks* 277

17 The Falklands. *A Quick Win (for the Mighty)* 297

18 Blair and Iraq. *The Dodgy Spinners* 309

19 The Social Media Revolution. *Trump, Tweets and Fake News* 328

20 The Future. *Wobbling On* 346

Acknowledgements 354

Index 355

1

THE TUDORS

Traitors and Heretics

God hath opened the Press to preach
whose voice the Pope is not able to stop
with all the power of his triple crown.

John Foxe (1516/17–1587)

Around Eastertime in the year 1525, during the reign of Henry VIII, in the village of Aldington, 65 miles south-east of London, a young servant named Elizabeth Barton suffered a sudden seizure. She collapsed, lost consciousness, her body stiffened and then began a violent jerking. It was reported that while in this state, she spoke about the nature of heaven, hell and purgatory, and correctly foretold the death of a child she'd met. When she awoke, she remained very ill. In the sixteenth century, prolonged sickness usually ended only one way. But Elizabeth didn't die. Not yet.

Uttering religious prophesies was a dangerous thing to do in the reign of Henry VIII. It could mean you were a heretic and might have to be burned at the stake. So, an episcopal commission was set up to investigate, headed by a learned friar named Dr Edward Bocking. He cleared Elizabeth of any heresy. But Bocking himself had some views that were controversial in

An early nineteenth-century representation of Elizabeth Barton in a seizure.
Her elaborate clothing is a fanciful idea – she was a servant girl. It's not recorded
which of the men is Edward Bocking, although the shifty-looking one keeping a
written record is the most likely candidate.

England of the 1520s, and he now realised that he could use Elizabeth Barton to help him convert others to his own beliefs.

That autumn, Bocking arranged for the still sick young woman to appear before a large crowd at the nearby Chapel of Our Lady in the hamlet of Court-at-Street. There she spoke in a mysterious voice, declaring to the people that she'd made a promise to God during a vision she'd experienced at the time of her seizure. After that, she stood up and – miraculously, it was believed – was cured. Elizabeth then entered the Convent of St Sepulchre in Canterbury and became a nun, with Bocking acting as her advisor, or – as her detractors said later – her 'ghostly father'.

Elizabeth Barton now became a pawn in a momentous and dangerous national and international contest between the king and the pope. Henry VIII's marriage to Catherine of Aragon had become a disappointment to him. After two stillbirths, two miscarriages and two deaths in infancy, Catherine finally produced a baby that survived in 1516. But it was a girl, christened Mary – and daughters were risky. Queens were more likely to be overthrown.

Henry, who'd already fathered an illegitimate son, concluded that the marriage was the problem. It had been cursed by God. And he could see another – more attractive – way forward. He'd fallen in love with an English commoner's daughter, Anne Boleyn. He decided he would marry her and she would bear him the longed-for son and heir. But he needed to get a divorce from Catherine first.

Divorce, in the sense we understand it, was impossible in the sixteenth century. Legal separation could be achieved only by the pope's ruling. So, the king's representatives would have to negotiate a deal with Pope Clement VII.

There was opposition in the country from conservative Catholics to the king's planned marriage, and one of the opponents was Dr Bocking, Elizabeth's 'ghostly father'. By 1528 Bocking had the young nun firmly under his influence, and he managed somehow to get her close enough to the king to confront him face to face. She told His Royal Majesty to burn English translations of the Bible and to remain faithful to the pope and all he represented. She then warned the king that if he married Anne Boleyn, he would die within a month and that within six months the people would be struck down by a great plague. Henry was disturbed by her prophesies and ordered that she be kept under observation. She wasn't punished, however – something that would soon change as her fame as a holy prophetess spread.

By 1533, political events were moving fast. In January that year, Henry lost patience with the papal negotiations, and he married Anne. Now it was necessary to pass laws which would justify Henry's marriage. And in rapid succession, Acts of Parliament removed the English Church from the pope's jurisdiction and made Henry its head instead. Other acts declared his marriage to Catherine void, and his offspring by Anne to be his legitimate successors.

The king's enemies were enraged, and royal advisors identified a conspiracy to overthrow him, with Elizabeth Barton, the 'Nun of Kent', its chief inspiration. It was at this point that printed books and pamphlets began to appear on the streets of London, and beyond, which told of the Nun of Kent's miraculous cure and the revelations she'd uttered, revelations that made difficult reading for Henry and his courtiers.

Henry now came to the view that Elizabeth's words, as reported in print, were heretical and treasonous – the two, amid the politico-religious dramas of Henry VIII's reign, wrapped up in each other. She was guilty of heresy because, according to the books being circulated, she'd delivered a dead man from the terrors of hell, companies of angels and martyrs had paid homage to her, the Devil himself had come 'like a jolly gallant' to woo her to be his wife, and she'd been sent a letter from heaven by Mary Magdalen.

The treasonous element of the nun's words was even more dangerous. Her prophesy that the king would die one month after marrying Anne Boleyn had turned out not to be true, and Elizabeth Barton's followers were now claiming this meant Henry was no longer a monarch in the eyes of God, and that he'd die a 'villain's death'.

The king's advisors condemned these claims in words that might have come straight out of Donald Trump's White House. The prophesies were 'false fables and tales', said Henry VIII's men. And a 1533 Act of Parliament claimed that the nun's reputation had been built up in order to put the king in the 'evil opinion of his people'. The treasonous and heretical printed works were to be used, said the official account, in sermons to be preached throughout England on a signal from the nun, in order to put the king, 'not only in peril of his life but also in the jeopardy, loss and deprivation of his crown and dignity royal'. The problem for the government was made far worse because these books and pamphlets were becoming – by sixteenth-century standards – bestsellers.

* * *

And so it was that a war began. Not a conventional war, with armies fighting in the field, but a war of words. Whoever said 'The pen is mightier than the sword' was wrong. If you write a letter and send it to a friend who reads it and then puts it in a drawer, there's little power in it. The old adage should have said, 'The *press* is mightier than the sword'. Print lots of copies of what you wrote and distribute them, and then your words can reach a multitude of people, prompt debates, cast doubts, make converts, even maybe stir up rebellion.

And this war didn't die with Henry VIII. It's been fought, century in and century out, ever after. Not over the same ground, of course – that's changed countless times according

Johannes Gutenberg

to the great issues of the day and how the government has dealt with them – but from 1533 onwards, those in power have always had to worry about 'the press' (what would soon be newspapers, and then, nearer our own time, would expand to include broadcasting and the Internet, all nowadays under the label 'the media'). It's a term that's come to mean the people who control and use it, as much as the technology itself. At stake in this war has always been a prize more valuable than any land won by force of arms. It's a war to win possession of the minds of the people. And that threatens the power of those at the top.

The technology that triggered this war – the printing press – had been around for a century before the anti-government books and pamphlets appeared in Henry VIII's day, and in its first decades it had been used for largely peaceful purposes. It was born sometime around 1439, when a German goldsmith, named Johannes Gutenberg, realised there might be a way of making hundreds – if not thousands – of copies of a handwritten page. This was a leap of imagination in an age when the only way of reproducing such a document was by laboriously copying it out again and again with quill and ink, or possibly by making the odd smudgy re-version of an illustration with a primitive carved stamp. Mass production was out of the question – until Johannes Gutenberg had an idea.

Gutenberg, like all talented inventers, built on existing technologies but with the tweaks, modifications and combinations of mechanisms that can only come from the mind of a genius. In his workshop in Mainz, he took a screw press, a device which had been used since Roman times to squeeze olives into oil and grapes into the makings of wine, and he added to it 'movable type'. That is, small metal blocks with the raised, reverse shape of a letter on one side. He didn't invent movable type – it had been around, though not much used, for at least 200 years – but he did make his type from a special hardwearing alloy, and at the same time he devised a mould that could

Replica of a Gutenberg Printing Press from around 1450 on display at the International Printing Museum in Southern California. The massive frame was needed to withstand the force of the tightening screw as it pressed the paper onto the inked type.

mass-produce the metal letters in the kinds of numbers needed for a document that might have hundreds of pages.

Now, in Gutenberg's press, each page was separately set, with the letters held firmly in a tray known as a 'coffin', before ink – another first for Gutenberg, it was oil-based – was applied with balls of sheep's wool. A sheet of paper was then fixed onto a flat surface, and the coffin – with the inked letters face down – was placed on top. This was pushed hard onto the paper by means of the screw press. The result was text printed on paper.

Over the next sixty years, Gutenberg's invention slowly caught on across Europe, and by the end of the fifteenth century was turning out pamphlets and books in 110 cities. It's been estimated that 20 million volumes, of various lengths, had by this stage been pressed and bound.

Although there was a market for ballads and romances, it was mainly religious works that were printed. In the 1450s, Gutenberg himself had produced around 180 copies of the Bible in Latin, a work that still bears his name.

In London, because the Church was the biggest customer of the printing business, the presses were set up in workshops around St Paul's Cathedral, and that's where the presses were still to be found until the 1980s. If you stand today on Ludgate Hill with the great west door of the cathedral behind you, and look ahead, you can see down the length of Fleet Street, for centuries a synonym for the national newspaper industry in Britain.

Gutenberg could not have guessed that the device he'd created in his workshop would change the world forever. The so-called digital revolution of our own age can't compete with the invention of the Gutenberg press. In effect, he'd invented mass communication.

It's almost impossible for us today to imagine living in the world before Gutenberg when, for 99 per cent of us, 99 per cent of the time, all we would have known would be either happenings in our own village or town, or occasionally some oft-repeated – and undoubtedly oft-embellished – rumour of great events far away. And because knowledge is power, the printing press would, step by step, change forever the structure of society. It started to break the hold of the elite on learning and education, and so it boosted the rise of middle-class merchants and tradespeople. There was also an increase in the number of those who could read during the first half of the sixteenth century, encouraged by the availability of printed books.

But literacy levels were only part of the reason for the growing popularity of whatever the presses could produce. There'd always been a strong oral tradition throughout the Middle Ages, with storytelling around the fire being the main way that legends and traditions were passed from generation to generation. However, word of mouth didn't now die out. In fact, it gave more power to the press, because those who could read often did so out loud, telling friends, family and neighbours what was in the latest book or pamphlet.

This newfound ability to spread information relatively rapidly made possible mass movements in politics and religion. Ideas could more easily cross borders. And all of this would soon be a terrible threat to the most powerful institutions, the Church and the monarchy. Heresy, treason and sedition could suddenly catch on right across the country.

In the early sixteenth century, Europe was becoming increasingly split between those who followed traditional religious practices defined by the pope in Rome, and newcomers who chose the beliefs of Martin Luther and the Protestants. The press was the means of disseminating these new ideas.

The first attempt in England to stop them flooding in from across the Channel had come in May 1521, when a pile of Lutheran volumes, considered heretical, was burned outside St Paul's. But smuggling continued, and the Bishop of Norwich, wringing his hands in despair, declared, 'It passeth my power or that of any spiritual man to hinder it now, and if this continue much longer it will undo us all'.

Henry VIII would have sympathised with the bishop's frustration. As he was about to discover – like many a king, president and prime minister who came after him – there was no easy way to stop the onslaught from 'the press'.

***

Henry tried. In July 1533, under fire from these treasonous and heretical printed volumes, he fought back on two fronts. He attacked the source of the 'false tales and fables', while at the same time trying to suppress the mechanism that had published them.

The source was Elizabeth Barton, and the king now ordered his secretary, Thomas Cromwell, and the Archbishop of

Canterbury, Thomas Cranmer to take action against her. Royal agents entered the Convent of St Sepulchre in Canterbury, seized the nun, and brought her before the archbishop for questioning. Cranmer adopted a soft, manipulative approach in his interrogation, pretending he believed her every word – and it paid off. He won her confidence, and by November she'd confessed to a conspiracy against the king. Names were named. Arrests were made.

Those accused were thrown into the Tower of London, and on 23 November they were subjected to a staged public humiliation. While they stood, heads bowed, on a scaffold before a huge crowd outside St Paul's Cathedral, the Abbot of Hyde read out extracts from a printed book of Elizabeth Barton's revelations. He reviled both them and the nun herself. She'd lived it up while in the convent to become 'fat and ruddy', said the abbott – and what's more she'd had sex with Bocking the night before her revelations. However, no evidence was produced to support these allegations.

But all this was not enough. The king wanted the conspirators condemned in the eyes of the law as traitors and heretics. Henry and his secretary Cromwell, however, were worried that a jury might let them off. So, Parliament was persuaded to pass an Act authorising punishment without trial.

On 20 April 1534, Elizabeth Barton, her ghostly father, Bocking, and four other priests were transported in shackles on an open cart across London to the west and over the fields to the village of Tyburn – today this is where Marble Arch stands at the end of Oxford Street. In front of another huge crowd, the five of them were hanged, then cut down and decapitated. Elizabeth's head was put on a spike at London Bridge. It's believed she was the only woman ever subjected to this dishonour.

Meanwhile, Thomas Cromwell had his spies out. A compilation of some of the Barton books and pamphlets, called *The Nun's Book*, was now being circulated. Henry and Cromwell considered it inflammatory and dangerous. Cromwell tracked down the printer who, under pressure, confessed to having 200 copies of the book and revealed that Bocking was his paymaster and had a further 500 copies. All 700 were seized and publicly burned. At the same time, Cromwell got hold of other treasonous books and pamphlets, which were also thrown on a bonfire.

And in the same month that Elizabeth Barton was hanged, Parliament – loyal to the king – was persuaded to pass a law that made it high treason to print and publish anything that argued against Henry's marriage to Anne Boleyn, and treason was punishable by death.

But the burning of a few objectionable volumes – or, indeed, of women and men – no longer seemed to have the power to deter others. Those who might have been scared off in a previous age, now – because of the printing revolution – could feel they were not alone, but part of something bigger. Cromwell's actions caused little more than a stutter in the torrent of words, hostile to the king and his actions, pouring off the printing presses at home and abroad.

Thomas Cromwell, however, had learned one very valuable lesson. He realised that the weapon wielded by the king's enemies could be turned back on them. The press could be just as powerful in the hands of the government. He recognised that if the plot by the nun, Bocking and their accomplices could be exposed to the population at large as evil, then that would boost popular support for the king. So, Cromwell, through his contacts in London's burgeoning printing industry, encouraged and patronised writers and printers to publish works not only to destroy the reputation of Elizabeth Barton and the other traitors, but also to promote the benefits of the new independence from Rome of the Crown and England's religion.

A chance to use the new weapon at a time of crisis came two years later. A dangerous rebellion against the king broke out in Lincolnshire and Yorkshire. Cromwell persuaded the king to have a pamphlet printed that answered, point by point, the rebels' complaints about Henry's break with Rome and his dissolution of the monasteries. It was distributed in the rebel areas.

We'll see this happen often on our journey through the centuries – the 'mighty' hijacking the media. And they'll do it in many ways – some subtle and some crude. And what's more, sometimes those who control or work in the media will help the mighty do it.

* * *

Henry VIII's two successors on the throne, however, had no Cromwells at their sides, and the lesson of using the press to promote the royalist cause, for the moment, was forgotten. After the old king's death in 1547, his Catholicism without the pope vanished during the two short reigns of Edward VI and Mary – the first an evangelical Protestant, the second the complete opposite, an uncompromising supporter of the papacy. Although Edward and Mary had little in common when they knelt to pray, they faced similar problems from their enemies, and both failed in pretty much an identical fashion. Neither were press savvy, and government use of printing for propaganda purposes during their reigns was almost non-existent.

Meanwhile, more and more material, threatening to those in power, was being printed or brought into the country from overseas. Sometimes these printed attacks were carefully argued academic treatises against the Protestantism of Edward or the Catholicism of Mary, but they were also often short pamphlets – relatively cheap to produce and buy – lampooning the personal foibles and beliefs of the monarchs.

Some of the defamatory attacks on Mary and her religion were printed to further a specific conspiracy. And some were part of a general campaign to besmirch her name. The Protestant opponents of Mary seemed more imaginative in their vitriol against her than the Catholics against Edward, and were more effective users of the press. Printed papers often described her as a 'jezebel', which meant, to those who knew their Old Testament, a false prophetess, a whore and – in a spirit of hope – someone who was killed when her courtiers threw her out of a window, her corpse then eaten by stray dogs. And the most celebrated assault came from the Scottish Protestant Reformer, John Knox, in his book on *The Monstrous Regiment of Women*, which described Mary as a 'horrible monster' who 'compelled Englishmen to bow their necks under the yoke of Satan'.

Both Edward and Mary and their advisors reacted in a similar way to such attacks against them. They became more and more frenetic in their attempts to stamp out the hostile press. In 1549, a proclamation in Edward's name decreed that nothing – it's worth stressing – nothing at all, written in the English language could be printed or sold unless it had first been approved by a member of the Privy Council. An ambitious, not to say unachievable, aim.

Mary was extra vulnerable because of her marriage to the King of Spain. She could see that Edward's proclamation hadn't worked, and 'very lewd and rude songs against the Mass, the Church and the Sovereigns' continued to spread throughout the kingdom. So, a new Act was passed with the stated aim of quashing those 'diverse heinous, seditious and slanderous writings, rhymes, ballads, letters, papers and books' which were stirring up discord.

Now if you were found guilty you would be pilloried, that is, locked in the stocks or a similar device as a humiliation, where any idle or incensed citizen could throw eggs or stones at you. You'd then have your ears cut off, unless you could afford to pay the mountainous sum of £100. The law further said that if the crime was an attack in print against the queen or her Spanish husband, then the penalty was having your right hand chopped off. When these threats failed to have much effect, it was decreed in 1558 that possession of any heretical or treasonable book, whether printed in England or imported, would be punishable by death.

The ferocity of these penalties was a sign of desperation, a confession of failure by the authorities. In fact, no record of a single successful prosecution has been traced. Not because seditious and blasphemous works weren't out there – we know they were – but because so few journalists, publishers and printers were caught and convicted. One of the main problems was that enforcement of these laws depended on local Justices of the Peace, and they often let their own personal sympathies override their duty to uphold the law of the land. The state was discovering that an effective, anti-democratic dictatorship (as we might see it) needs a widespread efficient bureaucracy to impose its will on the people, especially in an age when uncontrolled mass communication can spread discontent relatively fast and far. Tudor England had no such bureaucracy.

* * *

In 1558, Catholic Mary died and was succeeded by her Protestant half-sister, Elizabeth.

In the popular imagination today, there's a stark contrast between the two queens. Mary, still remembered as 'Bloody Mary', for the way she presided over the brutal execution of hundreds of Protestant heretics. Elizabeth, 'Gloriana', for the way she defended the nation against the Spanish and brought peace and prosperity to a previously divided people. The truth is, of course, much more complicated than that.

For a start, the executions for heresy didn't stop under Elizabeth – 190 priests and lay Catholics were burned at the stake during her reign, and torture was more common under her than at any time in English history. But what's revealing is why this image of the bad queen and the good queen arose in the first place and then stuck in the popular mind for 400 years.

In part, it's because Elizabeth herself was cleverer than her half-sister. Elizabeth knew far better than Mary how to play the politics game. She knew when to compromise, and when to show sympathy for those she didn't agree with. And these tactics benefitted her image. But there was something more – and that was a favourable press. Protestant authors, now released from the oppression of Mary's reign and always more adept than their Catholic opponents at using the power of printed propaganda, set to with a will.

The most effective of them all was John Foxe, an academic who rejoiced at the accession of a queen who would defend the Protestant cause. His *Book of Martyrs* became a classic. It gave a flame-by-flame, dying-scream-by-dying-scream account of how the most famous bishops, abbots and lay Protestants had been burned as heretics during Mary's reign. He it was who coined the nickname that's lived on – 'Bloody Mary'. His writing is highly biased. He made no pretence at objective journalism. He didn't need to. It was a concept unknown in the sixteenth century. Foxe dedicated his book to Queen Elizabeth, and she in turn recognised its huge value to the nation's Protestant faith and her role as its defender. She commanded a copy of Foxe's *Martyrs* be placed in every church in the land. Now, that was a real contrast with her sister. Elizabeth, unlike Mary, knew the power of the press.

So, did that mean that she was also more successful at suppressing opposition pamphlets and books? Here the answer is not so clear. She certainly tried. The threat to her crown was very real. In 1570, Pope Pius V gave clear and open instructions to those of Elizabeth's subjects who still practised the Catholic faith. He absolved them of their loyalty to her. The government now feared that the sprinkling of Catholic citizens left in the country was a fifth column, ready and waiting to assist any attempted invasion by a foreign Catholic army. And so, the following year, Elizabeth made it treason to import, publish or put

Archbishop Cranmer being burned at the stake, from *Foxe's Book of Martyrs*.
Elizabeth I learned that she could use the press to hit back at her opponents, and
she decreed that a copy of Foxe's work, with its graphic illustrations of Catholic
brutality, should be placed in every church in the land.

into effect any printed account of the pope's words, or anything
asserting 'that the Queen is a heretic, schismatic, tyrant, infidel
or a usurper'.

Did this deter rebels from printing and circulating treasonable
or heretical books and pamphlets? It's impossible to judge how
many people during Elizabeth's reign, who might otherwise
have got involved with publishing rebellious works, decided
against it for fear of getting caught and punished. But historians
today do think that, despite having her own Cromwells around
her – Sir Francis Walsingham and William Cecil with their network of spies and informers – she may not have done much
better than Edward or Mary in controlling the hostile press.

Certainly, one of the most famous cases during Elizabeth's
reign was hardly a massive victory for the government.

The accused at its centre was more loyal dunderhead than dangerous insurgent. In 1579, the queen was contemplating marriage to the Duke of Anjou, a Catholic, and brother of the King of France. It never came to anything, but while it was on the cards, a puritan lawyer called John Stubbs put his objections into a pamphlet which he had printed and distributed. It went by the explicit – if not catchy – title of *The Discovery of a Gaping Gulf whereunto England is like to be swallowed by another French Marriage, if the Lord forbid not the banns, by letting her Majesty see the sin and punishment thereof.*

Stubbs described the proposed wedding as 'an uneven yoking of the clean ox to the unclean ass'. Clean or not, 'ox' was hardly the most diplomatic name for your monarch. And he added that the union would draw the wrath of God down on England, and leave 'the English people pressed down with the heavy loins of a worse people and beaten as with scorpions by a more vile nation'.

He was simply being a good, patriotic Englishman, he argued. It was a sign of the government's nervousness that Stubbs, his printer and publisher were all seized and put on trial. Although Stubbs protested his loyalty to the Crown, he was found guilty of 'seditious writing', and sentenced to have his right hand chopped off. Elizabeth herself had to be talked out of ordering the death penalty for him.

In the moment before he received his lesser punishment, Stubbs had sufficient equilibrium to utter what may have been intended as a joke, 'Pray for me, now my calamity is at hand' – a bad pun can be forgiven in the circumstances. Then, once his right hand had been removed by a meat cleaver driven through the wrist with a mallet, he raised his hat – with his left hand – and declared, 'God Save the Queen!', then fainted.

A much more serious threat than John Stubbs came from the Jesuits, who were becoming increasingly active in the country. They made good use of the printing press to spread their beliefs. Their most celebrated member, Edmund Campion, worked underground to promote the Roman Catholic ministry. He was arrested by priest-hunters. Although he protested, 'We travelled only for souls. We touched neither state nor policy', he was still considered too dangerous – as were many other Jesuits – and he was convicted of high treason, before being hanged, drawn and quartered at Tyburn.

Nevertheless, the tide of Catholic printing was not turned back, and Elizabeth faced several serious Catholic rebellions and plots during her reign. Her ability to defeat them and stay on the throne is more down to the fact that Catholics were finding it difficult now to raise widespread support, rather than because of any effective control of the hostile press.

***

But the battle lines in the war between the press and those in power had been drawn, and the first volleys had been fired. Once the Nun of Kent's prophesies had been set in type, inked and pressed onto paper, nothing in politics would ever be the same again.

Following Queen Elizabeth's death in 1603, those at the top could not now ignore the threat from this monstrous machine. The press – the technology and those who wrote what it published – could loosen their grip on power. As we'll discover on our journey through the centuries, all rulers, everywhere in the world – one way or another – would have to deal with that threat.

The advantage – as in most wars – would often shift from one side to the other. Sometimes, monarchs, elected politicians and military leaders in wartime would gain the upper hand by banning, threatening, bribing, cajoling, discrediting, taxing or even imprisoning or executing those who might publish things they didn't like. Or they'd simply censor what the people could be told. Then the mighty would be free to seize control of the media and use it to push their own propaganda on the masses.

Throughout this long war, it would be the job of journalists to resist, and to report with accuracy what they found out. As we'll soon see, they'd sometimes fail. Truth wouldn't always be their weapon of choice. But many times, it would, and then through the determination and bravery of individual editors and reporters, the truth would flash home like a sword in the sunshine, targeting the misdeeds, the mistakes and the secrets of the mighty.

And over four centuries, as society itself was to change, so would the nature of this war. Developments in technology, in beliefs about democracy and freedom, and in the very definition of journalism itself, as well as the rise and fall of political leaders, the outbreak of rebellion and wars, the need to make a profit, would all play their part in pushing the battle lines this way and that. But through all this turmoil and sometimes bloodshed, one thing wouldn't change. The media and the mighty will always be natural enemies.

It's going to be a long, messy, at times bloody, conflict. And that – with all its many battles over the centuries – is what we're now going to investigate. We shall criss-cross the Atlantic on our journey between Britain and America, even visiting the Soviet Union, and we'll meet the men and women caught up in the fighting. And as we reach the twenty-first century, we'll face some tricky questions. Is the world today – when fake news, Donald Trump and social media dominate the fight – experiencing something new in the media–mighty conflict? Or is it the same old war, the same old opponents, fighting for the same causes as ever, but just with different weapons?

* * *

There's a long road to travel before then, though. So let's return to what happened after the death of Queen Elizabeth I. The next eighty years were to be arguably the most tumultuous in English history, marked by civil war and the execution of a king, followed by a military dictatorship. It would all be ammunition for the printing press, which would be as powerful a weapon as any musket, sword or executioner's axe.

One short, stocky man with an odd name would know better than anyone how to wield that weapon, and – as we'll discover next – how to persuade whoever happened to be in power to pay him to be their journalist.

2

CIVIL WAR AND
OLIVER CROMWELL

The Poisoner of the People

The pen is a virgin, the printing press a whore.

William Cavendish (1592–1676)

On 20 August 1620, in the market town of Burford in
Oxfordshire, the daughter of the landlord of the George Inn,
Margery Nedham, gave birth to a boy. Though he looked a
healthy baby, the family wanted to take no risks. In the seventeenth century, many an infant died in those first days, and it was
best to get them baptised quickly. So the next day, the family
and their friends processed down the hill to the Church of St
John the Baptist. Burford was a wealthy place, which had made
its money from the wool trade, the profits of which had helped
to build its magnificent cathedral-sized place of worship.

We don't know whether the mother was recovered enough
to be there at the church, but the father – described as a 'genteel
man' – now stood before the ancient font, and advised the vicar
that the child was to be christened 'Marchamont', the same as
the father himself. Why the Nedhams called their sons such an
odd name is a mystery. In fact, Marchamont is so unusual as a

Christian name that it doesn't appear in the *Oxford Dictionary of National Biography*, other than in the entry for Marchamont Nedham – this latest addition to the family.

He was going to make his mark on history. His extraordinary career and unpredictable character would take him to the front line of a war of words that would be fought between different sets of governments and rebels over the next sixty years.

Within months of young Marchamont's birth, his father was dead and his mother remarried, this time to the Vicar of Burford himself, the Reverend Christopher Glynn. Marchamont's step-father was also master of the local free grammar school, and he made sure the boy got a thorough education, not only in reading, handwriting, the Bible and a certain amount of Latin, but also in mathematics and the sciences such as magnetism and chemistry. And Marchamont would have had seen something quite new, printed textbooks.

Then, at the age of 14, he went off to Oxford, 20 miles away, as a chorister in the chapel of All Souls' College, while he continued his studies there. At the age of 17, he graduated with a bachelor's degree – this was the normal age to get your BA in the seventeenth century. After that, he went off to London where he worked as a junior master at the Merchant Tailor's School for four years. At this point, he seems to have got restless. He didn't know what he wanted to do with his life. He briefly studied medicine, and worked as an under-clerk to the lawyers at Gray's Inn.

At the age of 23, Marchamont Nedham got his first big break. He was invited to become chief writer of a publication called *Mercurius Britannicus*. This was one of a new breed of printing press productions, the periodical newsbook. It was the forerunner of today's newspaper, though it looked more like a small magazine. The key difference from the one-off books and pamphlets we saw during Tudor times, was that newsbooks came out in regular editions, usually once a week, which meant they could build up a readership.

What young Marchamont Nedham had done to win this position, or who he'd met that had swung it for him, we can only guess. Those who've examined in detail the writing style of the various editions of *Mercurius Britannicus* at this time, can't detect any change with Nedham's appointment, which has led to the theory that maybe he was already writing for the publication before, perhaps on a trial basis.

But if we're looking for an explanation for why, around 1643, Marchamont Nedham switched careers to become a journalist, we need look no further than what was happening in the country. These were turbulent days in England, some of the most violent and uncertain in the country's history. King Charles I, who'd come to the throne in 1625, was trying to put back the clock. He believed kings were answerable to God alone, so ignoring the past 350 years of Parliament's rising power. And what's more, he was suspected of nurturing an ambition to return England to Roman Catholicism.

The country's religious divisions were pushed to extremes under Charles. On one side, the Presbyterians and Puritans who sought to exercise their influence through Parliament. On the other, the High Church Anglicans who backed the king. Tension between them was such that it would take only the merest jolt to turn peaceful disagreement into violent rage. And jolt it Charles did.

On 4 January 1642, stung by his openly Catholic wife's accusation that he was a coward, the king marched into the Palace of Westminster with 200 armed courtiers to arrest one peer and five MPs suspected of plotting against him. But it was a botched job. The six men escaped, and Parliament pronounced the king a 'public enemy to the commonwealth'. It was the start of the most bloody and divisive civil war in England's history. And as armies marched and battles were fought on home territory, there was an unprecedented demand among the populace for news of what was happening and opinions as to what to make of them.

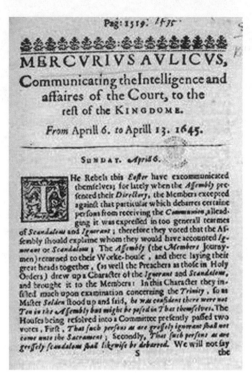

Mercurius Aulicus, a newsbook supporting the royalist cause, was printed in Oxford and Bristol during the Civil War. This issue from April 1645 begins, 'The rebels, this Easter, have excommunicated themselves...' The parliamentarians hit back with *Mercurius Britannicus*, whose chief writer was Marchamont Nedham.

Exciting times for a 23-year-old, trying to find his place in the world. The war was getting into full swing as Marchamont Nedham was appointed chief writer at *Mercurius Britannicus*. *Britannicus* was firmly on Parliament's side in the conflict. It had been founded to counter the propaganda being pedalled by a Royalist newsbook called *Mercurius Aulicus*. King Charles, earlier in his reign, had refused to indulge in anything so demeaning as communicating with his subjects – such action hardly befitted a king with a divine right to rule. And he'd tried to impose the same restraint on his opponents by banning the printing of domestic news. But that prohibition had collapsed by 1641, when Charles lost control of Parliament. The many Presbyterian-owned printing presses immediately started churning out an estimated twenty different newsbooks, most with a pro-Parliament and anti-Royalist bias. Even Charles now realised he had no alternative. He'd have to do the same and swallow his I-only-talk-to-God principles.

And that was the start of *Mercurius Aulicus*. It specialised in systematic smearing of opponents and scandalous news stories. We can get a flavour of its style from this entry in the edition of 17 December 1643. In it, *Aulicus*, after reminding its readers that the Parliamentary rebels were always boasting about how they held Sundays sacred, went on – with lip-smacking irony – to describe what one Parliamentary prisoner had got up to in Shrewsbury:

> On Sunday last, while His Majesty's forces were at church, one of the prisoners was missed by his keeper, who searching for him and looking through a cranny in the stable, he saw a ladder erected and the holy rebel committing buggery on the keeper's own mare.

That's what *Britannicus* aimed to combat. And Marchamont Nedham's writing style must have been what appealed to its owners. One contemporary critic of his said Nedham was 'transcendently gifted in opprobrious and treasonable droll'. In other words, he could be witty and vicious in his seditious attacks on the country's rulers.

One of his first targets, for instance, was the Church hierarchy. He wrote:

> Bishops are the big-bellies, the red nose tribe of priests [who] preach and exercise nothing else but broad-sword divinity to hack and hew down the main pillars of reformation and liberty.

In these early days, he held off from any full-on assault against the king, instead complaining in a roundabout way of it being 'unlawful to speak plainly to the king in his ways'.

In 1645, he managed to get hold of Charles' private papers which had fallen into enemy hands after the Battle of Naseby. He published them, adding satirical notes of his own. And then in a subsequent issue, he hardened his line against the king with personal insults and a spot of fake news. Nedham began by putting out a mock appeal for anyone to come forward who'd spotted the king anywhere, and he mentioned in passing that they'd know him by his stammer:

> If any man can bring any tale or tiding of a wilful king, which hath gone astray these four years from his Parliament with a guilty conscience, bloody hands, a heart full of broken vows and protestations – if these marks be not sufficient there is another in the mouth, for bid him speak and you will soon know him – then give notice to Britannicus and you shall be well paid for your pains ... As sure as can be, King Charles is dead, and yet we never heard of it: I wonder we have not his funeral sermon in print here.

By May 1646, Nedham was writing an editorial describing the king as a tyrant, and suggesting he was trying to overthrow Parliament by setting the Scots and English against one another. This time, he'd gone too far. The Royalist authorities shut down *Mercurius Britannicus*, arrested Nedham and threw him into London's Fleet Prison. He got himself released two weeks later by agreeing to desist from publishing anything further, and he paid a £200 surety against his future good behaviour. However, there's some evidence that – despite this – he just carried on writing under a false name, while he supported himself by practising as a physician.

***

Over the next few years, several of these 'Mercuries' – all with high-sounding Latin names, some pro-Parliament, some for the king – sprang into being, and often died just as suddenly. Although it's been estimated that only around 30 per cent of England's population could read at this time, that figure jumped to 70–80 per cent in London. The public demand for news and comment on current events seemed insatiable, and in 1641 the government was forced to lift the ban on printing domestic news. Within four years, over 700 different newsbooks and other news-sheets were in circulation. Two years later, Parliament decided that all this publishing was getting out of hand, and introduced a system of licensing. Printers and writers who flouted the new rules could be fined, whipped or imprisoned and their presses confiscated.

It was at this moment that Marchamont Nedham pulled off his next coup. He somehow inveigled his way into Hampton Court Palace, and got himself introduced to the king. He knelt before the monarch, kissed his hand and begged the royal forgiveness, which – despite all the very rude and treasonable things he'd written about Charles – was 'readily granted'. Whether or not he offered at this meeting to commit his talents to the Royalist cause, we don't know, but that's precisely what he did. He began to publish, and of course to write for, a new Mercury, *Mercurius Pragmaticus*. And he packed its pages with commentaries on the events of the day, as well as witty and vitriolic attacks, now against the king's enemies. Oliver Cromwell, for instance, was mocked as 'Copper-Nose', 'Nose Almighty' and 'The Town-bull of Ely'.

So instantly successful was *Pragmaticus* that many others counterfeited it. No fewer than seventeen other Pragmaticuses regularly appeared on the streets, each pretending to be the real thing. Some just wanted to make money by sneaking a share of its market, while others aimed to blacken the reputation of the real *Pragmaticus* by printing outrageous libels in its name.

But it was Nedham's own enthusiasm for journalism that now got him into trouble. He started to include in the real *Pragmaticus* accounts of proceedings in Parliament. Parliamentarians didn't like that. They saw it as highly dangerous, because debate, disagreement and quotes out of context could be used by Royalists to discredit them. So, within a month of its first appearance, the printer of *Pragmaticus*, one Richard Lownes, was thrown into jail, and Nedham himself fled London.

For a while, Nedham managed to keep publishing and to stay one step ahead of the Parliamentary spies. But then in January 1649, he lost his royal patron. In one of the most momentous events in English history, King Charles I was found guilty in Parliament of 'being a tyrant, traitor and murderer, and a public and implacable enemy to the Commonwealth of England', and had been executed. By June that year, Nedham's luck ran out. He was arrested, and he found himself back in prison.

But then there was a remarkable intervention by no less an important Parliamentary personage than the Speaker of the House of Commons, William Lenthall. Nedham's talents were still in demand. Master Lenthall pleaded his case and won him a pardon, on condition that Nedham switch sides a second time. England was now a republic, and its leaders in Parliament reckoned that Nedham had just the skills to persuade the people of its righteousness.

And so, on 8 May 1650, just released from jail, Nedham published a pamphlet entitled *The Case of the Commonwealth of England stated ... with a Discourse of the Excellency of a Free State above a Kingly Government.* In the prologue, Nedham felt he had to defend his latest U-turn. He told his readers:

> Perhaps thou art of an opinion contrary to what is here written; I confess that for a time I myself was so too, till some causes made me reflect with an impartial eye upon the affairs of the new government.

Oliver Cromwell: Marchamont Nedham insulted him as 'Nose Almighty,' and 'The Town-bull of Ely.' When Cromwell became Lord Protector, he forgave Nedham, and employed him as his own press propagandist.

And Nedham was not only free to practise his profession again, he also received a more tangible reward. The Council of State voted him a one-off fee of £50 and a pension of £100 a year 'whereby he may be enabled to subsist while he endeavours the service of the Commonwealth'. Nedham set about his new commission, and on 13 June 1650 he brought out the first edition of yet another Mercury, *Mercurius Politicus*. It opened with a heated attack on the institution of monarchy and ended with a 'Hosanna to Oliver Cromwell'.

Cromwell, now hailed as the successful Civil War general, was fast rising to the top. And in 1653, he became ruler of England, not as a king but with the title Lord Protector. In effect, it was a military dictatorship. 'Government,' said Cromwell, 'is for the people's good, not what pleases them.' But he and his army grandees were practical men, and they could see that opposition was less likely if the people were also *told* what was good for them.

Cromwell recognised the usefulness of the printed word. So it was that this otherwise ruthless autocrat turned to the same man who'd insulted him as 'Nose Almighty' and the 'Town-bull of Ely'. In fact, Cromwell was so impressed by what he read in *Politicus* that he not only overlooked the old smears he'd suffered, but he awarded Nedham a £50 a year pension. And what's more, he granted him a one-off gigantic payment of £500.

Then, in 1655, *Mercurius Politicus* was adopted as the official mouthpiece of the government, with its editor Marchamont Nedham, in effect, chief propagandist to the Lord Protector. At the same time, the government passed laws subjecting the rest of the press to stringent censorship – nothing was permitted to be published that showed the new regime in a poor light or that could be seen as stirring up revolt. The ban wasn't totally effective because, by 1655, England's postal service was delivering mail three times a week, and some of Cromwell's opponents were taking advantage of it to send out regular anti-government newsletters.

However, Nedham's *Politicus* was far and away the front runner in the propaganda race, so Cromwell now heaped even more responsibility on him. Nedham was handed the editorship of another official government newsbook, titled the *Public Intelligencer.* He was a busy man, with *Politicus* coming out every Thursday and the *Intelligencer* each Monday. And he was now becoming a celebrity in his own right, though hardly in a way to be welcomed. He was attracting the personal venom of those outside the ranks of Cromwell's supporters. An independent-minded preacher called John Goodwin denounced Nedham as having 'a foul mouth, which Satan hath opened against the truth and mind of God', and being 'a person of an infamous and unclean character'.

Nedham's position was shaky. As it had been with the king before, he was dependent on the fortunes of one man. And when Cromwell died in 1658, and Richard, his weak and ineffective son, took over, Nedham's detractors felt even more free to gun for him. They accused him of being 'a lying, railing Rabshakeh' – an Old Testament character who used promises and lies to try and turn the populace against their ruler – 'and a defamer of the Lord's people'. There were increasingly loud demands now for Nedham to be fired from all public employment. But when Parliament was recalled in May 1659, the two houses dithered about what to do with him.

At first, they fired him as editor of the *Public Intelligencer*. Nedham was unbowed. He started yet another paper, called *The Moderate Informer*, and published a one-off pamphlet to prove that the whole country, high and low, of every party, would suffer if King Charles II returned from exile and was put back on the throne. Parliament liked that, and so changed its mind and put Nedham back in charge at the *Intelligencer*. But, the mood of the country at large was shifting. By early 1660 it was becoming clear that popular support was growing to bring back the king. So Parliament – seeing which way the wind was blowing – did another backtrack and stripped Nedham of his editorship of both *Politicus* and the *Intelligencer*.

Now Marchamont Nedham was in deep trouble. He'd run out of options, and the Royalists issued a pamphlet of their own which argued that the restoration of the monarchy wouldn't be complete unless Master Nedham were indicted for treason and hanged. Its writer, Roger L'Estrange, a strong supporter of Charles II, wrote that Nedham had:

> with so much malice calumniated his Sovereign, so scurrilously abused the nobility, so impudently blasphemed the Church, and so industriously poisoned the people with dangerous principles, that the Devil himself (the father of lies) … could not have exceeded him.

Nedham knew when to run, and he high-tailed it across the Channel to Holland. Two weeks later, at the end of May 1660, Charles II crossed back the other way and England was a monarchy again.

But Nedham, it seemed, was irrepressible. Within a few months, he'd obtained the new king's pardon, bought – according to his enemies – with 'money given to a hungry courtier', and he too came back from exile. Now, though his writing days weren't over, he steered clear of politics – for the moment anyway.

For the next few years, he maintained what for him was a low profile. He practised as a doctor, but couldn't keep away from the printing press. He did a bit of pamphleteering on the side, making rather less controversial points on matters of education mixed with attacks on the College of Physicians. But his political journalism was to make one last big splash.

In 1676, King Charles II – like Charles I and Oliver Cromwell before him – conveniently forgot that Nedham had so attacked and insulted him, and now paid him £500 to publish a tirade against one of his enemies, the Earl of Shaftsbury. Nedham showed that his taste for acid vitriol was far from dulled. The earl, he wrote, was:

> ... a man of dapper conscience, and dexterity, that can dance through a hoop ... a pettifogger of politics, ever ready to shift principles like shirts and quit an unlucky side in a fright at the noise of a new prevailing party ... a will-o-the-wisp that uses to lead men out of the way then leaves them at last in a ditch and darkness, and nimbly retreats for self-security.

The irony of this invective is nothing short of delightful. It could be a perfect summary of Marchamont Nedham himself. But the attack on Shaftsbury was to be his swansong. Anthony Wood, an Oxford academic who'd lived through Nedham's years in the public eye, wrote:

> This most seditious, mutable, and railing author died suddenly in the house of one Kidder, in Devereux Court, near Temple Bar, London, in 1678, and was buried on the 29th of November at the upper end of the body of the church of St. Clement's Danes, near the entrance into the chancel.

Two years later, when the chancel was rebuilt, Nedham's monument disappeared.

***

Marchamont Nedham has been described as 'the world's first great journalist', though reporters and editors in the twenty-first century might not relish being lumped in with a man whose cynical opportunism meant he was ever ready – in his own words – to 'shift principles like shirts'. Clearly, though, what you can't dispute is that he knew what his readers wanted to hear, and he knew how to write it in a way that made them come back for more.

So, was there any consistent guiding light behind his side-switching career? Some historians have argued that he never changed his passionate hatred of 'priest craft', in other words, the way that clerics of all churches were hungry for power. The Presbyterians and Catholics, he wrote in 1650, were all the same, and he complained of:

> ... the popish trick taken up by the Presbyterian priests in drawing all secular affairs within the compass of their spiritual jurisdiction... [bringing] all people into the condition of mere galley slaves while the blind priests sit at the stern and their hackney dependents, the elders, hold an oar in every boat.

Nedham was also a fan of Machiavelli, who most certainly would have approved of his lack of moral scruples when it was expedient to go back on your word and slip over to the other side.

But there was something else going on with Nedham that might strike a chord with the world's great media owners of the twentieth and twenty-first centuries. He was perhaps the earliest exponent of the benefits of a society where you were free to make money, and he acted on it. He was one of the first, if not *the* first, to introduce paid advertising into journalism, and it made *Mercurius Politicus* throughout the rule of Oliver Cromwell a profitable, as well as a popular, success. In 1652, he wrote that commercial interest 'is the true zenith of every state and person ... though clothed never so much with the specious disguise of religion, justice and necessity'.

And whatever else we may say about Marchamont Nedham, he did not lack courage. He came very close to being hanged in 1660, and that risk did not go away over the following decade, when others were not so fleet-footed or smooth-tongued as he, as the case of John Twynn showed.

In 1663, Twynn sat in a cell in London's Newgate Jail awaiting his execution. He'd been involved in publishing an anonymous pamphlet justifying the people's right to rebel. It was 'meddle-some stuff', according to the official state censor. There was no suggestion that Twynn had written the treasonable words himself; he was just the technician who'd set up the press and printed the booklet. The authorities offered him a deal. Reveal the name of the journalist behind it and Twynn would be spared the death penalty.

He refused. He told the prison chaplain, 'it is not my principle to betray the author'. And so he was taken to the place where martyrs to the press had met their end in Tudor times – Tyburn. And there he was hanged, cut down while still alive, so his guts could be drawn out with a hook, before his body was cut into four parts and distributed around the gates of the city. His head was hoisted on a spike at Ludgate. It was a terrifying warning to anyone who might contemplate writing or printing anything which could be thought treasonous against the new king. It's worth repeating John Twynn's words – 'Not my principle' to reveal the name of the author.

So, is there any sign in the seventeenth century that the concept of the right to a free press was beginning to be recognised? In 1644, one of England's greatest poets, John Milton, published a pamphlet with the scholarly title *Areopagitica*. On the face of it, the document may look like a statement in favour of a free market in ideas, the first of its kind. He writes:

> Who kills a man kills a reasonable creature, God's image; but he
> who destroys a good book, kills reason itself.

But down in the detail, it becomes clear, he's saying that if seri-ous-minded men are exposed to both good and evil ideas, they will be able to distinguish one from the other. Milton declares:

> a wise man, like a good refiner, can gather gold out of the dross-iest volume, and ... a fool will be a fool with the best book.

In other words, a free press is OK for intelligent men, but not for the hoi polloi who are easily misled. For that reason, Milton never concealed his contempt for the popular press. *Areopagitica* makes no statement supporting the abolition of censorship and, in fact, seven years later Milton accepted the job of Licensor of Newsbooks, i.e. the official censor.

Something closer to what we might begin to recognise as a demand for a free market in news and opinion came in 1648, not from a great thinker like Milton, but from the hoi polloi that Milton disparaged. That year – at the point when Civil War con-ditions were at their most anarchic – a popular movement sprang up across the country among a group of labourers and their supporters, calling themselves 'the Levellers'. They presented a petition to Parliament with 40,000 signatures. It demanded a republic, and promised to support the Parliamentarian Army as long as it followed the will of the people. The key words in the petition stated that it was 'absolutely necessary' for those in government 'to hear all voices and judgements, which they can never do but by giving freedom to the press'. It went on:

> To refer all books or pamphlets to the judgement, discretion or
> affection of licensers, or to put the least restraint on the press, seems
> altogether inconsistent with the good of the Commonwealth, and
> expressly opposite and dangerous to the liberties of the people.

The Levellers movement faded and came to nought. But this statement shows that the benefits of a free press were starting to be recognised. And, we should note, it was the readers not the journalists who were demanding it.

* * *

The Levellers, in their demands for greater democracy, were of course centuries ahead of their time. Fine ideas, but naïve too. Those in power were still a long way from making such a powerful weapon as the press available to opponents and rebels. Nevertheless, power itself was, bit by bit, starting to shift, and this brings us back to Marchamont Nedham.

Even more extraordinary than his successive U-turns was how he got away with them. The three most powerful figures in seventeenth-century England – King Charles I, Oliver Cromwell and King Charles II – plus the most powerful institution, Parliament, all of whom Nedham had insulted and viciously attacked in full public glare, forgave him. And not only forgave him, but then paid him vast amounts of money to write for them. It seems to say that those in power, the mightiest of the mighty, had now come to realise that 'getting a good press' was so important that they were prepared to go to any lengths for it, even allowing themselves to be manipulated and humiliated by an inky wretch like Marchamont Nedham.

The conclusion is inescapable: the most powerful in the land had now come to understand that the humble people could no longer be kept in the dark. The printing press had seen to that. Governments and anyone else in positions of power could huff and puff all they liked and whinge about His Majesty's subjects being poisoned by the press, but there was no getting away from it, the mighty could no longer ignore those many hundreds of thousands of ordinary people who could read what was printed. The press – as a medium of communication, if not always the individual journalists themselves – had become a force for democracy.

But we shouldn't get carried away. The terrible fate of John Twynn in 1663 showed that the restoration of the monarchy under Charles II had been far from the dawning of some sort of age of democratic enlightenment. And, of course, little of what people read in newsbooks, pamphlets and newsletters throughout the century came close to what we might describe as objective reporting about the actions of government or the opposition. It was partisan politics. Even something that seems to us so innocent as the right to report the proceedings of Parliament would have to wait another 100 years.

The road to that particular modest objective had to be fought over every mile of the way. And again, one man's story would dominate the struggle. John Wilkes – like Marchamont Nedham – was not exactly the classic shining hero. His character and political views were at times unpredictable and, what's more, his sexual morals were very dubious. But he knew how to fight, as we'll discover on the next stage of our journey.

3

JOHN WILKES

The Terror of all Bad Ministers

The sentiments of one of these scribblers
have more weight with the multitude
than the opinions of the best politicians in the kingdom.

Sir Joseph D'Anvers (1686–1753), independent MP for Totnes

John Wilkes, politician, journalist, radical campaigner and rake, was said to be 'the ugliest man in England'. According to contemporary accounts, he was cross-eyed and had a protruding jaw. A sketch by the cartoonist Hogarth showed him with a malicious grin, fit to terrify any small child. Wilkes himself made fun of his own diabolical appearance, which he more than made up for with a fast wit and renowned charm.

He used to boast that it took him 'only half an hour to talk away his face'. On one election campaign, a constituent told him he'd rather vote for the Devil. Wilkes replied, 'Naturally. And if your friend decides not to stand, can I count on your vote?'

Remarkably, given his looks, he was a big hit with the opposite sex. He claimed his bent features gave him an advantage in any sexual conquest, declaring he could get 'a month's start on his rival on account of his face'. Even by the permissive standards of the eighteenth century, he was a libertine. When

John Wilkes, 'the ugliest man in England', by William Hogarth, 1763.

John Montague, the 4th Earl of Sandwich, told him, 'Sir, I do not know whether you will die on the gallows or of the pox', Wilkes replied, 'That depends, my Lord, on whether I embrace your lordship's principles or your mistress'.

Wilkes was born in Clerkenwell, London, in 1727, the second son of Israel Wilkes, a successful businessman who could afford to keep a carriage and six horses. Young John received a private education at a school in Hertfordshire, whose master, a Presbyterian minister, had a taste for mildly heretical views. John then went to university in republican Holland, where he found himself debating with fellow students in a free-thinking atmosphere.

He didn't compromise on his patriotism, however. In 1745, the Scottish Jacobite rebels invaded England, with the aim of restoring the Catholic Stuart dynasty to the throne. Wilkes promptly interrupted his studies and returned to London to join a militia there ready to defend the capital. The rebels made it as far as Derby, but were then turned back, and Wilkes returned to Holland.

By 1747, he was back in England, and now, at the age of 20, at his father's insistence, he married a wealthy woman, ten years older than him. They had a daughter. Wilkes' inclinations, however, were not those of a home-tied family man. He was gaining a reputation as a tearaway with questionable sexual morals.

In 1754, he joined something called the Sublime Society of Beefsteaks, a dining club for young gentlemen who usually ended their sessions with a visit to the whorehouses of Covent Garden. He was also a member of the Hellfire Club, known as the Medmenham Monks. The great eighteenth-century writer, Samuel Johnson, wrote that none there 'surrendered himself to the orgy with more of the true Rabelaisian abandon than Wilkes'.

Wilkes was, however, less keen on some of the Monks' rituals which he regarded as childish, and on one occasion when the drunken young men were planning to hold a black mass, he hid a baboon decked out with devil's horns in a back room. Then, at the height of the celebration, he released it, thus – says Johnson – terrifying his fellow members out of their wits.

Such shenanigans were hardly likely to endear any man to his wife, and Wilkes' spouse was a strict Christian Dissenter. So, in 1757, the couple separated. Strange as it may seem to our twenty-first-century sensibilities, Wilkes was granted custody of their young daughter, though, to his credit and by all reports, he was devoted to her and remained so for the rest of his life.

His attention now turned to politics. He wanted to get into the House of Commons, which at this stage of democracy often involved more than just courting a majority of the narrow electorate of privileged men in your constituency. Payments had to be made to secure the backing of those on high, and it's recorded that Wilkes forked out the huge sum of £11,000 before he could take, and then hold on to, his seat as the MP for Aylesbury. Then in 1762, he added a new strand to his many other vices and occupations. Journalism.

***

By now, the battle between the English press and the government was being fought out in very different circumstances from those that Marchamont Nedham had known. The old system of licensing newspapers and punishing those who flouted the regulations had lapsed. And so, in the years leading up to Wilkes bursting on the journalistic scene, successive governments had resorted to a mix of old and new tactics in their fight to control a hostile press.

In 1712, stamp duty was introduced – in other words, a tax on newspapers and pamphlets. Publishers had to pay a penny per page per edition and a shilling on every advertisement. For newspapers to survive they had to pass on the extra cost in the price, and some of the cheaper popular papers were driven to the wall – which was precisely what the government wanted.

Rebellion among the masses, stirred up by the press, was what they most feared.

However, although it was a decent revenue-raiser for the government, as a means of controlling the opposition press, stamp duty had limited success. Many publishers simply ignored the law and produced unstamped papers. So, in 1743, a new law was passed, aimed not at publishers or journalists, who often hid their identities behind pseudonyms, but at a softer target, the street-side newspaper vendors. Anyone selling an unstamped paper could now be sent to prison for three months.

Another new government device for securing a sympathetic press was rather more underhand: bribery. With blatant bias, publications sponsored by the government were exempted from stamp duty. And Sir Robert Walpole, for instance – the leader of the government in Parliament, and prime minister in all but name from 1721 to 1742 – provided a free mail service and subsidies for papers that supported the government, and even pensions and paid sinecures for loyal writers and editors. This roused strident opposition from other papers, in particular the *London Journal*, run by a couple of dissident Whig politicians. They'd offended the government by calling for an investigation into ministers, who – they claimed – were guilty of insider trading during the so-called South Sea Bubble, a public–private investment scheme that collapsed, bankrupting thousands of ordinary citizens. Walpole's reaction was simple and direct. He bought the paper, fired the editor and changed it to a pro-government stance.

Ministers had a few old tricks up their sleeves too. They could still invoke the libel laws to cower editors and reporters, and – in a tradition dating back to Henry VIII's time – they could accuse publishers, authors and printers of sedition. In 1719, for instance, a freelance printer who'd been paid to produce a pro-Jacobite pamphlet, was hanged for treason.

But despite official efforts, the eighteenth century saw an increasing demand among general readers for news and comment. Political debate in the pages of opposing pamphlets and newspapers flourished, with the great writers of the day pitching in. Daniel Defoe, author of *Robinson Crusoe*, produced the first influential political periodical, the *Review*. And Jonathan Swift, creator of *Gulliver's Travels*, started a rival paper with a Tory leaning, the *Examiner*. Defoe tried to steer an independent political line. But despite that, his comments could still get him into trouble, and on two occasions he ended up in Newgate Prison for comments he'd made about the line of royal succession.

***

The press, then, was an obvious outlet for John Wilkes' rebellious spirit. And it was the appointment in 1762 of John Stuart, 3rd Earl of Bute, as leader of the government in Parliament, that drove Wilkes to the press. Bute's new exalted position was an affront to Wilkes' patriotism. The man was not only a Scot, but a member of that same aristocratic Jacobite house which, a mere seventeen years earlier in 1745, had invaded England. And what was more, in Wilkes' view, this Scottish interloper had sold out the country in a peace deal he'd made with the French.

Added to all of this was a dash of personal venom. Under the previous government, Wilkes had been all but promised a promotion either as Ambassador to Constantinople or Governor of Quebec. Under Bute that wasn't going to happen. Wilkes was determined to stir up popular opposition across the country, and so he turned to the press.

He published a couple of pamphlets attacking the French peace deal, and when they caught the popular mood, he went further and set up his own newspaper. He titled it *The North Briton*, a direct jibe at the Scots, who – it was implied – weren't worthy of a separate identity, but were simply the inhabitants of the furthermost part of Britain. In the columns of his paper, he vilified Bute, not only for the French treaty but also with allegations that he was sleeping with the king's mother. And that wasn't all, Wilkes also attacked King George III himself. In the columns of *The North Briton*, he compared the monarch to his famously weak predecessor, Edward III, and he likened Bute to that king's much-despised influential favourite, Roger Mortimer.

One of Bute's loyal supporters, William, 1st Earl Talbot, challenged Wilkes to a duel. The two men met at night – to evade the authorities, duels being illegal – on Bagshot Heath in Surrey, and at a range of 8 yards fired their pistols at each other. Both missed, then they shook hands and went off to the nearest inn to share a bottle of claret.

But most of Wilkes' shots at his enemies – the ones in print – were not so easily shrugged off. He wrote that Bute was a 'despotic minister' who was 'dazzling his prince with high-flown ideas of the prerogative and honour of the crown'. And he added that 'Royalty' had 'sunk even to prostitution'.

By April 1763, popular and parliamentary sentiment against Bute – largely whipped up by Wilkes in *The North Briton* – had reached such a pitch that he was forced to resign. This is believed to be the first case where the press played the major role in bringing down such a powerful politician, a notable media victory in the war with the mighty.

But Bute, although out of office, had one last say. Wilkes recognised Bute's hand behind the king's speech at the adjournment of Parliament, in support of the French peace treaty. In Issue 45 of *The North Briton*, Wilkes attacked the speech as 'the most abandoned instance of ministerial effrontery ever attempted to be imposed on mankind'. And he even went so far as to suggest that the king himself had colluded in a lie.

George III was furious. He was advised that this was seditious libel, and he ordered two warrants of arrest to be issued against the authors, printers and publishers. But the king and his supporters in Parliament hit a stumbling block, and it was one they would trip up on time after time in the battles ahead.

When it came to executing the law, the power of the monarchy and Parliament was not supreme. There was a justice system – courts, judges and other legal officers – all part of Magna Carta's 'due process of law'. So, now Justices of the Peace refused to be government pawns. They wanted proof against named individuals, and there was no such proof that Wilkes had written the defamatory piece.

The unfortunate printers of the seditious libel, however, were not so lucky. It was known who they were, and they were apprehended. And now one of them pointed a finger at Wilkes as its author.

So, on the afternoon of 30 April, Wilkes was seized by officials in the street near his home in Westminster. His lawyers immediately started proceedings to get him freed by writ of habeas corpus. Meanwhile, Wilkes was grilled by the king's secretaries and managed to stall them for a time. But before his release came through, he was thrown into the Tower of London and kept as 'close prisoner', which meant he was allowed to see no one, not even his legal advisors. His house was ransacked and all his papers seized. The arrest of a Member of Parliament, however, had by this stage in the eighteenth century become a very grave matter. It was a breach of parliamentary privilege, and on 6 May, Wilkes was freed.

Issue 45 of *The North Briton* has another claim to significance in our charting of the media–mighty war. It contained an uncompromising definition of the value of a free press. Wilkes wrote:

The liberty of the Press is the birthright of a BRITON, and is justly esteemed the firmest bulwark of the liberties of this country. It has been the terror of all bad ministers; for their dark and dangerous designs, or their weakness, inability, and duplicity, have thus been detected and shown to the public generally in too strong colours for them long to bear up against the odium of mankind.

The statement portrayed Wilkes as much more than a victim of the system. He had positioned himself as a champion of constitutional freedom. And that gave him a popularity that he could rely on during the coming fight.

**

Wilkes' restored position in the House of Commons didn't last long. And this time it was not politics, but pornography and his past pranks that got him into trouble. He'd published a risqué poem dedicated to a courtesan named Fanny Murray (although we today might not think it too offensive to talk of Fanny showing 'the coral centre of her snowy orbs' or her rivals getting their corset stays 'cut an inch or two lower' to display 'the whole lovely circumference'.)

The verses also lampooned Fanny's lover, the Earl of Sandwich, who now had two reasons to be affronted by Wilkes, because he'd also been one of the Medmenham Monks and still harboured a grudge against Wilkes for the baboon outrage. Sandwich read out the verses in the House of Lords. Their lordships judged it obscene and blasphemous. On the same day, the House of Commons decided to get in on the Wilkes-bashing act, turning its attention to Issue 45 of *The North Briton*. In response to a request from the king, the Commons condemned it as seditious libel and ordered that all available copies be consigned to the common hangman who would, with due ceremony, burn them. The Speaker of the Commons ordered Wilkes to answer before the House.

Meanwhile, a disgruntled supporter of the king challenged Wilkes to a duel, and with a better aim than Wilkes' last duellist opponent, shot him in the stomach. That provided Wilkes with an excuse to avoid appearing in the Commons. He sent in a sick note, which the Speaker read out, commenting that it was 'entirely unauthenticated', and the House duly expelled him.

As soon as he was well enough, Wilkes slipped off to Paris, where he fell into the arms of a famous courtesan named Corradini. Then, as soon as he was fit enough, he toured Italy. Meanwhile, he was convicted in his absence.

By 1768, he'd run out of money and he returned to England. Although he was still an outlaw, the government hesitated to arrest him on the old sedition charges. The widespread acclaim in the country for his anti-Establishment fight, which his witty, campaigning journalism had made so popular, was still strong even after his four-year absence, and on 28 March, he stood again as MP for Middlesex and won by an immense majority. At this point, he decided to try his luck before the courts and to prove himself innocent. So, he surrendered to the Court of King's Bench. The judge was not sympathetic and he committed Wilkes to prison.

A huge mob of supporters had gathered in the street outside the court, and as Wilkes was led off to jail, they surged forward, overwhelmed his guards, and freed him. But Wilkes, not wishing to be guilty of absconding, managed to slip off and surrendered himself again.

For the next two years, he conducted a spirited campaign from his prison cell. First, he smuggled out a written speech, thanking his supporters. It was read aloud to the growing mass of people who daily gathered outside the jail. They now started chanting, 'No liberty, no king!' That sounded like the makings of a revolution to the government, so, on the 10 May, troops were called out, and they opened fire on the unarmed demonstrators. Seven were shot dead and another fifteen were wounded. It became known as the St George's Fields Massacre. The Secretary of War, Lord Barrington thanked the soldiers – a clumsy mistake.

It was now open warfare between Wilkes' growing number of sympathisers and the government. Inside prison, Wilkes seems to have got himself a degree of freedom in communicating with the outside world, and he pursued two lines of attack. He made a formal appeal to both Houses of Parliament to have his convictions reversed, and at the same time he turned again to the press. He'd managed to get hold of a copy of orders issued by a government minister, Lord Weymouth, to the chairman of the magistrates for the district around the prison where Wilkes' supporters had been gathering. The document ordered the magistrates to make prompt use of the military if it looked like a riot was threatened. It was dated three weeks before the St George's Fields Massacre. Wilkes persuaded the editor of the *St James's Chronicle* to publish the damning instructions accompanied by his own outraged comments. Both the Lords and the Commons voted the *Chronicle's* coverage to be libellous, and at the same time, yet again, stripped Wilkes of his membership of Parliament.

There then followed a battle, at times farcical, between the government and the voters of Middlesex. They promptly re-elected Wilkes. The House of Commons then declared the ballot invalid, adding that Wilkes 'was and is incapable of being elected a member to serve in this present Parliament'. The Middlesex electors weren't so easily deterred. They voted twice more in favour of their man, and twice more had their decision annulled. In fact, Parliament had to resort to falsifying the voting numbers in order to get a replacement MP returned.

The whole affair now sparked a press war for and against Wilkes. The government, relying on some dull and academic articles written by Dr Johnson, soon found itself on the back foot. The leading political commentator of the day, who wrote under the name 'Junius' in the *Public Advertiser*, backed Wilkes. He even addressed the king himself through its columns:

Sire – it is the misfortune of your life that you should never have been acquainted with the language of truth, until you heard it in the complaints of your people. It is not, however, too late to correct the error.

Sir William Blackstone, the most respected judge of the eighteenth century, tried in his *Commentaries on English Common Law* to steer a middle course in the argument. He wrote in 1769, 'The liberty of the press is indeed essential to the nature of a free state', but, he added, if anyone 'publishes what is improper, mischievous, or illegal, he must take the consequence of his own temerity'.

On 17 April 1770, Wilkes completed his prison term and was released. He'd gone to jail a bankrupt, but now, thanks to the generosity of his supporters – some of them in America, who admired his fight for constitutional rights – he was now well off. And the press campaign fought over many years, both by him and by other newspapers on behalf of his cause, meant he was now the idol of the populace. Shop windows sported posters of his unforgettable face, which also decorated punch bowls, snuff boxes, jugs, teapots, buttons and medals, while several inns renamed themselves The Wilkes Head.

An organisation had even been formed with the specific objective of backing Wilkes and all he stood for. It went by the splendid title of The Society of Gentlemen Supporters of the Bill of Rights.

Wilkes himself, unable to sit in Parliament, now turned to local politics. He became an Alderman of the City of London and was soon invited to stand for mayor. But his influence on national politics and the press had one last – shining – victory to come.

* * *

As well as using bribery, bullying and the libel and sedition laws as tactics to control the press, governments also still had the legal power to prevent the reporting of debates in Parliament. The legal ban had been in place since the restoration of the monarchy in 1660.

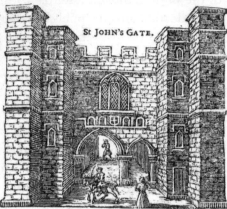

The Gentleman's Magazine:

St John's Gate.

Lond Gazette
Lond. Jour.
Fog'' Journ.
Applebee's
Read's :: ::
Craftsman
D. Spectator
Grubstreet J
W.ly Register
Free = Briton
Univ = Doctor
Daily Court.
Daily = Post
Dai. _ournal
Da. Post-boy
D. Advertiser
Evening Post
St James's Ev.
Whitehall Ev.
Lõdon Ev'g
_rving = Post
Weekly Mis-
cellany.

York 2 News
Dublin 6 :::
Edinburgh 2
Bristol :: : ::
Norwich 2 ::
Exeter 2 ::
Worcester
Northampton
Glouceſter : :
Stamford : :
Nottingham
Bury Journ
Chester ditto
Derby ditto
Ipswich dit.
Reading dir.
Leeds Merc.
Newcaſtle C.
Canterbury
Manchester :
Boſton ::: ꝗ
Jamaica. &c
Barbados :

Or, MONTHLY INTELLIGENCER.

For JANUARY, 1731.

CONTAINING,

(more in Quantity, and greater Variety, than any Book of the kind and Price.)

I. A VIEW of the WEEKLY ESSAYS, *viz.* Of Queen *Elizabeth*; Ministers; Treaties; Liberty of the Press; Riot Act; Armies; Traytors; Patriots; Reason; Criticism; Versifying; Ridicule; Humours; Love; Prostitutes; Musick; Pawn-brokers; Surgery; Law.

II. POETRY. The Ode for the New Year, by *Colly Cibber*, Esq; Remarks upon it; Imitations of it, by way of *Burlesque*; Verses on the same Subject; ingenious Epitaphs and Epigrams.

III. DOMESTICK OCCURRENCES; *viz.* Births, Deaths, Marriages, Preferments,

Casualties, Burials and Christenings in *London.*

IV. Melancholy Effects of Credulity in *Witchcraft.*

V. Prices of Goods, Grain, Stocks, and a List of Bankrupts.

VI. A correct List of the Sheriffs for the current Year.

VII. Remarkable Advertisements.

VIII. FOREIGN Affairs, with an Introduction to this Year's History.

IX. REGISTER of Books.

X. Observations on Gardening.

XI. Table of CONTENTS.

By SYLVANUS URBAN, Gent.

The FIFTH EDITION.

LONDON: Printed for the AUTHOR, and sold at St *John's Gate*: By F. *Jefferies,* in *Ludgate-street*; all other Booksellers; and by the Persons who serve Gentlemen with the News-papers: *Of whom may be had* Compleat Sets, *or any* single Number. A few are printed on ROYAL PAPER, *large Margin,* for the CURIOUS.

The Gentleman's Magazine of January 1771, the year it began to report proceedings in parliament by getting its correspondent to memorise what he heard then write it down back at the office.

Publishers were driven to finding more and more ludicrous ways of working around the law in order to satisfy their readers' hunger for parliamentary news. For a start, information about what was said by MPs had to be smuggled out of the Chamber. Clerks and other parliamentary minions were paid for the odd snippets that they'd overheard. But, as the following extract from the magazine titled *The Political State of Great Britain* shows, they weren't always too enlightening:

> After the King had delivered his speech in the House of Lords, the Lord Chancellor reported upon it, after which the Duke of Devonshire said something, but so low that nobody could hear him, and it was supposed that he was speaking in praise of His Majesty's policy.

The Gentleman's Magazine managed to go one better. In 1731, it employed a man named William Guthrie, who apparently had a remarkable memory. Guthrie would bribe the parliamentary doorman to let him in, memorise the whole debate, then rush back to the magazine's offices where he wrote it up. The magazine's editor, Dr Samuel Johnson, then added the kind of rhetorical flourishes he imagined the speakers would have used. The result was the closest to anything resembling reports of parliamentary debates since the Civil War, eighty years earlier.

This routine went on for seven years, until – under threats from the government to shut the magazine down – Johnson had to change tack. By now the *Gentleman's Magazine* was selling 30,000 copies an issue and parliamentary reporting was its biggest selling point. So, instead of recounting debates in the Westminster Parliament, he started to publish accounts of proceedings in the fictitious parliament of Lilliput. In 1741, for instance, the magazine reported a speech in the House of Lords by 'The Hurgo Adonbing', in which he was reported to say:

> We have been amused, my Lords, on this occasion with great pro-
> fusion of mirth and ridicule, and have received the consolation of
> hearing that Lilliput is an island, and that an island is not to be
> invaded without ships.

It didn't take a reader with much expertise in doing anagrams to
work out that 'The Hurgo Adonbing' was the Earl of Abingdon, and
just in case there were any doubts about the whole charade, Johnson
added with a wink, 'Mr Gulliver was astonished at the wonderful
conformity between the constitution of England and Lilliput'.

In 1738, a rival publication started up, *The London Magazine*,
and its parliamentary reporting dressed up the Westminster
Parliament in the disguise of the Roman Senate, with speeches
by such notables as Cicero and Cato. The editor helpfully added
an index of who was who.

But it was for only so long that the public demand to know what
those who governed them said to each other could be satisfied by
such childish gimmickry, and in 1771, Wilkes threw his weight
behind the campaign to free parliamentary reporting, and won.

It began with what seemed an inconsequential row about
reinforcing the embankment along the River Thames close to
where today the Adelphi Theatre stands. Parliament tried to insist
on how the work should be carried out, and the City authorities took offence and accused the Westminster Government of
interfering where it had no right to do so. In clear defiance of
the ban on parliamentary reporting, the *Middlesex Journal* published an account of the debate on the matter in Parliament,
and the resulting publicity further enflamed opposition in
the City, and – at the same time – outraged government MPs.
So, the Speaker of the House of Commons summoned John
Wheble, the printer of the report, to appear before the bar of
the Commons. The order was backed up by a proclamation
from the king with a reward of £50 for anyone who arrested
the unfortunate Wheble and brought him in.

This was just the sort of fight Wilkes relished, and he hatched a plot to defend the printer. It was again 'due process of law' that was to trip up Parliament. In his capacity as an alderman and magistrate, Wilkes ordered Wheble to be brought before him, and when he appeared, Wilkes dismissed the charges against him. Wilkes himself was then summoned to appear before the House of Commons. Wilkes countered by arguing – perhaps not entirely seriously – that since Parliament itself had banned him from its proceedings, he had every right to refuse to turn up there.

Wilkes saw this fight as more than a battle for justice in the case of one unfortunate printer. It was something more fundamental. In a letter he sent to the Secretary of State, Lord Halifax, he wrote, 'Wheble was apprehended in violation of the rights of an Englishman, as well as of the chartered privileges of a Citizen of London'.

Another of the printers at the *Journal*, John Miller, then faced similar charges. He was brought before the lord mayor himself, Brass Crosby, who then followed Wilkes' lead and dismissed all charges against Miller. Crosby was seized by parliamentary officers and thrown into the Tower of London. Wilkes and his Society of Gentlemen Supporters of the Bill of Rights came out in public support of Crosby.

Now came a crucial turning point in the battle. The country's judiciary failed to support Parliament, and instead recognised the justice of the fight for freedom to report proceedings in Parliament. One after another, judges were lined up by Parliament to hear the case against Crosby, and one after another they threw out the case.

The government was defeated. It had no other options left, and both the House of Commons and the House of Lords quietly dropped all opposition to the reporting of their debates. It was a mammoth victory for the press. From now on, newspaper readers – and in later centuries those who watch TV and listen to the radio – could always be well informed about the divisions, squabbles, promises and threats uttered by those they'd chosen to govern them in the chambers of Parliament.

This new freedom marks another milestone on our journey, too. Up to this point, there'd been little or no recognition of the difference between comment and facts. Objective reporting had been more or less unknown. Accounts of the Nun of Kent's revelations in Henry VIII's day or of King Charles I's activities at the time of the Civil War had been printed and circulated – not to enable readers to be informed and to make up their own minds, but to stir up devotion or hatred or some other reaction. Facts were not sacred.

But now, in the late eighteenth century, for the first time, with the lifting of the ban on reporting parliamentary debates, we have an example of the media telling it like it is, without distortion, and with the simple aim of relaying the truth about those in power to the population at large. It was a significant victory for the people in the media–mighty war. But before we go over the top with our celebrations, we shouldn't imagine that, from now on, only the truth would be printed in newspapers and pamphlets. Far from it, as we'll soon find out.

* * *

So, what happened to Wilkes? In 1774, he was elected unopposed again as the Honourable Member for Middlesex, and in the same year he became Lord Mayor of London. His old charm never faded. He was presented to King George III, who announced that he had never met such a well-bred lord mayor. But in 1780, many of his erstwhile supporters started to ask where was 'the man of the people' they'd known. During the Gordon Riots, in which the rioters were opposed to ending discrimination against Roman Catholics, Wilkes commanded a force of soldiers defending the Bank of England and ordered his troops to fire into the crowd. Wilkes' action was consistent with his championing of the cause of greater tolerance, but the violence of his actions shocked many. Some of those who'd once worshipped him now called him 'hypocrite'.

In 1790, he retired from both politics and journalism, and divided his leisure between his villa on the Isle of Wight and his two London houses. He died in 1797. His memorial inscription reads, 'The Remains of John Wilkes, a friend to liberty'. These last four words are as good as any to sum up a man of such complex and controversial character. We could add that one of the liberties he befriended and advanced was the freedom of the press to attack, criticise, hold to account and simply report on the government of the day.

* * *

One of the great issues of the time that caught Wilkes' attention during his last spell in Parliament was the threatened breakaway by the American colonies. In the lead up to the American Revolution, Wilkes was consistent and ardent in opposing the government's war against the colonists. He failed to stop it.

The American Revolution and the war that followed was a conflict in which, it's been said, newspapers played as powerful a part as did any gun in securing victory for the colonists. It was the press as much any other weapon that defeated the British Government in America. And that's where we're going next, to find out more.

4

THE AMERICAN REVOLUTION

Forge of Sedition

Were it left to me to decide whether we should have a government without newspapers, or newspapers without a government, I should not hesitate a moment to prefer the latter.

Thomas Jefferson (1743–1826)

Isaiah Thomas began his career as a printer at an age when we today would be just starting our first school. His father, Moses Thomas, farmed land to the east of New York City on Long Island. He was bankrupted in 1755 and died soon after, leaving his widow, Fidelity, with Isaiah and four other young children to support on her own. In desperation, she gave away the two youngest to nearby friends, while she and the rest of the family, including Isaiah, boarded a ferry across to the mainland then headed north to Boston, where she hoped to make enough money to feed them all.

However, she soon found she couldn't do it, so Isaiah – now aged 6 – had to go elsewhere. She apprenticed him to a local printer named Zechariah Fowle. This meant he'd be provided with food and a bed while working at the printing shop, although no pay.

Isaiah's job was to set the type, which would have required him to learn to read and write as well. He was so small that he needed to stand on a bench in order to reach the double frame of Roman and italic letters which he had to fix and arrange in the right order. He must have been a bright lad who soon took to the work, because within a year he'd completed his first job on his own, which – he wrote with pride later – was to set the type for a ballad called *The Lawyer's Pedigree*.

At the end of his apprenticeship, Isaiah stayed on to work for Fowle. But in 1765, when he was 16, he had an argument with his boss and decided to head off for England, where he hoped to learn more advanced printing techniques. For reasons that aren't clear, instead of taking a passage from Boston or some other New England port, he went to pick up a ship 600 miles north in Nova Scotia.

When he reached Halifax, however, he got sidetracked, and it was here that his rebel politics emerged. He met the only printer in the town, a Dutchman named Anton Heinrich, and was shocked by what he found at Heinrich's shop. Not only was the Dutchman ignorant of a printer's basic skills, but he was lazy as well. It was an affront to Isaiah's professionalism and he offered to help. Heinrich's main business was producing the local newspaper, the *Halifax Gazette*, and he was only too happy to hand over sole responsibility for its production to Isaiah.

Almost straightaway, he had what would be the first of many brushes with authority. In 1765, the Parliament in Westminster, which had supreme authority over the people of the American colonies, introduced a Stamp Act, not unlike those we saw over the previous half-century in Britain itself. This one applied specifically to the American colonies and was a tax on all printed matter produced there, including everything from legal documents, to playing cards, pamphlets and newspapers.

The law stated that all printing presses must use special embossed paper which could be purchased only from the British authorities and, what's more, only by paying in British – rather than the local – currency. There were different tax rates for each category of printing. For newspapers, it was a penny on every page of each copy of the paper.

It was no secret that the money raised from the tax would be used to fund British troops stationed in the colonies, so it was hardly likely to be popular among Americans, and they soon came to see it as a means of making them pay for the instruments of their own oppression. Nova Scotia, like the colonies further south, was also subject to the tax. Isaiah took exception to it, and he printed a piece in the *Gazette* stating that the people of Nova Scotia were disgusted by this Stamp Act.

British Government officials in Halifax couldn't tolerate such rebellious comments, and they summoned Heinrich before them as the paper's owner. He denied all knowledge of

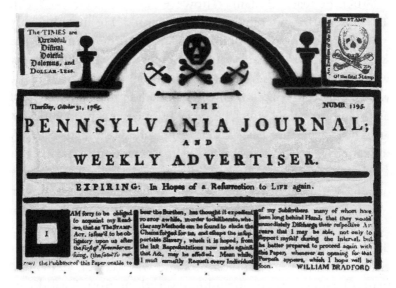

The Pennsylvania Journal mourning its impending death by the Stamp Act. To the top left of the masthead, it says, 'The Times are Dreadful, Dismal, Doleful, Dolorous and Dollar-less.' Under the death's head to the right, it reads, 'O! the fatal Stamp.'

the article, and when a second piece appeared in the *Gazette* attacking the Act, it was Isaiah who found himself standing before the most senior local British official, the Secretary of the Province. According to Isaiah's own account, his interview went like this:

> Mr. Secretary: How dare you publish in the *Gazette* that the people of Nova Scotia are displeased with the Stamp Act?
>
> Isaiah Thomas: I thought it was true.
>
> Mr. S.: You had no right to think so. If you publish anything more of such stuff, you shall be punished. You may go; but, remember, you are not in New England.
>
> I.T.: I will, sir.

The implication to Thomas was clear. According to the secretary's words, opposition must be much more outspoken back in his homeland of New England. And Thomas soon had evidence in his hands that rebellion was stirring in an even wider area, not just around Boston.

A ship put into Halifax Harbour carrying recent copies of the *Pennsylvania Journal*. The edition was in full mourning. Thick black lines surrounded the pages, and had been placed between the columns. There was a skull and cross bones above the title, and at the bottom of the last page was a large illustration of a coffin. Beneath it were printed the age of the paper and the words, 'Died of a disorder called the Stamp Act'. Instead of the required embossed stamp to show that tax had been paid, there was a death's head.

Thomas loved it, and he immediately wanted to do something similar in the *Halifax Gazette*. He realised, however, that it would bring the British officials down on his head again, so he looked for a way to make a protest that might avoid getting him into trouble. He put a paragraph in the *Gazette* which said:

We are desired by a number of our readers, to give a description of the extraordinary appearance of the *Pennsylvania Journal* of the 30th of October last, 1765. We can in no better way comply with this request, than by the exemplification we have given of that journal in this day's *Gazette*.

And he then reproduced all the same black lines, death's heads and a coffin on the same page.

A few nights later, a group of locals hanged the effigy of the stamp master – the British official in charge of administering the tax – from a gallows on top of the hill overlooking the harbour, where it could be seen across the town next morning. The British took the threat seriously, and stationed a twenty-four-hour guard on the stamp master's house.

The officials believed that Thomas himself was the ringleader behind the outrage, and the sheriff came to see him, accusing him of being a 'printer of sedition' and threatening to throw him in prison. Thomas responded by showing the sort of courage that, time after time, would serve him well. He challenged the sheriff for some proof that he had 'the king's authority' for his allegation, and the official backed off.

Isaiah Thomas, by the artist Ethan Allen Greenwood, 1818.

In March 1767, Thomas left Halifax and headed back south. For the next three years, he worked for various printers around the American colonies, in New Hampshire, the Carolinas and Rhode Island, before he pitched up again in Boston, where he ended up buying his old boss Zechariah Fowle's printing equipment, as well his newspaper, *The Massachusetts Spy*. Thomas was now more than a freelance printer. He was a newspaper owner and publisher. And he found himself in the midst of a bitter and violent media war that reflected the broader political battle lines now being drawn up.

***

The thirteen American colonies had become split between two warring factions, each adopting the names of the political parties in London's Westminster Parliament: the Tories, who favoured the status quo of British rule in America, and the Whigs, who supported reform and greater political freedom for the colonies. Boston's two principal newspapers were on opposing sides. The *Chronicle* was Tory, while the *Gazette* supported the Whigs.

The battle between them had started to turn nasty when the noted Whig and radical, James Otis, wrote an anonymous article in the *Gazette* slandering the *Chronicle*'s Scottish owner, John Mein, as a Jacobite. Mein burst into his rival's office, and in an angry outburst demanded that Otis tell him who'd written the offending piece. Otis refused to say. Then, when Mein met the *Gazette*'s publisher, John Gill, in the street and could get no answer from him either, he proceeded to club Gill with a walking cane.

Samuel Adams, who was emerging as one of the chief leaders of the anti-British faction, wrote in the *Gazette* that this was no private feud, but an attack on the principle of freedom of the press. Mein was charged with assault and fined, but this did nothing to dampen his attacks on his enemies.

Parliament at Westminster now introduced another law guaranteed to raise the hackles of American radicals – it imposed a
set of taxes on the import into the American colonies of certain
products, including glass, lead, paints, paper and tea, the so-called
Townshend Duties, after the British minister who dreamt up
the scheme.

Opposition in Boston was led by a group calling themselves the Sons of Liberty, and they organised a boycott of all
goods imported from Britain. This time, Mein thought he'd
got some juicy evidence of corruption by the radicals, and he
published in the *Chronicle* a list of Boston merchants who, he
said, in public supported the boycott while secretly continuing to import British goods. The boycott, said the *Chronicle*,
was nothing more than a sly attempt by these so-called radical merchants to get one up on their commercial competitors.
The Sons of Liberty were incensed, and they persuaded an
open meeting of the town's citizens to condemn Mein as 'an
enemy of his country'.

Gangs of vigilantes now started to take the law into their own
hands, and Mein and his business partner decided to stuff loaded
pistols into their pockets before they ventured outside. They had
good cause to be worried. When an angry crowd gathered outside the *Chronicle* office, Mein was set upon and beaten. He was
rescued from a worse fate only by the intervention of a troop of
British soldiers with bayonets fixed. But for Mein, enough was
enough, and he fled to England.

Such clashes between crowds and troops were becoming
more and more common, and they were meat and drink to the
radical press. The *Gazette* chronicled each one, often with a dash
of exaggeration. The shooting dead of an 11-year-old boy in
February 1770 had inflamed feelings, and now radicals roamed
the streets looking for soldiers to harass, while the soldiers, for
their part, were often up for a fight. The climax came during the
following month in an incident at the Boston Customs House.

According to the *Gazette*'s report, a group of boys was suddenly set upon by a troop of soldiers:

> The Captain commanded them to fire; ... He again said, 'Damn you, fire, be the consequence what it will!' One soldier then fired, and a townsman with a cudgel struck him over the hands with such force that he dropped his firelock; and, rushing forward, aimed a blow at the Captain's head which grazed his hat and fell pretty heavy upon his arm. However, the soldiers continued the fire successively till seven or eight or, as some say, eleven guns were discharged. By this fatal manoeuvre three men were laid dead on the spot and two more struggling for life; but what showed a degree of cruelty unknown to British troops, at least since the house of Hanover has directed their operation, was an attempt to fire upon or push with their bayonets the persons who undertook to remove the slain and wounded!

It became known as the Boston Massacre.

✳ ✳ ✳

It was into this frenzied atmosphere that Isaiah Thomas in 1770 now relaunched his newly acquired newspaper, the *Massachusetts Spy*. The British authorities had at first been slow to recognise the power of the press to influence the people, but they now started to see how wrong they'd been. So, they approached Thomas and tried to persuade him to give the *Spy* a pro-government, Tory stance. When he refused, they tried to bankrupt him by getting the man who'd lent him the money to buy Zechariah Fowle's printing presses to call in the debt. Thomas managed to raise another loan and to keep the *Massachusetts Spy* in print. Both Thomas and the *Spy* were now firmly on the side of the Whigs and against what was increasingly seen as British oppression.

It would be only so long before Isaiah Thomas and the *Spy* would clash head on with the authorities. And when it did happen, it had two far-reaching effects. It roused popular support for the Whig, anti-government cause, and it advanced the fight for the freedom of the press.

In November 1771, Thomas published in his paper an attack on the most powerful British official in Massachusetts, Governor Thomas Hutchinson. The offending article was written under the name of 'Mucius Scaevola', the name of a young ancient Roman famous for his bravery and patriotism. It revealed that Hutchison drew his pay directly from customs duties, in other words, out of the pockets of local people who had no say in the matter. Without that, wrote Mucius Scaevola, Hutchinson 'is no legal governor ... he is a USURPER. A ruler, independent of the people, is a monster in government.'

This attack was a forerunner of what was to become the battle cry of the American Revolution: 'No taxation without representation'. The article ended by demanding that the Massachusetts Council of elected representatives should therefore replace the governor and 'take upon itself the government of this province'.

Hutchinson read this as a dangerous challenge to his authority, so he decided to sue Thomas, as the printer and publisher of the article, for seditious libel. The *Spy* and the town's other radical newspaper, the *Boston Gazette*, both published a series of pieces defending Thomas. And when Hutchinson ordered him to appear and answer the charge against him, Thomas' reply was – to say the least – cheeky, 'I am busily employed in my office, and cannot wait upon your excellency and their honors'.

The Chief Justice of the Supreme Court now got involved and fared no better. He ordered Thomas to be brought before a grand jury for publishing 'an obnoxious libel', then lectured the jurymen on what he called 'the present licentiousness of the press' and 'the necessity of restraining it'. But the jury were not impressed, and they threw out the charge. The council then advised the governor that he'd be better to drop the case against Thomas because it risked provoking a violent popular uprising.

It was a clear victory for Thomas. And the press was becoming what governments since the time of Henry VIII in England had known and feared: a powerful mechanism able to radicalise and unite ordinary people in their opposition to those who rule them.

***

After his battle with Governor Hutchinson, Isaiah Thomas became the arch-villain in the eyes of the British and their Tory supporters. And he, in turn, took a leading role in fomenting rebellion. In 1772, for instance, he told his readers:

The Massachusetts Spy, or *Thomas's Boston Journal*. Note the figure of Liberty in upper left, and below, a rattlesnake labelled 'Join or Die' symbolising the thirteen colonies, challenging the British in the form of a griffin.

Liberty has taken deep root, and will reign in America. Five
millions of people, born and nourished in freedom and
enlightened by learning, cannot, unless Heaven is against
them, be enslaved.

By 1773, the government in London had realised that the
Townshend Duties, the taxes on certain imports to America,
were the source of more trouble than they were worth, so the
Act was repealed, though not entirely – tea was still subject to
the duty. And tea – that innocuous, polite drink, often regarded
by the English as a mark of civilisation – was converted into the
watchword of rebellion. Thomas' *Massachusetts Spy* played a part
in that metamorphosis. On the 2 December 1773, it reported
that a ship had docked in Boston Harbor carrying 114 chests of
the stuff, and that posters had gone up all over the town, whose
wording the *Spy* now diligently reported:

Friends! Brethren! Countrymen!
    THAT worst of plagues, the detested TEA shipped for this port
by the East India Company, is now arrived in this Harbor: the
hour of destruction or manly opposition to the machinations
of tyranny stares you in the face. Every friend to his country,
to himself and posterity, is now called upon to meet at Faneuil
Hall at nine o'clock THIS DAY (at which time the bells will ring)
to make a united and successful resistance to this last, worst
and most destructive measure of administration.

The result, two weeks later, was one of the most iconic events in
American history, the Boston Tea Party. Certain members of the
Sons of Liberty, some disguised as Native Americans, secretly
boarded the ship and threw all the chests of tea into the harbour. The *Spy* and the *Gazette* published articles defending the
action as 'a principled protest and the only remaining option the
people have to defend their constitutional rights'.

The British Government's response was harsh, and had an impact they hadn't bargained for. The port of Boston was closed and laws put in place which took away any right of the citizens of Massachusetts to participate in their own government. To the British, they were known as the Coercive Laws. The colonists called them the Intolerable Acts. They helped unite and strengthen the resolve of the colonists, and war was now inevitable.

Isaiah Thomas, like other prominent radicals became a target, and British soldiers on the streets of Boston openly threatened to tar and feather him (not the gentle punishment suggested by the word 'feather'; having boiling tar poured over you could cause lasting injury). He became deeper and deeper involved with the activities of the Sons of Liberty, and his printing shop started to be referred to as 'The Forge of Sedition'; not only the place from which the message of revolution was sent out to the people, but also where Bostonian patriots met to plan acts of rebellion. Thomas placed above the *Spy*'s masthead the words, 'Americans! – Liberty or Death! – Join or Die!'

The struggle between the American media and the British mighty followed a pattern during the build-up to the War of Independence itself. First, the press would attack some widely recognised injustice on the part of the British. Then, the British authorities would accuse those who'd published the attack of sedition, or some other crime, and try to punish them. They'd fail – largely because of widespread opposition stirred up by the press. Next, it was left to British soldiers or pro-British vigilantes to try to mete out unofficial justice to the rebel publishers. Finally, this often led to street battles between patriots and pro-British gangs or regular troops. And this, in turn, would provide the printers and publishers – who'd started the whole thing off in the first place – with more ammunition for their publications with accusations of British atrocities against defenceless citizens. It was a virtuous circle, as far as the American patriots were

concerned. The British were unable to break it, and so the
media defeated them.

***

Boston had become the front line in the conflict, and Isaiah
Thomas realised that the town would soon be swamped with
British troops, so he'd soon need to get out if he wanted
to continue publishing his paper. In the dead of night on
16 April 1775, he packed up his printing press and type blocks
and loaded them on a boat which took them over the Charles
River and – with the help of allies – on to the patriot strong-
hold of Worcester, 50 miles west. For the moment, Thomas
himself didn't follow his equipment. He was about to add
another role to his experience as printer, publisher and editor
– that of war reporter.

On 18 April, British troops were spotted embarking in boats
on the river near Boston Common. The radicals now were preparing for war, and organising themselves into armed militia
bands. They'd amassed stores of weapons and ammunition at the
town of Concord, 18 miles from Boston, and it was clear that this
was going to be the target of the troops seen crossing the river.
At daybreak, Isaiah left the town, and joined the local militiamen
at Charlestown. They did not have to wait long for the fight.

The next day saw the first battles of the American War
of Independence. In the early morning light at the town of
Lexington there was an exchange of musket shots between the
two sides. Eight militiamen and one British soldier were killed.
The militia fell back to Concord where, by now, they outnum-
bered the British soldiers four to one. After some skirmishing, the
British retreated and the patriots claimed a victory.

Isaiah Thomas witnessed the action and may himself have
taken part, but he must have thought that in future he could
better serve his country with the skill he knew best, and the next

day he travelled to Worcester where he assembled his printing press. On 3 May, the *Massachusetts Spy* was on sale again. Thomas himself wrote its lead story. This is how it began:

> Americans! forever bear in mind the BATTLE of LEXINGTON! where British Troops, unmolested and unprovoked wantonly, and in a most inhuman manner, fired upon and killed a number of our countrymen, then robbed them of their provisions, ransacked, plundered and burnt their houses! Nor could the tears of defenseless women, some of whom were in the pains of childbirth, the cries of helpless babes, nor the prayers of old age confined to beds of sickness, appease their thirst for blood! – or divert them from the DESIGN of MURDER and ROBBERY!

Thomas had discovered that battles could make powerful propaganda, and he ended his detailed account of the fighting with a sentiment designed to make the hearts of American patriots proud:

> We have pleasure to say, that notwithstanding the highest provocations given by the enemy, not one influence of cruelty, that we have heard of, was committed by our Militia; but, listening to the merciful dictates of the Christian religion, they breathed higher sentiments of humanity.

Rumours of the battles at Lexington and Concord reached Britain over a month later. The *London Gazette*, by now the official British Government mouthpiece, gave a simple response. Battles! What battles? Or, as it told its readers:

> A report having been spread, and an account having been printed and published, of a skirmish between some of the people of the province of Massachusetts Bay and a detachment of His Majesty's Troops; it is proper to inform the public that no

> advices have as yet been received in the American Department,
> of any such event.

But it was no use the government in London denying that hostilities had started. It was now all-out war between the British
and the rebels in the American colonies.

***

The *Massachusetts Spy* continued to publish in Worcester throughout the war. By 1776, Isaiah Thomas himself had become a patriot
celebrity. The British published the names of twelve American
rebels who, if captured, should be summarily executed. They
included renowned American leaders such as Samuel Adams and
John Hancock, and Thomas too was on this death list.

In 1781, he acquired a new printing press, and he relaunched
the *Spy*. His fame now was such that it could help sell the paper,
whose title was changed to *Thomas's Massachusetts Spy or the
Worcester Gazette*. And below were the words, 'The noble Efforts
of a Virtuous, Free and United People, shall extirpate Tyranny,
and establish Liberty and Peace'. Its new masthead was a figure
representing America, holding the cap of Liberty with the left
hand, and in the right, a spear aimed at the British Lion, with the
motto above, 'LIBERTY DEFENDED FROM TYRANNY'.
Alongside it was a chain of thirteen links, with a star in each,
representing the union of the thirteen colonies.

This chain of thirteen links is significant. It tells us everything
about the power of the press during the struggle for independence in America. At every stage of the fight, the biggest challenge
for the radicals was how to form the thirteen American colonies
into some sort of united, cohesive force. Americans, especially
in the build-up to hostilities, were deeply divided over what
to fight for, who would do the fighting, and often whether to
fight at all. John Adams, who'd helped draft the Declaration of

Independence and would be the second president of the new nation, explained it like this:

> The colonies had grown up under constitutions of government so different; there was so great a variety of religions; they were composed of so many different nations; their customs, manners, and habits had so little resemblance; and their intercourse had been so rare and their knowledge of each other so imperfect that to unite them in the same principles in theory and the same system of action was certainly a very difficult enterprise.

The American historian, Michael McDonnell even suggests that the War of Independence was 'by any measure the first American civil war'. And the challenge wasn't just how to bolster the Whigs against the Tories. It's estimated that tens of thousands of ordinary colonists didn't much like what either side stood for, and, by some reckonings, as many as three-fifths of Americans at this time supported neither the British Crown nor the patriotic radicals.

So, how could rebellion succeed, given such divisions and such a level of apathy among the people? The answer lay in the activities of Isaiah Thomas at the *Massachusetts Spy*, and all the other newspaper publishers who were doing a similar job across colonial America: William and Thomas Bradford in Philadelphia, Ebenezer Watson and George Goodwin in Connecticut, John Holt in New York and many more. Not only did they publicise the local patriot campaign in their area, they also swapped news stories and comment articles with each other. This helped give a sense that the struggle was gaining momentum across all thirteen colonies. And this feeling was strengthened further when many newspapers – thanks to an improved postal system – started to be circulated outside their home base. Thomas himself boasted that the *Spy*, for instance, was 'read by people not only in Boston and Massachusetts but throughout all thirteen American colonies'.

And so Whig papers such as the *Massachusetts Spy*, the *Pennsylvania Journal*, the *Connecticut Courant* – more than thirty newspapers in all – tended as a result to present a uniform stance on American liberty and the best way to achieve it. This had the effect of creating among the vast and growing legion of newspaper readers an impression that they were part of a united community of resistance to British 'tyranny'. And that legion was far bigger than just those who sat of an evening before their home fires reading the paper to themselves. Just as had happened in England, the latest issue of the *Massachusetts Spy* or the *New York Journal* was read aloud in taverns, coffeehouses and at public meetings. Those who couldn't read or couldn't afford the paper became radicalised too through the columns of the Whig press.

And what about the Tory, pro-British side? There were Tory-leaning papers, such as the *Boston Chronicle*, but they were fewer in number, and as tensions rose with the approach of war, Tory papers in patriot areas were driven out and could operate only in towns controlled by British troops.

It was the Whig-supporting, anti-British newspapers who won the press war. As David Ramsay, a South Carolina senator who fought against the British and was captured by them, wrote later, 'In establishing American independence, the pen and press had merit equal to that of the sword'.

***

The War of Independence was a war of attrition. It took eight years for the two sides to wear each other down. In the end, there was little appetite among the British to fight on, and America achieved her aim and was free of the imperial yoke. Now it had to define how it would govern itself. And in crafting the Constitution of this new nation, the founding fathers did not forget the role that the press had played in winning them their liberty.

And so, in December 1791, Congress adopted the First Amendment, which defined access to a free press as one of the fundamental rights of Americans. It stated:

> **Congress shall make no law** respecting an establishment of religion, or prohibiting the free exercise thereof; or **abridging the freedom** of speech, or **of the press**; or the right of the people peaceably to assemble, and to petition the Government for a redress of grievances. [My emphases.]

So, here was a government — the mighty — declaring that, for all time to come, the media was free to attack it, and that the mighty would not, ever, pass any laws to restrict that freedom. This was a remarkable commitment. And although, as we shall discover later on our journey, American governments have often sought to bend that law to their own benefit, the First Amendment's declaration on the freedom of the press was a landmark, not only in America, but in world history.

* * *

And what became of the man who, alongside other printers during the build-up to and during the War of Independence, laid the groundwork for this freedom, Isaiah Thomas? After the war ended in 1783, he continued to publish the *Massachusetts Spy*, with many extra pages and a new motto: 'Knowledge of the world is necessary for every man'. The boy who'd had no formal education and had started work at the age of 6, had grown up to become one of the heroes in the long story of the media. He developed a new passion: history. He founded the American Antiquarian Society and wrote a *History of American Printing*. He died in 1831 at the age of 82, and is buried in the Rural Cemetery at Worcester, Massachusetts.

The Boston Massacre, as portrayed by Paul Revere, published by Isaiah Thomas in the *Royal American Magazine* in 1774..

* * *

Among his many achievements, Thomas was one of the first to recognise the benefits of pictures in spreading the message of rebellion. In 1774, he'd started a new publication called the *Royal American Magazine*, which was richly illustrated. And its favourite contributor was one of America's most celebrated patriotic heroes, Paul Revere. He was a talented artist, and

Thomas' publication of Revere's dramatic image of British troops firing at unarmed civilians during the Boston Massacre, played a key part in stirring up hatred of the British among all classes of Americans.

Back in Britain itself, the technique of using illustrations to hit out at governments was developed further over the next decades. The political cartoon was born. No target among the mighty was too high for satirical attack. And no slander was too low or loathsome for this new generation of the media. So, let's go to the most fashionable quarter of King George III's London to find out more.

5

THE POLITICAL CARTOON

Poking Fun

I don't understand these caricatures.

King George III (1738–1820), reigned from 1760

Hannah and James were an ill-assorted couple. He came from a poor family, suffered a brutal childhood and was put to work at 11. She was brought up in a comfortable middle-class home, and in her twenties chose to help her elder brother in his business. She became a steady-minded, well-organised entrepreneur, while he turned out to be a temperamental artist. But by the rule that opposites attract, they became a couple, although exactly what that meant was always a mystery. Their enemies, back at the end of the eighteenth century, said their relationship was scandalous.

And enemies they made aplenty, because together Hannah and James attacked those in positions of power in a way that's still going strong today. They didn't threaten revolution on the streets, nor shatter the screen of secrecy that politicians like to hide behind. Instead, they vilified the greed, idiocy and corruption of those at the top with a device as ancient as human laughter – ridicule. And there are few things the mighty hate more than being made to look fools.

Hannah Humphrey was much older than James Gillray. We know little about her earlier life. She was born sometime around 1745 to comfortably-off parents in west London. The first we hear of her was in her twenties, when she was helping her elder brother William to run a print shop in St Martin's Lane. His business was not the printed word, but illustrations.

Multiple copies of drawings were produced at this time by the process of engraving. This involved scoring or scratching the design on a metal plate – usually a copper sheet. Ink was then rubbed into the carved out lines and the flat areas were cleaned. Moistened paper was next placed on top, and both plate and paper were pressed together between rollers, so that the image on the copper was printed onto the paper. If a brighter effect was wanted, coloured ink or a paint wash could then be added by hand. The printed pictures which resulted were not incorporated into newspapers or pamphlets but were sold as separate items in specialist shops, like that of William Humphrey.

It's a mark of Hannah's independent and unorthodox spirit that, unlike most of her peers, she didn't allow herself to be toted around the eligible young men of the neighbourhood in the hope that one of them might marry her and take her off her brother's hands. She must have shown talent and enthusiasm for the print business, and in 1772 records show her as the accredited publisher of the prints from two engraved plates.

It was in 1779, when she was in her mid-thirties, that her career took off. She opened her own shop in London's Old Bond Street, selling printed illustrations. This may sound unremarkable to us today, but in the late eighteenth century it was rare for a woman to run her own business. By this stage, Hannah had already met young James Gillray some years earlier when he became a client, then a friend, of her brother.

James had been born eleven or so years after Hannah, in 1756, in what was then the village of Chelsea, not much more than a handful of cottages, small farms and an inn on the north bank of the Thames, just west of London. The family were poor. His father, also James, had been a private in the army, and as result of a wound received in 1745 at the Battle of Fontenoy in Flanders, had had his right arm amputated. He then received a pension of 9 pence a day to support himself, his wife, Jane and their growing family of five children. James would be the only one of his siblings to live into adulthood.

About the time James was born, his father joined an obscure religious sect called the Moravians. Their unbending faith – which was grounded in the belief in the essential depravity of humankind – dominated James junior's early years. He was sent to the Moravian school where, although he was taught reading, writing, mathematics, German, Latin and music, he was also exposed to Moravian doctrine and practices. The children were made to sigh and cry out for mercy from the Saviour. They were isolated from the contamination of the outside world, and rules even forbad them from gathering together themselves without the supervision of a master. Four-year-olds were taught to welcome thoughts of death, and to desire passionately *not* to recover from illnesses. We can only guess what impact this terrifying upbringing would have had on James' art, his character and his tragic final years.

At the age of 11 or thereabouts, James was released from the grasp of the Moravians and had his first taste of what they'd condemned as a depraved, other world. He was apprenticed to an engraver in Holborn on the edge of the city. There he learned the basics of the trade, which included scoring copper plates with lettering, although not with illustrations. He found it boring, and claimed later that he and his fellow apprentices ganged together, quit and joined a touring theatre group, though we've no further evidence of that.

Nevertheless, whatever else he did, he now discovered he had some talent as an artist. He started to produce engraved illustrations. And when, at the age of 19, he turned up at the

Humphreys' shop with a couple of them, William bought them, printed and sold them. One, called *Six-pence a day*, showed a pregnant woman and her small children pleading with her husband, a thin, knock-kneed soldier, to stay home. It was an early sign of Gillray's talent, as well as the direction of his art – he'd chosen to point out the suffering of a poor family. It wasn't a direct attack on those in power, but it came close to it. And of course, given his father's war injury, there was a personal element to the theme.

It was at this time that James first met Hannah. At the age of 21, he won a place at the Royal Academy of Arts, and was taught there by one of the most renowned artists of the day, Sir Joshua Reynolds. Within a year, he sold his first engraving to Hannah Humphrey. She had just set up her own shop, and he was one of her first suppliers.

* * *

Caricatures – illustrations exposing by ridicule and exaggeration the weaknesses of those in power or the society we live in – were nothing new. William Hogarth, who lived earlier in the century, excelled at social satire with sets of drawings such as *The Harlot's Progress* and *Marriage a la mode*, and with warnings against the rising abuse of alcohol in his *Beer Street* and *Gin Lane*. And closer to Gillray's time, Thomas Rowlandson also became famous for his satirical caricatures, though he too concentrated more on the evils he saw in the streets around him than on politicians.

As Gillray's own career as a caricaturist developed, he produced caricatures on both social and political themes, but it was the latter that brought him into head-on clashes with those in power and began a tradition that's lasted ever since.

The twelve years from his first job for Hannah Humphrey until she became his exclusive publisher in 1791 were turbulent times in Parliament, and Gillray played his part in churning up

A March to the Bank, 1787. Note a baby among the victims (bottom left) and where Gillray couldn't resist a bit of scurrilous imagery (bottom right).

the mayhem. In 1783, William Pitt became Britain's youngest ever prime minster at the age of 24, and was to remain in power for most of the following twenty-three years.

During much of the 1780s, Gillray's caricatures were directed against both government ministers and the opposition. In 1787, an incident in the City of London provided him with the subject for one of his most lively lampoons. The military guard that marched each morning through the streets to protect the Bank of England had become regarded as a public nuisance, and when one citizen made a formal complaint that the soldiers had knocked him off the pavement, the lord mayor requested they march in single file. The Minister of War refused and so Gillray produced *A March to the Bank*.

Gillray worked for as many as twenty-five different print shops during this period, but his association with Hannah Humphrey was beginning to take root. It's been suggested that she formed a financial relationship with some members of Pitt's government in the mid-1780s, and in 1788 she commissioned seven illustrations from Gillray specifically attacking Charles James Fox, leader of the Whig opposition. The record of Tory election expenses for 1788 shows an entry of '£20 for Mr Gilwray'.

He switched sides several times during this decade, and the assumption must be that he was accepting paid commissions wherever they came from. He was not fighting some principled war against those in power. Rather, he'd discovered that the shenanigans in Parliament provided subject matter that he enjoyed lampooning and, what's more, the publishers and the public wanted more, which in turn provided him with a comfortable living.

* * *

By 1791, Gillray's work was so much in demand that there was a bidding war for his exclusive services between rival print shops. Gillray chose Hannah Humphrey. It was a decision which would change both their fortunes. She, largely because of her monopoly on the sale of Gillray's drawings, soon became London's leading print seller, and he benefitted from the new partnership financially, domestically and even in the direction of his art.

We know few details about Hannah Humphrey's character or life, but we can glean odd glimpses of her and her importance in Gillray's career from correspondence at the time and the comments and diaries of those who knew them. There's only one portrait of her, and that's her playing cards in *Two-penny Whist* by Gillray himself. She's the bespectacled figure second from the left. Beneath her flouncy bonnet, she looks astute, determined, and perhaps not someone to mess with. One of her neighbours in Bond Street, a fashionable gentleman called Henry Angelo,

Two-penny whist, 1796. Hannah Humphrey is second from the left. (© National Portrait Gallery)

said of her, 'Old Mother Humphrey was not much given to the melting mood'.

She was a shrewd businesswoman. In the early 1790s, most caricatures were affordable by the average middle-class household, but Hannah decided that a better business model would be to put up the prices of Gillray prints. They might sell fewer but the profits would be greater. As it turned out, she'd judged the market well.

Within two years of their exclusive business arrangement, Gillray had moved in over her shop in Old Bond Street. We shouldn't jump to any conclusions from this about their personal relationship – not at this stage anyway. It is certain that she guided him in the management of his financial affairs, and made sure that he was well fed and housed in comfortable surroundings. He showed his gratitude in 1793 by presenting her with a mahogany fire screen decorated with miniatures of his caricatures, and inscribed with the words:

For his old friend and
Publisher H. Humphrey,
as a mark of respect
and esteem.

When she moved premises to St James' Street in 1797, he went with her. Their enemies – of which his lampoons made many – accused the couple of a scandalous arrangement, in other words that they were living together without the benefit of sacred wedding vows. To protect her respectability, she started to call herself Mrs, rather than Miss Humphrey.

Gillray did apparently propose marriage to her more than once, and on at least one occasion, she agreed, and they even got as far as the door of the nearby St James' Church, when he whispered to her, 'This is a foolish affair methinks, Miss Humphrey. We live very comfortably together, and we had better let well alone.' Whereupon, it was said, he turned around and returned to his rooms above the shop to get on with his latest engraving.

There's no evidence that this snub caused the slightest cooling in their relationship. In fact, it warmed over the years. In 1798, she'd started a letter to him, 'Dear Gillray', and signed off, 'Yours sincerely'. By 1804 she was writing, 'Dear Gilly', and ending, 'Your affectionate friend'.

In terms of his work, her greatest impact came in the way she got him to focus his talents on sharp-witted, sometime savage satire, which of course was what would sell. The leading Gillray biographer, Draper Hill, notes that once he was under Mrs Humphrey's influence, he 'acquired a steadiness and a sense of purpose, settling down to comment as a matter of routine'. She got him to concentrate on attacking well-known politicians and other figures at the top of society. She persuaded him that if his caricatures were to succeed – strike their targets and sell well – he needed to apply the same approach he'd use on a serious work of art. And that's what he did. Now in his mid-thirties, he became wholly committed to the satirical cartoon, and began to employ a consistently high level of artistic design, something which had been sporadic in his earlier work.

* * *

During the early 1790s, there was a market for lampoons of the royal family. Whether it was Mrs Humphrey who pointed Gillray in this direction, we don't know. King George III was suffering recurring bouts of mental illness. Various treatments were tried, such as opening up his veins to bleed him, putting a pepper mixture on his skin to raise a blister and dosing him up with morphine-rich laudanum, none of which helped.

Paradise Lost: Sin, Death and the Devil (1792). The insulting image of the queen, in the middle, caused great offence to the royal family.

His sickness was a political issue. It threatened Pitt's government, because there was a strong argument that the king's son, Prince George, should take over as regent, and he was a close friend of the Whig opposition leader, Fox (he called the prince, 'Prinny'). Once in power, the prince was likely to dismiss Pitt as prime minister.

So, Pitt played for time, hoping the king would recover. In the row that followed, the queen sided with the prime minister. The battle divided loyalties on both sides, and was portrayed in one of Gillray's most savage caricatures, *Paradise Lost. Sin, Death and the Devil*. In a parody of Milton's epic poem, it showed a naked, saggy-breasted queen with serpents for legs, protecting Pitt – the figure of Death, wearing only a crown – against an attack by Satan, the Lord Chancellor Edward Thurlow.

* * *

So, were caricatures in the late seventeenth and early eighteenth centuries an effective means of attacking those in power? Was Gillray anything more than a foot soldier in the long war between the media and the mighty, unable to influence the course of the battle? Or was he a general?

It's true that a cartoon, printed a few at a time and sold at a high price, would have been seen by many fewer people than those who read, or were read to, from newspapers. So, we might expect a drawing to have much more limited impact. However, that's not the whole story. Gillray's caricatures became must-have items for the titled, moneyed and political classes.

Mrs Humphrey's shop was close to the fashionable gentlemen's clubs, White's and Brooke's, and only 200 yards from the gates of St James' Palace, at that time still the chief residence of the royal family. His latest outrageous attack on some personage well known inside these institutions would have been passed around the moment it was published, with much tittering and tutting, no doubt. And in 1802, a visitor to London was astonished at the reaction when a new Gillray came out. It was like first day of the sales in our day. He wrote, 'The enthusiasm is indescribable when the next drawing appears; it is a veritable madness. You have to make your way in through the crowd with your fists.'

What's more, the lower classes — at least those who found themselves in the neighbourhood of Mrs Humphrey's shop — could enjoy Gillray's jokes and jibes too. In a print of 1808, he showed us how her window was covered from top to bottom, and side to side with his drawings — all identifiable Gillrays. And among those crowding round to look are not only a gentleman and a naval officer but a coachman and a frog-eyed street urchin too. In *Very Slippy Weather*, they're all so wrapped up in the cartoons that they don't notice the elderly chap falling on his bottom. Even clergymen — there are two inside the shop — are customers.

And if the outrage that Gillray's political satires provoked is any measure of their effectiveness, then they score high. On at least one occasion, one of Gillray's victims smashed Mrs Humphrey's windows when a caricature of him appeared there, and several times the caricaturist himself was manhandled by some of the St James' beaus who took exception to the way he'd ridiculed one of their heroes.

However, it was the reactions of those at the political summit of the nation that best illustrate the power of Gillray's satire. Around 1798, he became friendly with the 77-year-old Viscount Bateman, a Pittite. Bateman was also a favourite of George III, and he persuaded Gillray to stop his assaults on the royal family.

This was not just an act of friendship by Gillray. He, like Marchamont Nedham before him and many a journalist after, was happy to work for the highest bidder. He was offered, and accepted, an annual fee of £200, in return for holding off from targeting the king, the queen and the Prince of Wales, as well as Pitt himself. Instead, Gillray agreed to go for the Whigs.

Very Slippy Weather, 1808. Hannah Humphrey's shop; the window, displaying all Gillray's latest caricatures, became a magnet for all classes.

Bateman was pleased with the result. He wrote to Gillray, 'The Opposition are as low as we can wish them. You have been of infinite service in lowering them, and making them ridiculous.' It was the ultimate proof of the power of the caricature in the hands of a skilled artist like Gillray.

The agreement to hold off on the royal family lasted six years until 1803, when presumably the fees dried up. The following year, Gillray produced one of his most colourful compositions, *L'Assemblee Nationale*. The plump couple in the centre-right are Fox and his wife entertaining other members of the Opposition. Giving the meeting a French title added insult to ridicule. However, it was a barely noticeable detail on the edge of the picture that caused a ruckus. On the far right is a figure chopped in half by the edge of the picture. It is recognisable, to those in the know, as the Prince of Wales, and the portly woman on the sofa looking at him is Mrs Fitzherbert. It was a scandalous – and badly kept – secret that the pair had married, an illegal act under the laws of succession because Mrs Fitzherbert was a Catholic.

The prince was so offended by Gillray's portrayal of her that he offered a large sum of money – we don't know how much – to get the print suppressed. However, his agent was slow in

L'Assemblee Nationale, 1804. The figure half seen on the far right was the Prince of Wales. To show him close to Mrs Fitzherbert, the voluptuous woman with the fan on the sofa, caused a scandal.

paying up, and there are enough copies of *L'Assemblee Nationale* still around today to back up the theory that prints continued to be sold for some time before Gillray and Humphrey destroyed the plate, presumably when the cash came in.

The king seemed more able than the prince to shrug off Gillray's attacks on his family. He even used to buy the prints and send them to a university library in Germany, his ancestral home. But then, with his mental health declining, many of his actions were surprising. His son, the Prince of Wales also collected Gillrays, especially the ones that included some savage attack on him. He even had an account running for a number of years at Mrs Humphrey's shop. But the prince's action was more rational – every Gillray portrayal of him would be a talking point among his courtiers, so he needed to keep one step ahead of them.

Sometimes – and we might think this truly bizarre – politicians were desperate to be *included* in Gillray's satires. This was the case with George Canning, elected an MP in 1793 and later to become prime minister. In 1795, he wrote, 'Mr Gillray, the caricaturist has been much solicited to publish a caricature of me and intends doing so', as if the 'soliciting' was nothing to do with him. Canning, however, didn't want his appearance to be a nasty one. 'A great point,' he added, 'to have a good one.' It had become, in Canning's eyes at least, a sign that you'd arrived at the top if you featured in Mrs Humphrey's shop window.

A vicar called John Sneyd acted as Canning's go-between and, in 1795 was making suggestions to Gillray as to how he might present the young MP in one of his caricatures. Nothing happened at first, and Canning wrote to Sneyd, asking, 'Have you heard anything from Mr Gillray lately? And do you know how soon after my *coming in* I am likely to *come out*?' The following year, he became a government minister and revealed his motives in another letter to Sneyd. What he liked best about his new position, he wrote, was 'the sort of consideration that it gives one in the eyes of the country'. And he went on to bemoan the fact that when he'd peered into Mrs Humphrey's shop window that morning, he couldn't find himself in Gillray's latest caricature.

Gillray was spurred into doing something for Canning by a sudden shock. On 23 January 1796, he was arrested and brought before a magistrate on a charge of blasphemy for a drawing he'd done called *The Wise Men Offering*. This showed the Whig opposition leader, Fox, kissing the bottom of the Prince Regent's newly born daughter, Princess Charlotte. Nothing came of the case. There's a suggestion that Canning intervened to save Gillray.

Whether or not that's true, the young minister did then finally turn up in a Gillray caricature, but it was hardly a big splash. In a patriotic illustration with dozens of jumbled characters called *Promis'd Horrors of the French Invasion*, Canning is one of two figures hanged from a lamppost – apparently by the French

More Pigs than Teats, 1806. Its alternative title was 'The New Litter of Hungry Grunters Sucking John Bull's Old-Sow to Death.' Greedy ministers in Lord Grenville's government are sucking the country dry.

– somewhere near the back. He made one more appearance three months later, and that was it. Was Gillray, in his relations with Canning, making a principled stand against pressure from the mighty? Probably not. It's more likely that he just wasn't inspired by anything Canning had done, so he didn't bother including him.

In his last few productive years, Gillray was much more independent of political sponsors or paymasters, and there was a late flowering of his artistry and imagination. It was the only time in his career that his satire was directed with zeal against the party in power. Pitt – after his long reign over Parliament – had died in 1806, and the Whig government of Lord Grenville was now in charge of the country. With derision and irony, it was known as the 'Ministry of all the Talents'. Over a period of sixteen months, Gillray produced twenty-five plates attacking the government. The new leaders were shown driven by greed, egoism and self-interest. One of the most telling of these prints was *More Pigs than Teats*.

*** *** ***

Gillray's character has always been a mystery. By one account, 'His natural temperament was excitable'. By another – from Henry Angelo, his near neighbour – 'Poor Gillray was always hypped.' The word then meant depressed. It's led to the theory that he may have suffered from bipolar disorder, with occasional bouts of manic activity followed by depression.

We can't know, 200 years later, if that's true, but Hannah Humphrey was certainly a constant in his life. Her stability helped him through the bad times, and gave him steady focus at others. She was often alongside him at fashionable social events. Viscount Bateman's letters to Gillray invariably contain some such phrase as, 'Give my kindest compliments to Mrs Humphrey'. She was an anchor of normality and

ordinariness in a life devoted to images of craziness and savagery.
When she was separated from him, usually because of a holiday
at Brighton, she'd pop into her letters to him some practical
reminder. In 1798, it was, 'P.S. Don't forget the pigeon pie'.
In 1804, it was, 'I hope you take care of the cat'.

By 1806, the years of eye-straining work over the copper
engraving plates began to take their toll. Gillray started to wear
spectacles. He took to drink and, by one account, tried to lose
himself 'in strange scenes and rough company'. He missed several
delivery deadlines for the latest engravings. His eyesight became
worse and, increasingly deprived of the work he loved, in 1807
he had a mental and physical breakdown. Mrs Humphrey, who
realised he needed to be given time and space to recuper-
ate, arranged for him to take a room close to the seafront at
Margate, 80 miles east of London. She wrote to him with details
of when she would join him, and asked if he could meet her at
Canterbury. The letter ends:

> I pray God grant believe me when I say I am your affectionate friend.
> H. Humphrey
> PS Canterbury not Rochester remember.
> I enclose a two pound note for fear you should run short.

He recovered enough to do sporadic work, but by 1810 he'd
become both blind and – by contemporary accounts – insane.

The following year, he tried to commit suicide. However,
it was a grotesque and sad failure. He felt his way upstairs to
the attic of Mrs Humphrey's shop, opened the window and
threw himself forward. What he didn't know in his blindness
was that iron bars had been fitted in front. His head became
jammed between them. The chairman of White's Club, some
of whose senior members had suffered the caricaturist's
fiercest attacks, happened to be passing, and he rescued the
unfortunate Gillray.

Hannah Humphrey cared for her 'Gilly' during these last years, until he died in 1815. He was buried at St James' Church, where the two of them had almost got married. At her direction, a flat stone covered his grave with the inscription:

In memory of Mr James Gillray
THE CARICATURIST
Who departed this life 1st June 1815
Aged 58 years.

Three years later, Mrs Hannah Humphrey followed him. She was in her early to mid-seventies – we don't know her exact age.

***

James Gillray was not the only political caricaturist in this period. Others, such as Thomas Rowlandson and George and Isaac Cruikshank, owed much, as did Gillray, to the tradition begun in the previous generation by William Hogarth. But Gillray's lively imagination, venomous wit, diligent craftsmanship and a sense of design that took his work at times into the realm of high art, set him apart.

Focus, application and determination were needed too. These qualities were not totally lacking in Gillray, but it was Hannah Humphrey who kept him on track. Without her, fewer of those in power would have found themselves looking ridiculous in the eyes of their peers, and without Hannah Humphrey, we today might not have had quite so many Gillrays of such high quality to appreciate.

James Gillray has become known as the 'father of the political cartoon', and nearer our own time, satirical artists such as David Low, Ralph Steadman and Gerald Scarfe have all acknowledged their debt to him.

***

In the last year of Gillray's life, there was a revolution. For the first time, the press became truly an instrument of mass communication. Before 1814, newspapers, satirical prints and any other printed information or comment was produced by a slow, laborious process. The machines in Mrs Humphrey's shop, like others at the time, could manage at best a meagre twenty printed sheets an hour. But in that year, *The Times* newspaper of London introduced the steam-powered press, which could turn out tens of thousands of copies in the same amount of time. Suddenly, newspapers and magazines, soon to include illustrations, could reach a mass readership.

And it wasn't just a technological revolution. Now it was within the power of newspapers, with their huge popular circulations, to bring thousands of people out onto the streets, threatening a political revolution, and at the same time able to spread the word quickly to many more across the land. That's what the mighty were frightened of. So, let's go to Manchester on a sunny Monday in the year 1819 to find out more.

6

NINETEENTH-CENTURY RADICALS

Guerrilla Journalism

> As the 'Peterloo Massacre' cannot be otherwise than grossly libellous, you will probably deem it right to proceed by arresting the publishers.
>
> *Home Office to Manchester Magistrate, 25 August 1819*

Whitworth, Joseph – killed by a musket ball in the head. Downes, Margaret – dreadfully cut in the breast. Buckley, Thomas – sabred and stabbed with a bayonet. Fildes, William – infant, trampled by the cavalry when his mother was knocked down. Jones, Sarah – beaten by constables' truncheons, left seven children motherless. Rhodes, John – a cut on the head, by which he lost much blood. Heys, Mary – mother of six children, pregnant, trampled by a cavalry horse, suffered fits almost daily until she died giving birth to a premature baby (fate unknown).

Sixty thousand people had gathered at St Peter's Fields in Manchester on 16 August 1819 to demand the right to vote. They were attacked by cavalry, volunteer yeomen and special constables. We still don't know exactly how many were killed. It was somewhere between eleven and fifteen. Between 420 and

Peterloo Massacre: A detail from a contemporary print titled 'Dreadful Scene at Manchester Meeting of Reformers 16 August 1819'. Top left, the yeomen are on the speakers' platform making arrests. Down below, the mounted cavalrymen are shown among the crowd hacking at random with their sabres.

500 were injured. What the *Manchester Observer* christened the 'Peterloo Massacre' sparked one of the bitterest wars in history between those in power and many of Britain's newspapers.

Conditions in Britain at the time were a perfect breeding ground for revolution. The end of the Napoleonic Wars in 1815 had left many in the now fast-growing cities without jobs and starving. The war had been financed by burdensome taxes. Wartime trade restrictions had seen food prices shoot up, while the introduction of labour-saving machinery had put many out of work, with the only option often to join the army or the navy. But come the peace, they were no longer needed and hundreds of thousands were jobless again. The Tory Government had then added to the misery of the poor by passing the first of the Corn Laws in 1815 in an attempt to help British agriculture by imposing tariffs on imported grain. The result was a leap in the price of bread and flour.

Radical Whigs, especially in the most industrialised areas of the north of England, now started to believe that the political system itself was the problem, and these radicals pointed to the gross unfairness of the parliamentary voting rules which hadn't changed for almost 400 years. So, for example, the tiny village of Old Sarum in Wiltshire – which had only one voter – was represented by two Members of Parliament, while the Lancashire urban centres of Manchester, Salford, Bolton, Blackburn, Rochdale, Ashton-under-Lyne and Oldham, with a combined population of close to a million, were also represented by just two MPs. And what's more, the only people who could vote were men who owned freehold land with an annual rental value of 40 shillings or more, which was about 2–3 per cent of the population.

The injustice of the system was highlighted in the columns of a growing number of radical newspapers. The *Manchester Observer*, for instance, set up in 1818, was aimed at those in the lowest ranks of society, more and more of whom could now read, and it was soon selling 4,000 copies a week in the north-west. At the beginning of 1819, the paper's editors founded the Patriotic Union Society to campaign for parliamentary reform. It was the *Observer* and the Patriotic Unionists who organised the mass rally which was held on 16 August at St Peter's Fields. It was to be addressed by the best-known radical orator of the day, Henry Hunt.

By this stage, there was already mounting tension on the streets of Manchester. In July that year, the town's magistrates had written to the Home Secretary warning that a 'general rising' was imminent. The 'deep distress of the manufacturing classes', they declared, was being worked on by the 'unbounded

The radical activist Henry Hunt in a watercolour by Adam Buck, c. 1810.

liberty of the press' and 'the harangues of a few desperate demagogues'. And the magistrates admitted they were at a loss as to how to stop the flood of dangerous ideas.

The founder of the *Observer*, Joseph Johnson, wrote to Henry Hunt ahead of the rally, saying, 'Nothing but ruin and starvation stare one in the face. The state of this district is truly dreadful, and I believe nothing but the greatest exertions can prevent an insurrection.'

But unknown to Johnson and Hunt, the letter was intercepted by government spies and copied before being sent to its destination. Government ministers interpreted it to mean that an insurrection was being planned, and a cavalry regiment, the 15th Hussars, was put on standby in Manchester. To try to avoid the rally being classed as seditious, the *Observer* reported that its specific aim would be 'to consider the propriety of adopting the most LEGAL and EFFECTUAL means of obtaining a reform in the Common House of Parliament'.

The organisers were also determined to make the rally as respectable as possible. Earlier mass meetings had been mocked by government-supporting newspapers for the ragged, dirty appearance of the men taking part and for their disorganised conduct. So, instructions were sent out that 'Cleanliness, Sobriety, Order and Peace' and a 'prohibition of all weapons of offence or defence' were to be observed throughout the demonstration.

St Peter's Fields was a large, open piece of land, and as the crowds started to gather on that warm, sunny day, the magistrates took up their positions in a house on the south-west corner to observe what would happen. In case of serious trouble, they'd ordered an armed force to wait at the ready nearby. It consisted of 600 men and horses of the 15th Hussars, several hundred infantrymen, 400 men of the Cheshire Yeomanry, 400 special constables, and 120 cavalrymen of the Manchester and Salford Yeomanry. Two 6-pounder cannons had been wheeled out as well. The *Observer* had already written about the Manchester and Salford Yeomanry, a troop of part-time volunteers, describing them as 'a few fools and a greater proportion of coxcombs, who imagine they acquire considerable importance by wearing regimentals'. The military commander for the north-west, Sir John Bing, was absent, watching his horses race at York.

The crowds arrived in organised contingents from each village and town, many in their Sunday best clothes. Soon there were so many that, in parts, it was said, 'their hats seemed to touch'. Around midday, several hundred special constables were led onto the field. They forced their way in among the crowd. It looked like they were trying make a corridor through the throng between the house where the magistrates were watching and the main platform. Some of the demonstrators guessed it was part of a plan to arrest the speakers. They formed a human barrier around the platform to stop that happening.

Hunt himself arrived around 1 p.m., accompanied not only by a number of leading radicals but also by the managing editor and the publisher of the *Manchester Observer*, as well as several newspaper reporters, including John Smith of the *Liverpool Mercury*, Edward Baines of the *Leeds Mercury*, and from London, John Tyas of *The Times*. The profession of reporter was fast becoming established, and newspapers now wanted their own accounts of major events.

The crowd became excited, clapping and cheering when they saw Hunt. The chairman of magistrates, William Hulton must have let his nerves get the better of his judgement, because he jumped to the conclusion that the meeting was getting out of hand. So, he issued an arrest warrant for Hunt and three other well-known radicals with him on the platform. The chief constable advised him that he couldn't carry out the order without armed assistance, so Hulton summoned the military, explaining that the magistrates considered 'the Civil Power wholly inadequate to preserve the peace'.

The Manchester and Salford Yeomanry were the first to arrive. Sixty of them came at a gallop with their swords drawn. One trooper knocked down a woman as he approached through the street, killing her 2-year-old son when he was thrown from her arms. Some reports alleged that the yeomen were drunk. They were ordered to proceed to the speakers so they could be arrested. It was now 1:40 p.m.

The Yeomen's horses weren't accustomed to crowds, and they reared and plunged as people tried to get out of their way. As they closed in on the platform, the cavalrymen became stuck in the throng, and in a panic started to hack about them with their sabres. The deputy chief constable managed to get through, and he arrested Hunt and a number of others, including Tyas, *The Times* correspondent. In his report, Tyas wrote that the yeomen then started 'cutting most indiscriminately to the right and to the left'. It was only at this point, he wrote, that missiles were thrown at the military, and 'the Manchester and Salford Yeomanry lost all command of temper'.

Hulton, the chairman of magistrates, watching from the edge of the square, turned to the commander in charge of the rest of the troops and shouted, 'Good God, Sir, don't you see they are attacking the Yeomanry! Disperse the meeting!' The 15th Hussars formed themselves into a line stretching across the length of St Peter's Fields and charged into the crowd.

At the same time, the Cheshire Yeomanry surged forward from the opposite side. But the people on the field couldn't get out. The main exit route into Peter Street was blocked by the 88th Regiment of Foot, standing with bayonets fixed. One cavalry officer, at least, showed some compassion and he screamed at the yeomen, 'For shame! For shame! Gentlemen. Forbear, forbear! The people cannot get away!'

Eventually, the way out was cleared, but there was another ten minutes of blood and mayhem before most of the crowd managed to escape. Only the wounded, those trying to help them and the bodies of the dead were left behind.   Word spread quickly throughout the city and to nearby towns. Rioting broke out in the streets of Manchester, and in the New Cross area troops fired on a crowd. Calm wasn't restored until the next morning. In Stockport, Oldham and Macclesfield street disturbances continued through the next day.

* * *

The Times reporter, John Tyas, who'd been arrested along with Hunt, was held in prison for three days. He'd arrived at the rally as no supporter of parliamentary reform. But after what he had witnessed, he changed his mind. *The Times* itself mounted a campaign against the action of the magistrates at St Peter's Fields. It told its readers in an editorial, 'A hundred of the King's unarmed subjects have been sabred by a body of cavalry in the presence of those Magistrates whose sworn duty it is to protect and preserve the life of the meanest Englishmen'.

And the paper added on 19 August:

Was that [meeting] at Manchester an 'unlawful assembly'? Was the notice of it unlawful? We believe not. Was the subject proposed for discussion an unlawful object? Assuredly not. Was any thing done at this meeting before the cavalry rode in upon

it, either contrary to law or in breach of the peace? No such cir-
cumstance is recorded in any of the statements which have yet
reached our hands.

One of those who died of his wounds was John Lees, a former
soldier who'd fought with Wellington at the Battle of Waterloo
four years earlier. 'At Waterloo,' he told a friend on his deathbed,
'it was man to man, but there [at St Peter's Fields] it was down-
right murder.' The *Manchester Observer* picked this up and coined
the phrase 'the Peterloo Massacre' and it's stuck ever since. In its
issue of 28 August, it wrote:

> Just published No. 1 price two-pence of PETERLOO MASSACRE.
> Containing a full, true and faithful account of the inhuman
> murders, woundings and other monstrous Cruelties exercised
> by a set of INFERNALS (miscalled Soldiers) upon unarmed and
> distressed People.

The paper went on to claim that the Manchester Royal
Infirmary had been cleared of patients in advance of the rally,
thus showing that the authorities had planned the slaughter
beforehand. The *Observer*'s editor, James Wroe, also published a
pamphlet entitled *The Peterloo Massacre: A Faithful Narrative of the
Events*. It was priced at 2*d* a copy, and sold out on every print
run for fourteen weeks. And there was something new – it was
distributed around the country.

Government ministers were incensed, and they reacted
to printed words they didn't like as those in power had often
done since the days of Henry VIII – they prosecuted those
responsible, and even some of those who had nothing to do
with producing the offensive articles. Street newspaper sellers
were arrested, charged and thrown into jail. Wroe, the *Observer*'s
editor, faced fifteen counts of seditious libel, and in what must
have been nothing other than an attempt to intimidate him, the

The first edition of *The Manchester Guardian*, 5 May 1821.

same charges were brought against his wife and his two brothers. He handed over editorship of the paper to Thomas Evans. He too was prosecuted for seditious libel and imprisoned for eighteen months. The paper closed down one year after Peterloo.

But other radical papers sprang from its grave. In its final edition, the *Observer* recommended its readers now switch to a new member of the press, *The Manchester Guardian*, which, said the *Observer*, combined 'principles of complete independence, and zealous attachment to the cause of reform, with active and spirited management, [and] is a journal in every way worthy of your confidence and support'. *The Manchester Guardian* – today the national paper renamed *The Guardian* – has thrived ever since, still subscribing to those principles.

Another newcomer inspired by Peterloo was the *Republican*. The radical political journalist, Richard Carlile, had been scheduled to speak at St Peter's Fields after Henry Hunt. He witnessed the soldiers' first attacks on the crowd before being smuggled away by friends and put on the mail coach to London. He published his account of what he'd seen in the radical *Sherwin's Weekly Political Register*. The newspaper vendors' placards around London declared 'Horrid Massacres at Manchester'.

The government promptly shut down the *Political Register*. Within eleven days, Carlile had launched the *Republican*. Its motto was, 'From the bottom of my soul I hate despotic kings and ministers of state'. In its first issue, Carlile suggested, 'Every man in Manchester who avows his opinions on the necessity of reform, should never go unarmed – retaliation has become a duty, and revenge an act of justice'.

He also claimed that women had been singled out for attack by the soldiers during the massacre. Female reform societies had become common in north-west England. Many members came to the St Peter's Fields rally. They stood out, dressed all in white and carrying their own flags. Carlile claimed that fewer than 12 per cent of the crowd were female, whereas 25 per cent of the casualties were women.

Carlile was prosecuted and found guilty of blasphemy and seditious libel. He was fined the huge sum of £1,500 and sentenced to three years in Dorchester Prison. From his jail cell, he kept writing for the *Republican*, which was now published by his wife, Jane Carlile. It outsold even *The Times*, which had been established for forty-five years. Other radical journals – with fanciful names such as *Gorgon* and *Black Dwarf* – joined in the attacks on the government. Through the power of the press, horror at the terrible events of Peterloo spread across the country.

The government, meanwhile, started to believe that Britain was heading for an armed revolution. Ministers used the courts to suppress any likely insurgents, and within sixteen months of Peterloo, every significant working-class radical reformer was in jail. At the same time, the decision was taken to tighten up the law against dangerous meetings and radical newspapers.

The Six Acts, as the new laws were known, decreed much harsher punishments for those found guilty of seditious or blasphemous writing – they could now be sentenced to fourteen years transportation. Although the law wasn't enforced with much vigour and was repealed in 1824, during its short life it became, like Peterloo, a symbol of the despotic tendency of the government.

One of the Six Acts, however, hit home much harder. It extended stamp duty to those radical papers who'd previously avoided paying the tax by claiming their journals weren't newspapers but comment pamphlets. And at the same time, the tax was upped to 4*d* per copy sold. Radical papers, whose subscribers were the poor working classes, were hardest hit – as the government intended. It was reckoned they could afford to pay only 1 or 2 pence a time. To cover the tax, a price of at least 5 or 6 pence a copy would have to be charged, way beyond the pockets of most of their readers.

It was the beginning of the end for the radical press. What one commentator has called 'guerrilla journalism', for its ability to damage governments with attacks mounted from the sidelines of power, would soon be defeated. Over the next two to three decades, reformist and anarchist-leaning papers were driven out of business. It was left to some in the mainstream newspaper industry to represent a moderate form of radical journalism.

* * *

So how did this happen? The answer is – through a combination of economics and new technology.

Let's take the economics first. Newspapers had always been a business, regardless of whether the publishers saw their aim as pushing political opinions or not. It was expensive to print and distribute large numbers of papers, never mind having to pay the government's stamp duty. And the more pages to the paper, and the faster and more often you wanted to publish, the more expensive the work became. Thousands of tuppences paid by readers just couldn't cover the cost. Advertising was essential. And the simple fact was that the working-class readers of the radical papers didn't have the spare cash to be great consumers. So, the ads for shoe blacking, universal remedy pills or positions for ladies' maids were much more likely to appear in newspapers that appealed to a comfortable middle-class audience.

The experience of the extreme radical publisher Henry Hetherington tells it all. His *Poor Man's Guardian*, started in 1831, declared itself to be 'A weekly newspaper for the people, established contrary to "Law", to try the power of "Might" against "Right"'.

It was against the law because he refused to pay the stamp duty, and instead of using government-approved paper embossed with a stamp to show the tax had been paid, he placed the image of a printing press with the words 'Knowledge is Power' underneath. Hetherington made no secret of the paper's belief in revolution. 'It is property which has made tyrants,' he wrote. 'Down with property.'

At its height in 1833, the *Poor Man's Guardian* was selling 15,000 copies a week, a remarkable number given that it wasn't circulated outside London. Its popularity had been enhanced by the Reform Act of the previous year, which the radicals saw as a sell-out – it extended the vote only to a few more middle-class men.

The government hit back again with its oldest weapon. Eight hundred of the paper's street sellers were prosecuted, and Hetherington himself was jailed twice, once for six months and once for twelve. But it was the struggle to make ends meet, just as much as the prosecutions, that in the end did for Hetherington and his radical papers. This anarchist now surrendered to capitalism. In 1834, he launched a new paper called the *Twopenny Dispatch*. Though it billed itself as a supporter of the Chartist movement for political reform, Hetherington realised that reformist politics alone wouldn't sell enough to keep the paper going, so he promised something a bit more earthy as well – in the words of its first edition, 'Fun and frolic … murders, rapes, suicides, burnings, maimings, theatricals, races, pugilism', a formula that might warm the heart of any sensation-loving editor of a Murdoch-owned tabloid in the twenty-first century.

But, despite the newfound business skills of men like Hetherington, the competition was too much. And it was made worse by an unexpected government action in 1836. In that year, stamp duty was slashed from 4 pence to 1. This was not some sudden conversion to the cause of radicalism on the part of ministers – quite the reverse. They were gambling that the effect would be to swamp the market with popular papers so that the more dangerous sections of the press would be drowned by the competition and put out of business. And it wasn't just the anarcho-radicalist newspapers that the government was worried about. That pillar of respectability, *The Times*, had, after Peterloo, become an increasing problem too.

And that brings us to the second factor that was changing the newspaper industry forever, and leaving little room for the extremist press – technology.

* * *

On the evening of 28 November 1814, journalists and printers at *The Times*' London offices had been told that the next morning's edition was being held – delayed, that is – because a big news story was about to break. But it wasn't what anyone expected. The story was the paper itself.

At 6 in the morning, the staff were astonished to find that the complete day's paper had already been printed and was ready to hit the streets. It had been produced by a new steam-powered cylinder press which could turn out 1,100 double-sided sheets an hour. The whole operation had been kept secret to avoid any violence from the pressmen, whose jobs were now at risk.

A Koenig steam-powered press, the model used to print *The Times* in 1814.

Using cylinders to press paper against type was nothing new, but a series of inventions during the nineteenth century would speed up the process exponentially. The first use of steam to power the process in 1810 increased production fivefold. Then, in 1813, the old way of inking the plates by hand with a leather swab was replaced by automated inking with rollers fed from a small duct. Over the next decades, with further refinements to the technology, the printing process became more and more streamlined, until by 1844 it reached 8,000 copies an hour, by 1865 it was 12,000, and soon after, 40,000.

But of course, this newfangled machinery was expensive. It required owners to invest, and risk, large sums of capital, money that might not be recouped for several years. The kind of cash needed was beyond the means of most of the publishers of radical papers with their limited access to advertisers and their low selling price. But without a rotary press, they couldn't hope to compete with other popular papers whose sales figures were now rocketing into the tens of thousands and even the hundreds of thousands. And so it was that technology and economics came together to bring down the curtain on the brief spell in the spotlight that the radical press had enjoyed.

Newspapers like the *Republican* and the *Poor Man's Guardian* had, without doubt, strengthened the Whig demands for parliamentary reform, but it was a hollow victory. The meagre extension of the franchise in the 1832 Reform Act wasn't followed by significant growth in democratic representation until 1867. The Reform Act of that year for the first time extended the vote to some in the working classes. Around one and a half million better-off men were now enfranchised. But that still left two-thirds of all men without a vote, and of course gave nothing to women. Equal and universal suffrage didn't arrive in Britain until 109 years after Peterloo. In the nineteenth-century press campaign for political reform, the mighty had won hands down.

✳ ✳ ✳

However, that wasn't the whole story. Technology and economics did bring about one massive and unexpected change to what newspapers printed in their columns. And it was a change which benefitted the growth of democracy and, in its own way, threatened the mighty.

It was one thing for newspapers to be able to print 40,000 copies an hour; it was quite another to sell them all. To do that meant that what was printed in those papers, day after day, week after week, had to have a wide appeal. So, how would newspaper editors achieve that? One way – and we need to emphasise, one way among many – was to establish a reputation for accurate and unbiased reporting, whether of political debates, street riots, or even wars. This was something new.

As we've seen over the past three centuries, writers and publishers had been interested only in winning over readers to their cause, whether that was Catholicism, Cromwell's Republic, or the Whig opposition to Pitt's Tory Government, and they'd done it by skewing their accounts of events and mixing together facts and propaganda. Now, in the mid-eighteenth century, for largely economic reasons, some newspapers were winning respect by giving their readers the plain facts so they could make up their own minds. That was something that would capture the attention of readers regardless of their political views.

The way had been paved for independent truth telling during the previous century, when John Wilkes had won the right to report the proceedings in Parliament. But now, for the first time, objectivity spilled over into the other news columns. *The Times* had led the way. Under its first great liberal editor, Thomas Barnes, who presided over the paper from 1817 to 1841, it earned the nickname the 'Thunderer'. By the mid-1800s it had become a great moulder of public opinion, and its circulation had grown from 5,000 in 1815 to 40,000 in 1850.

However, objective reporting didn't mean that papers, like *The Times*, couldn't take up a partisan stance – most did, but more and more often over the decades ahead, they tended to keep opinion pieces separate from news stories. As, C.P. Scott, the influential editor of *The Manchester Guardian*, wrote in the paper's centenary year, 1921, 'Comment is free, but facts are sacred'. Of course, we can't pretend that all newspapers have always abided by this principle. But it has at least become one of the most cherished values of a free press.

***

In the United States, as we've seen, freedom of the press is enshrined in the Constitution. So, what about in Britain? Did the battles of the nineteenth century result in some kind of written or legal guarantee that journalists and newspaper publishers would no longer be persecuted for what they printed? The simple answer is: No.

The right to a free press was often discussed by campaigners and political philosophers. In 1819, the *Republican* printed a letter which claimed, 'Without the Liberty of the Press, the public authority can neither be enlightened or responsible'. And in 1869, John Stuart Mill wrote that free speech and a free press guaranteed that 'the most diverse set of voices will be able to compete in the marketplace of ideas'. But no law protecting that liberty has ever been passed in England, Wales or Scotland. It just became accepted practice that a democracy can't function unless voters have access to the facts and to a full range of opinions. Of course, once you've accepted the right to a free press – whether or not it's enshrined in law – you also have to accept that you're handing over huge power to the media.

In the eighteenth century, it had been declared that the mighty in the land were divided into three separate estates: the monarchy, the House of Lords and the House of Commons. In 1841, the philosopher and historian, Thomas Carlyle wrote that in the Reporter's Gallery of the House of Commons there now sat 'a Fourth Estate, more important far than they all'. Taken at face value, Carlyle was recognising the power and legitimacy of newspapers to influence popular opinion.

But there's another way of looking at it. You could say that reporters were no longer on the outside of the tent pouring in scorn on politicians. Instead, journalists had been sucked into the Establishment and were now drinking, dining and fraternising with those who should have been their enemies. But then that has, and always will be, the ambiguity of the relationship between the media and the mighty.

* * *

The newfound practice of objective reporting was about to be put to a severe test. In 1853, hostilities broke out between Russia and an alliance in which Britain played a leading role. With so many lives at stake, how would the Crimean War be reported back home? The pressures on a correspondent sent out to the front line, caught up in the dangers of the fighting, and often hated by the generals, would be far greater than on any parliamentary reporter. *The Times* took its responsibilities seriously, so let's go and find out how the world's first war correspondents managed the job.

THE CRIMEAN WAR

That Miserable Scribbler

I trust the army will lynch *The Times* correspondent.

Sydney Herbert (1810–61), Secretary of War 1852–55

Billy Russell was a street-fighting man. He'd wanted to be a soldier, and as a young lad growing up just outside Dublin in the 1820s he used to get up before daybreak and run down to the barracks in Jobstown to watch the men marching and drilling on the parade ground. As soon as he was old enough, he tried several times to enlist, but his grandfather, Captain Jack Kelly (Billy said he didn't believe he'd been 'captain' of anything) managed to stop him each time and drag him back home.

By the age of 18, Billy was a student at Dublin's Trinity College, and it was there that – deprived of his boyhood dream of serving in the army – he took to fighting in the sectarian street battles that were common in the city at that time. Trinity men were Protestants, and Billy Russell and his fellow students battled against the Roman Catholic lads. 'There were glorious doings,' he wrote later. 'We frequently parted with broken heads.'

In his more studious moments he was training to be a doctor, but the sight of dead bodies made him feel sick, so he soon gave that up. Strange, when we consider that later as a war reporter, he would often be landed in the midst of the freshly slaughtered corpses of soldiers.

At the age of 21, William 'Billy' Russell became a journalist. It happened by accident rather than as any planned career move, and it was the experience of his street-fighting days that tipped him into it. In 1841 his cousin, who worked for *The Times* of London, asked for his help reporting the Irish elections. Campaigning was a violent affair, with much brawling between supporters of the different parties. That was something Russell knew all about, and he was in the thick of it. His job was to write up what he saw, and he soon discovered he could do it with immediacy and passion. One of the first accounts he wrote for *The Times* read:

> I have to record an atrocious attack made this day upon a harmless young gentleman named King, who, while standing near his own house in the middle of the day not twenty yards from the barracks, and within a hundred yards of an immense force of military and police, was attacked by a number of pitiless miscreants, beaten, trampled under foot, and left helpless on the road. He is now, or rather his inanimate body is, lying in the Infirmary, his life despaired.

It was dangerous work, and he ended his report, 'I cannot procure accurate information as to the state of the suburbs; in fact, I have been warned that I am a marked man'.

The Times editor in London, John Delane, loved it, and he published it as well as an editorial condemning the violence. The paper now started to commission Russell directly to go wherever the action was. On one occasion in Athlone, he was talking to the Tory candidate when a crowd of women appeared and started screaming at him, then slapping, pinching and scratching him, before dragging him off towards the River Shannon. He only avoided a ducking by the timely intervention of the police.

He was so covered in mud that he had to be wiped down 'like a horse in the stable-yard'.

But Russell had made it. When the elections were over, Delane invited him to London, and gave him a contract to work for *The Times* as a correspondent.

In 1849, he got his first taste of war reporting. He was sent to cover the fighting between the Danish Army and the German-backed troops of Schleswig-Holstein. He arrived in time to report the Battle of Idstedt. But, despite the fact that he came under fire and received a flesh wound (he didn't bother reporting where exactly he was hit), he seemed – for the moment at least – to have lost the spark in his writing. His account of the fighting lacked the verve of his Irish elections writing. The Danes, he wrote, 'harassed the posts to the right of the Holsteiners soon after midnight, which kept the men under arms, and in some degree fatigued them before the battle itself commenced'.

* * *

By 1854, Britain itself was at war. It was fighting alongside the French and the Turkish Ottomans against the Russians, with the action centred on the Crimean Peninsula in the Black Sea. 'The war,' wrote Queen Victoria, 'is popular beyond belief.' And that meant a demand for news. Until now, newspapers had often paid officers to send them dispatches about what was happening – unsatisfactory because they were both too busy and too biased to do much of a journalist's job.

The Times had already broken new ground by sending its own man to cover the Schleswig War, and Delane now called Russell into his office and asked him to accompany the British forces who were about to embark. Russell was reluctant. He was now married with two children, and didn't want to be away from his family for long. But he accepted when Delane assured him it would only be for a couple of months, and 'depend upon it,'

William Russell in his makeshift military uniform.

he told Russell, 'you will have a pleasant trip'. In fact, it would be two years before he was home again. And 'pleasant' would hardly be the word for it.

Almost as soon as Russell arrived alongside the army, he was shocked by what he found. He wrote to Delane, 'The management is infamous. Could you believe it? – the sick have not a bed to lie upon' while their officer 'only seems anxious about the men being clean-shaved, their necks well-stiffened and waist belts tight'.

The expedition's leader was Lord Raglan, who'd shown himself to be brave when he'd fought alongside Wellington, but that was forty years ago, and he was now 65. The officers beneath him were a poor lot, whose qualifications often amounted to little more than noble birth and a dissolute lifestyle. Outstanding among them was the Earl of Cardigan, commander of the Light Brigade, a hard-drinking, arrogant adulterer, who'd stood trial – and been acquitted by his peers – of murdering a fellow officer in a duel. Cardigan and his colleagues brought with them a French chef, a selection from their wine cellars, their servants, as well as shotguns and hunting dogs. It was all going to be a frolic. And once they arrived in the Crimea, they were greeted by some of their gentlemanly civilian chums who'd turned up to watch the fun – i.e. the war.

Russell wrote to Delane, 'Am I to tell these things, or hold my tongue?' Delane told him to go ahead. However, Delane was less than honest in this reply. In the months ahead, he indulged in some self-censorship. If he felt that a report from Russell with information critical of the army might be seen as unpatriotic, he sometimes didn't publish it. So, *Times* readers were not always aware of the shortcomings and incompetence that Russell witnessed. However, he did see to it that Russell's work was not wasted. He would forward those of the correspondent's letters that didn't make into *The Times* columns to his contacts in the government. In addition, the 'unpatriotic' reports often provided ammunition that he could use in editorials.

The combination of Russell's witnessing of events and Delane's diplomatic manoeuvres would soon play a part in bringing down the government.

***

Russell was not alone in reporting the war, other newspapers had their correspondents on site too. The *London Daily News* had sent out a 22-year-old reporter named Edwin Godkin. Godkin had also spotted the incompetence. He reported that a British supply officer had been sent to Rumania and Bulgaria to organise the purchase of cavalry horses. 'The ignorance which dictated this step,' wrote Godkin, 'is scarcely conceivable.' A single enquiry of the local consul, he added, would have revealed that there were very few horses in the whole of that area.

The military hierarchy out in the Crimea were only too aware of the damage that Russell, Godkin and their kind could inflict. Their first-hand accounts of the army's blunders and secrets could undermine support for the war back home, not to mention the harm they'd do to the generals' own personal reputations. So, the army started to make life as difficult as it could for the press. Lord Raglan refused to recognise the correspondents, and gave orders they should be denied food or any other assistance. And when Russell pitched his tent within army lines, he soon found it had been cut down.

Russell tried to give himself some semblance of authority by cobbling together a sort of uniform: an officer's cap, a rifleman's jacket, what were described as 'butcher's boots', and from somewhere he got hold of a sword. He also bought a horse – 'a fiddle-headed, ewe-necked beast' – and during one of the first actions at the Battle of Malakoff, he rode up and down trying to attach himself to one of the divisional commanders, all of whom told him to clear off.

He missed most of the fighting, so he tried to piece together what had happened by interviewing those officers who agreed to talk to him. This was not always as difficult as the official policy of non-co-operation with journalists might suggest. He found men coming up to him, anxious to tell all about their own alleged bravery so they might look heroes in the eyes of friends and family reading *The Times* back home. But exaggerated tales of derring-do were hardly a guarantee of accuracy, and Russell accumulated a mass of contradictory versions of the fighting. With a lack of factual detail, the report he sent back to London about the assault on the Malakoff redoubt slumped into toe-curling cliché. His report read, 'The French, like a swarm of bees, issue forth from their trenches close to the doomed Malakoff, scrambled up its faces and were through the embrasures in the twinkling of an eye.'

***

Delane, back in the London office, appreciated the difficulties under which Russell was working, and he lobbied the War Office to improve the facilities granted to *The Times* correspondent. And he succeeded. That must be a credit to Delane's diplomatic skills in getting ministers to understand that Russell's objective accounts of the war were useful to them. And of course, the fact that Delane himself was acting as a low-level censor – withholding some of Russell's reports and routing them through to the government instead – must have helped.

Word was passed from the War Office in London to the high command in the Crimea that *The Times*' man should be assisted in his work. So, by the time the army had moved on to Balaclava, Russell was no longer being given the cold shoulder. As a result, on the morning of what was to become the most famous battle of the Crimean War, Russell found himself sitting astride his horse alongside Lord Raglan and his adjutants on a high plateau overlooking the troops on the plain below, in Russell's words, 'as the stage and those upon it are seen from the box of a theatre'.

Down in front of him, Russell could see a green valley, enclosed on all sides by mountains, with the ships in the harbour at Sevastopol just visible to the right. In the centre, at the mouth of the valley, nearest to Russell and the generals, squadrons of British cavalry were regrouping. It was clear to those watching from on high that these men had retreated before a vastly superior number of Russian troops. Raglan and his adjutants could also see that the Russians had captured a battery of guns on the right, and he wanted to stop the enemy removing the cannons for their own use. That was a job for the light brigade of cavalry who, under the command of the Earl of Cardigan, were among the troops in the valley below. So Raglan dictated an order to his secretary, which was then rushed down to the cavalry by a mounted messenger.

The order read, 'Lord Raglan wishes the cavalry to advance rapidly to the front, follow the enemy, and try to prevent the enemy carrying away the guns'. The trouble was that, while Raglan had a clear view of the gun battery, he failed to realise that Cardigan, from the bottom of the valley, couldn't see the position at all. Raglan's order was vague and – as it turned out – tragic in its consequences. It was claimed later that Cardigan and his fellow officers should have used their initiative and have realised that Raglan didn't want them to advance as they did straight into the face of an overwhelming enemy. Cardigan's defence was that he'd done what was expected of a British soldier: he'd obeyed orders, or rather, on that day at Sevastopol, he'd obeyed what he thought the order meant.

And so, Cardigan led his 673 men and horses on a charge into the mile-long valley. He knew it was suicidal, and is said to have muttered, 'Here goes the last of the Brudenells!' (Brudenell being his family name.) The men were sitting ducks for the 5,000 Russian troops and their guns atop the surrounding hills. Of the 673 cavalrymen who charged in, only around 200 came out alive. The officers around Russell watched in silent shock as the few survivors stumbled back through the wreaths of smoke.

So how did Russell report what he'd seen? Did he tell the bald facts and allow his readers to make up their own minds? Did he hammer the high command for the catastrophic mistake? He wrote later something that he gave no hint of in his immediate reports at the time:

> I am persuaded that whatever there was of disaster and misfortune on 25th October 1854 was due first to the distance of Lord Raglan from the field, and secondly to his failure to understand … that he saw more than his generals below could see; therefore … he did not take pains in wording his orders.

However, that was not what he told readers of *The Times*. Instead, he filed a story of pride and heroism:

> At ten minutes past eleven, our Light Cavalry Brigade advanced … As they rushed towards the front, the Russians opened on them from guns in the redoubt on the right, with volleys of musketry and rifles. They swept proudly past, glittering in the morning sun in all the pride and splendour of war. We could scarcely believe the evidence of our senses! Surely that hand-

ful of men are not going to charge an army in position? Alas! it
was but too true – their desperate valour knew no bounds ... A
more fearful spectacle was never witnessed than by those who,
without the power to aid, beheld their heroic countrymen rush-
ing to the arms of death.

He told of the overwhelming odds faced by the men:

At the distance of 1200 yards the whole line of the enemy
belched forth, from thirty iron mouths, a flood of smoke and
flame, through which hissed the deadly balls. Their flight was
marked by instant gaps in our ranks, by dead men and horses,
by steeds flying wounded or riderless across the plain. The
first line is broken, it is joined by the second, they never halt
or check their speed an instant; with diminished ranks, thinned
by those thirty guns, which the Russians had laid with the
most deadly accuracy, with a halo of flashing steel above their
heads, and with a cheer that was many a noble fellow's death-
cry, they flew into the smoke of the batteries, but ere they were
lost from view the plain was strewed with their bodies and with
the carcasses of horses.

He told of their bravery and professionalism:

Through the clouds of smoke we could see their sabres flashing
as they rode up to the guns and dashed between them, cutting
down the gunners as they stood. We saw them riding through
the guns... to our delight we saw them returning, after breaking
through a column of Russian infantry and scattering them like
chaff, when the flank fire of the battery on the hill swept them
down, scattered and broken as they were. Wounded men and
dismounted troopers flying towards us told the sad tale – demi-
gods could not have done what we had failed to do.

The result Russell presented in clinical terms, 'At thirty-five minutes past eleven not a British soldier, except the dead and dying, was left in front of those bloody Muscovite guns'.

Russell was rightly paying tribute to the bravery of the troops, but he'd fallen victim to the most alluring temptation for a war correspondent: he allowed himself to think like a good army man, not like a journalist. There is no mention in his report of the terrible casualty figures – two out of three men dead – nor any of the frightful details of slaughtered men and horses left on the battlefield.

The reaction back home in Britain can be judged from a cartoon published in *Punch* magazine. It shows a father brandishing a poker above his head, as though he too were a charging cavalryman, while he reads out Russell's report to his entranced and proud family. And Russell's account of the battle became the inspiration for one of the best-known poems in the English language, Tennyson's *Charge of the Light Brigade.* Its final stanza summarising the nation's pride at the soldiers' brave charge into the 'Valley of Death':

> When can their glory fade?
> O the wild charge they made!
> All the world wonder'd.
> Honour the charge they made!
> Honour the Light Brigade,
> Noble six hundred!

The fact that so many men were killed or wounded because of a sloppy, incompetent order issued by the commander-in-chief, Lord Raglan, was glossed over by Russell, by Tennyson and hence by the nation.

Back in the Crimea, at least some of those who'd survived the slaughter knew better, and Russell himself was aware of that. During the hours after the suicidal charge, he rode from tent to tent looking for officers he knew. He noted afterwards that many of them spoke of the loss of comrades with the damning words, 'All for nothing'. Instead of reporting that to *The Times*, Russell just noted in his private diary that these soldiers 'had not the least idea of the immense kudos they had gained for ever', as though the feelings and opinion of those in the front line didn't count.

* * *

In the months that followed the disastrous action in the Valley of Death, there was a change in the style of Russell's dispatches. And it was matched by the way that *The Times* editor John Delane backed up those reports in the paper's editorials.

As the harsh Crimean winter set in, the glory and pride which Russell had identified in the disastrous battle were no more. Now he reported on the unhealthy and filthy conditions in which officers and troops were housed. 'The officers are in rags,' he wrote. Most of the tents were destroyed in a storm, cholera was spreading. He'd seen that 'the roads were mere quagmires. Horses and cattle were scattered all over the country, and here and there a sad procession charged with the burden of an inanimate body wound its way slowly in search of a hospital marquee still standing.'

The Times editor, Delane, published these damning accounts, and he backed them up with increasingly harsh editorial comment attacking the conduct of the war. In late November he wrote, 'All posterity will cry shame upon this country and this generation. They will hold our country to have disgraced itself in the face of the whole world.'

Meanwhile, another front had opened up in the war between the press and the government. The British Army's base hospital was at Scutari, across the Bosphorus from Constantinople, and *The Times* correspondent there, Thomas Chenery, discovered another scandal. He revealed:

No sufficient medical preparations have been made for the proper care of the wounded. Not only are there no sufficient surgeons ... not only are there no dressers and nurses ... there is not even linen to make bandages for the wounded.

Chenery's next report added, 'The worn-out pensioners who were brought out as an ambulance corps are totally useless'.

Delane followed up Chenery's story with an appeal in the columns of *The Times* for a charity to come to the rescue. The government itself responded by setting up an official nursing service, and the Secretary of War, Sidney Herbert approached the nursing superintendent at the Institute for the Care of Sick Gentlewomen in London's Harley Street, to become its head, one Florence Nightingale. She immediately agreed and, within weeks of her appointment, she was working to bring comfort, cleanliness and appropriate treatment to the wounded soldiers at Scutari.

For the government, however, the relief was only temporary. It had been forced by a press revelation to give wounded heroes the medical care they deserved. The early popularity of the war had by now gone up in a storm of reports about incompetence and heartlessness. And Delane – with information gleaned from Russell's dispatches – upped the pressure on the government with the fiercest editorial yet:

The noblest army ever sent from our shores has been sacrificed to the grossest mismanagement. Incompetency, lethargy, aristocratic hauteur, official indifference, favour, routine, perverseness and stupidity reign, revel and riot.

Soon the army started to retaliate. Russell, whose lodgings had been a tiny room shared with horses and cattle, with a decomposing body in the only well, was thrown out of even this filthy shelter. On 5 January, he wrote to Delane:

This army has melted away almost to a drop of miserable, washed-out, worn-out, spiritless wretches, who muster out of 55,000 just 11,000 now fit to shoulder a musket, but certainly not fit to do duty against the enemy. Let no one at home attempt to throw dirt in your eyes. This army is to all intents and purposes, with the exception of a very few regiments, used up, destroyed and ruined.

Russell went further, with a head-on attack against the army's commander:

Lord Raglan has roused up when too late. He has seen at last, when too late, the terrible condition to which his army is reduced, and he now thinks to mend matters by issuing all kinds of orders for show and not for use, because it is impracticable to carry them out ... I am told on good authority that Lord Raglan felt the remarks in the paper very keenly.

Lord Raglan: This 1855 photograph was taken by Roger Fenton, who'd been encouraged to go to the Crimea by Prince Albert, Queen Victoria's husband, in an effort to counter *The Times'* adverse publicity. Photography back then required long exposure times and couldn't capture action. This staged pose of the British commander was typical of Fenton's work during the war.

And Russell himself was getting depressed by what he saw and the conditions he too was forced to work in, 'I don't know what to write about, and I confess I am losing health and spirits in this wretched affair'.

Delane's reply reveals a clear understanding of the difference between fact and comment, between reporting and editorial writing, 'Continue as you have done, to tell the truth and as much of it as you can, and leave such comment as may be dangerous to us, who are out of danger'.

The government was at a loss to know what to do. It publicly denied the accusations, and at the same time demanded Raglan do something about them. The general's answer was to try to get rid of the correspondents, and he sent word to a judge in London asking him to declare that Russell's dispatches were of assistance to the enemy and a breach of national security.

Nevertheless, Delane continued through his editorial comment columns to demand the recall of Raglan, as well as an official enquiry into the incompetent management of the war. Ministers in the Earl of Aberdeen's Tory Government resisted. Delane, through *The Times*, told readers the moment had come for Parliament to act, 'The duty of the House of Commons in this hour may be painful but it is certain'. And he added that, if they failed to act, there was a danger of something unthinkable in a democracy. Delane even hinted there might be a military coup.

In all histories, we find that war has required such exceptional powers, and that where governments have not granted them, generals have taken them. Far better, then, that Parliament finds someone to whom to grant these powers speedily before they are independently adopted.

The government was defeated in the subsequent parliamentary vote, and by the end of January 1855, Lord Aberdeen's administration fell. Later that year, the new Secretary for War, the Duke of Newcastle, told Russell, 'It was you who turned out the government'.

Lord Raglan, however, was still in post in the Crimea. So *The Times* didn't let up in its barrages against him. And after the failure of a British and allied attack on Sevastopol in mid-June, Russell blamed the general for allowing his battle plan to be influenced by the French. Ten days later, Lord Raglan fell sick and died.

The new commander-in-chief was Sir William Codrington, and he was determined not to suffer the same press attacks as his predecessor. To Codrington belongs the doubtful honour of being the founder of wartime press censorship. On 25 February, the following year, he issued a general order forbidding the publication of anything that he or his officers might consider of value to the enemy, and authorising the ejection of any correspondents guilty of the offence. But he was too late. The war was almost over, and a peace treaty was signed in April.

* * *

Russell returned home to a mixed reception. There was no doubt about his fame – he was the man who'd laid bare the failings of the army and the government. To many ordinary folk, who'd lost sons, brothers, fathers or friends in the fighting, that made him a hero.

But however popular Russell was in the country at large, he found himself damned by Britain's mighty. This was not just by supporters of the ousted Aberdeen government. Russell's dispatches in the later stages of the war, backed up by Delane's editorials, had concentrated on the perceived incompetence of the commander-in-chief, Lord Raglan. Those who knew Raglan regarded him as a decent man, and blamed Russell for driving him to his grave. The general's supporters pointed out that he'd asked London time after time for equipment and supplies in order to give his men safer, more comfortable lodgings in the camps and adequate medical care in base hospitals and front-line ambulance stations. His requests were ignored by the government.

But the British public wanted a scapegoat, and Russell gave them Raglan. For that, Russell and the paper were condemned by many of the most powerful in the land. On hearing of Raglan's death, Sydney Herbert the ousted Secretary for War wrote, 'I trust the army will lynch *The Times* correspondent'. Prince Albert dismissed Russell as 'that miserable scribbler', and the queen let it be known that she was displeased with *The Times*. There were even suggestions that Delane and Russell might be guilty of treason.

***

So, what became of Russell after the Crimean War? As the years rolled on, the acrimony and accusations from on high were forgotten. He reported, among other conflicts, the Indian Mutiny, the American Civil War and the Zulu Uprising. Towards the end of his life, William Russell was knighted, he became an honorary private secretary to the Prince of Wales, stood for Parliament, and married a countess. In other words, the mightiest in the land sucked him in to their own ranks.

Russell has been called 'the first great war correspondent'. Is that reputation deserved? Edwin Godkin, the *Daily News* reporter who worked alongside and in competition with Russell in the Crimea, wrote that in Russell's hands, 'correspondence from the field became a power before which generals began to quail'. And we should add that the partnership between Russell, Delane and Chenery made government ministers quail too. They had done this by daring to tell readers the truth about the incompetence of those who governed them.

Of course, as we've seen, Russell and Delane didn't always live up to that high ideal. Russell's account of the Charge of the Light Brigade honoured the bravery of ordinary soldiers, but – as a piece of objective journalism – was jingoistic nonsense that ignored the tragic stupidity of those in command, and failed to give any impression of the horrors and suffering left behind by battle. And Russell's later attacks on Lord Raglan, reinforced by Delane's editorials, were overstated and unfair. Then, too, Delane's reluctance to publish the more 'unpatriotic' of Russell's early reports can seem weak-hearted to us today.

Nevertheless, Russell's revelations about the neglect and fever-ridden conditions under which the men on the front line struggled, and Thomas Chenery's shocking accounts of the lack of proper medical care, both backed up by Delane's editorials, are worthy of acclaim. The power of the press was being used, not to push a political standpoint, but to improve the lot of ordinary soldiers who deserved better from those on high.

What, more than anything, distinguished the reporting of the Crimean War from other conflicts over the next decades, was that there was no attempt at censorship. And once – with the ill-reported Charge of the Light Brigade behind them – correspondents like Russell started to reveal hard facts in their dispatches, the Crimean War became a golden age for a press committed to holding the most powerful to account.

But it would be a brief golden age. A savage civil war was about to break out 5,000 miles west of Sevastopol in America. Freedom of the press was a right there, guaranteed 100 years earlier by the Constitution. Hundreds of war correspondents would be dispatched to report the fighting on both sides. The press would be a powerful force in the American Civil War. So, how would they use that influence? Were President Lincoln and the generals quaking in anticipation? That's what we're going to investigate next.

8

THE AMERICAN CIVIL WAR

Wild Ravings

With the press unfettered, as now, we are defeated
till the end of time.

General William T. Sherman (1820–91)

Nineteen months into the American Civil War, at dawn on 18 September 1862, a scruffy, bleary-eyed journalist climbed down from his horse and hammered on the door of the telegraph office in the small town of Frederick in the state of Maryland. He was George Smalley, chief 'special' correspondent for the *New York Tribune*. He'd not slept for around twenty-four hours, and had just ridden at a furious pace through the darkness from the battlefield at Antietam, 23 miles to the west. There he'd spent much of the previous day under fire in the front line of what the general in command of the Union Army described as 'the most terrible battle of the war, perhaps of history'.

Smalley was an unlikely reporter. He'd shown no aptitude for nor interest in journalism as a young man. He came from a relatively wealthy family, had been educated at Yale University, then graduated from Harvard Law School. By the time he was 28, when hostilities broke out between the Union forces of the North and the Confederate armies of the South, he was working in an established New York law practice.

For no other reason than a wish to see the fighting at first hand, he decided to abandon his comfortable, well-paid career, and instead turned up at the offices of the *Tribune* to offer his services as a correspondent. This well-educated young lawyer turned out to be determined, ingenious and brave, with an ability to write graphic and accurate reports. By any standards, he was an outstanding journalist. He was not, however, typical of reporters covering the war.

Smalley had seen more of the near suicidal fighting at the Battle of Antietam than any other correspondent. The military leaders on the Union side had banned reporters from getting anywhere near the action. Smalley, however, found a way round that. He volunteered to join the staff of one of the Union Army's divisional commanders. His job, which carried officer rank, was to act as a secretary or assistant.

He might have thought that this would allow him to observe the fighting from a safe distance. But it wasn't to be. As it turned out, he was often closer to the enemy than the corps commander, Brigadier General Joseph Hooker, and his staff. His position as aide-de-camp was far from being honorary. He found himself carrying orders and other messages to various parts of the line, and he came under fire himself several times. General Hooker would say about Smalley after the battle, 'I never saw the most experienced and veteran soldier exhibit more tranquil fortitude and unshaken valour than was exhibited by that young man'.

Somehow, amid all the risks of his military duties, Smalley managed to jot down notes of what he saw. In his later report, he wrote:

Forward, was the word, and on went the line with a cheer and a rush. Back across the cornfield, leaving dead and wounded

behind them, over the fence, and across the road, and then back
again into the dark woods which closed around them went the
retreating rebels ... But out of those gloomy woods came suddenly and heavily terrible volleys – volleys which smote, and
bent, and broke in a moment that eager front, and hurled them
swiftly back for half the distance they had won.

At around 9 in the morning, General Hooker was hit by a bullet
in the right foot. High on adrenaline, the general didn't realise what had happened at first, but then dispatched Smalley to
relay the news of his wound to the Union commander-in-chief,
General George B. McClellan. Smalley then found himself getting sucked into military politics at the highest level.

According to his later account, he was approached by certain
members of McClellan's staff, who believed their commander
was mismanaging his troops, and they asked Smalley to tell
Hooker that they wanted him to 'unseat' McClellan, in other
words to oust him and assume overall command of the army in
his place. Whether or not Smalley did get involved in the plot is
still being debated by historians. Regardless of that, his duties as
aide-de-camp continued throughout the day
until the fighting died down. He then
toured the battlefield. And when,
hours later, he came to write what
he'd seen, he avoided the kind
of glory-and-pride-of-war tone
of William Russell's dispatch
from the Charge of the Light
Brigade. Smalley observed with
moving accuracy:

George Smalley.

The field and its ghastly harvest which the Reaper had gathered in those fatal hours remained finally with us. Four times it had been lost and won. The dead are strewn so thickly that as you ride over it you cannot guide your horse's steps too carefully. Pale and bloody faces are everywhere upturned. They are sad and terrible, but there is nothing which makes one's heart beat so quickly as the imploring look of sorely wounded men who beckon wearily for help which you cannot stay to give.

* * *

At the end of the day, Smalley swapped his military cap for his journalist's pen, and met up with the other reporters from the *New York Tribune*. None of them had anything much to match his own eyewitness accounts, and he nearly came to blows with one fellow journalist who he thought hadn't shown enough courage and determination.

Then it was the night ride, before his banging on the door woke up the telegraph operator in Frederick. Smalley had not yet had a chance to write his story, so he did it now, handing over to the telegrapher each page as it was finished.

But there was something Smalley didn't know. The operator wasn't sending the words to the *Tribune* office in New York. He was under orders not to co-operate with journalists, so he was actually transmitting Smalley's copy to the War Department in Washington. There, members of Abraham Lincoln's Cabinet were waiting, desperate for any news about the day's fighting. Soon President Lincoln himself was reading Smalley's exclusive report.

At some point during the telegraph transmission, Smalley realised what the operator was doing, and he confronted the man, but he refused to send the report to the *Tribune*'s New York office. So, now almost collapsing from lack of sleep, Smalley decided that he was going to have to find another way of filing his story. He rode off to the railroad station. There was no train for two hours, so he carried on writing his report, sitting on a log by the side of the tracks. Then he hopped aboard a military train heading for Baltimore.

For the first time in thirty-six hours he slept, and that was nearly his undoing. He almost missed his connection at Baltimore for New York. When he scrambled on board, he got back to his story, this time standing beneath an oil lamp at the end of the railroad car. Halfway between Philadelphia and New York, he scribbled the closing paragraph.

Back in the War Department in Washington, and of course unbeknown to Smalley, Lincoln's staff, after passing Smalley's early report over to the president, then – for reasons we'll explore in a moment – obligingly forwarded it to the *Tribune* newsroom. A full crew of typesetters and proofreaders had been kept on standby there all night, ready to receive reports of the battle. It was 5 a.m. when Smalley staggered into the building. The *Tribune*'s journalists and pressmen broke into a spontaneous round of applause. Within an hour, a special edition of the newspaper was on the streets, headlining Smalley's scoop.

His report made it clear that the battle had ended in stalemate:

Fierce and desperate battle between two hundred thousand men has raged since daylight, yet night closes on an uncertain field. It is the greatest fight since Waterloo – all over the field contested with an obstinacy equal even to Waterloo. If not wholly a victory tonight, I believe it is the prelude to a victory tomorrow.

The words were noted by President Lincoln, and when McClellan failed to resume the battle next day, Lincoln sacked him.

* * *

Few, if any, of the hundreds of other reporters during the Civil War would match George Smalley's bravery, determination and devotion to journalistic accuracy. Nevertheless, his experience during the Battle of Antietam and in the hours afterwards tells us a lot about the extraordinary relationship between the press and those in power on the Union side of the war. It was a relationship marked by confusion and incompetence.

Those in command were at odds among themselves about whether, how and how far to go in controlling what newspapers reported of the war. That hesitancy gave the press a let-in to run riot. And run riot they did. War correspondents used every trick in the book to get around such half-hearted restrictions as there were, rejoicing in a kind of wild freedom to write anything they wanted, often even throwing to the winds any semblance of truth or objectivity in what they told their readers.

Several factors came together to hand unprecedented power to the press in 1860s America. New technology, as ever, was all important. The country had the most extensive railroad system in the world. That meant reporters like Smalley could get from Maryland to New York in a few hours, but also that the hundreds of thousands of newspapers printed each night could be rapidly distributed to readers throughout their region. Then there was the telegraph, which meant that – unlike in the Crimean War, just a decade earlier – reports of battles no longer took weeks to get from correspondent to editor. What happened on the battlefield today was often being read over breakfast next morning. By the 1860s, there were 50,000 miles of wires strung between poles across the eastern states, and an army of strategically placed operators who were trained to tap out messages in Morse code. The result was a product that millions of readers wanted to buy.

Newspapers had become big business, and the outbreak of a civil war created a nation with a desperate hunger for news of their loved ones caught up in the fight, and of events which would have a profound effect on their futures. So, the hostilities gave newspaper owners the chance for big profits.

Competition, however, was fierce. There were between 2,500 and 3,750 newspapers across America. To win, editors had to be first with the news, and they had to have scoops. No fewer than 500 'specials', that is, war correspondents, were dispatched to cover the fighting, 350 for newspapers on the Union side in the North, and 150 for Southern Confederate papers.

As well as being driven by profit, the press had come to have a high-flown idea of its own importance in democratic America. Samuel Bowles, the editor and publisher of the Massachusetts-based *Springfield Republican*, wrote, 'The brilliant mission of the newspaper is to be the high priest of history … It is the great enemy of tyrants and the right arm of liberty.' This mission was enshrined in the First Amendment of the Bill of Rights which had decreed that Congress should make no law to abridge the freedom of the press. So, it was the constitutional duty of correspondents and editors to reveal the shortcomings of those in power.

The near sacred force of the First Amendment left President Lincoln and the elected government in a quandary. From one side, it had the army's top brass screaming in its ear that journalists were revealing sensitive, harmful information which would inevitably reach the enemy. But at the same time, the government felt its hands were tied by the Constitution.

When Union generals complained that reporters were damaging national security, they had a point. So, for example, in May 1862, General McClellan complained:

My order of the 25th May, directing the order of march from the Chickahominy and the disposition to be made of the trains and baggage, is published in full in the *Baltimore American* of the 2nd instant. If any statement could afford more important information to the enemy I am unable to perceive it.

Major General Hooker, during the Gettysburg campaign the following year, suffered a similar security breach. He tried to win over newspaper editors by sending them a confidential letter asking for discretion in preparing their reports. But he was too late. On that same day, the *New York Herald* revealed the location of all the units in Hooker's entire army of 90,000 men.

But the conflicting pulls between the right to a free press and the needs of national security were further complicated by other more practical and selfish considerations. Lincoln and his Cabinet also recognised that the press had a useful role to play in persuading voters – newspaper readers – to support government policies. So, editors and publishers also had to be courted because of the influence they had over the minds of the people.

* * *

The press, however, was not all powerful. The government and the military hierarchy made several attempts to rein in correspondents and editors. If, because of the First Amendment, it was difficult for the president or Congress to impose any outright ban on the press, they could do something about the technology which correspondents now depended on. In 1862, Congress passed a law that allowed Lincoln to take control of the railroad and telegraph networks when necessary to ensure public safety. Railroad and telegraph companies would continue to operate their networks, but Congress warned them that company officials would be punished – even with the death penalty – for failing to co-operate.

The Secretary of War, Edwin Stanton, who saw himself as chief guardian of sensitive military information, seized on these new powers and instantly decreed that telegraph operations should come under a newly formed Military Telegraph Corps. Newspapers that published unauthorised military information were to be cut off from the telegraph and forbidden to send their reports by railroad.

Edwin Stanton, Secretary of War.

Stanton's action explains why the Frederick telegraph operator rerouted George Smalley's dispatch to the War Office. But the fact that the War Office, having delivered it to Lincoln, was happy then to pass it on to the *New York Tribune* shows the authorities wobbling to keep their balance between controlling the press and not offending them at the same time. It was often an impossible trick to pull off. And when, later in 1862, Congress passed the Treason Act, which made it illegal to aid the enemy in any way, no editor or reporter was ever convicted nor even brought to trial.

The generals themselves also had a go at imposing their own censorship, but they discovered it wasn't that easy. At the Battle of Bull Run in July 1861, it seemed, as the day wore on, that the North was winning, so correspondents scurried off to Washington to write their reports. Meanwhile, in their absence, fortunes turned on the battlefield and the Northern Army was routed. The Associated Press, the news agency jointly owned by all the major papers to give them a basic reporting service, got the real story, but when its correspondent arrived at the telegraph office in Washington, General Winfield Scott stepped in and stopped the dispatch being transmitted. The result was that the earlier – wrong – accounts of a northern victory were what hit the headlines, rather than the truth that Bull Run was a disaster for the Union Army.

Out in the field, the military leaders tried another means of reining in the 'specials'. They threatened to use their powers under martial law to prosecute any reporter who failed to comply with the rules the local commander had laid down for how they were to operate. Correspondents were required to sign a lengthy document.

General William Sherman used his martial law powers when he got annoyed by repeated newspaper allegations that he was insane, and he court martialled the *New York Herald*'s Tom Knox as a spy. In the end, Knox was found guilty of the lesser charge of violating transport restrictions, and his punishment was merely being barred from covering the Union Army of the Tennessee, and he was still free to report elsewhere. And even Knox's mild slap on the wrist was an exception. Few reporters faced trial for martial law infringements.

The generals too, however, were far from united and consistent in their attempts to control the correspondents who flocked to their side. It was common for officers to try and become buddies with reporters in order to get glossy accounts of their actions written up. And if you got on the wrong side of the 'specials', they could do serious damage, as the army commander General George Meade discovered in 1864. Meade got so irritated with the *Philadelphia Inquirer* reporter, Edward Crapsey, that he mounted him facing backwards on a mule, hung placards on his front and back labelling him a 'Libeller', and then paraded him among the troops while the band played 'The Rogue's March'. Crapsey, however, got his own back. He organised a boycott by journalists who were infuriated at what had happened, and Meade found that any military successes he now achieved failed to get a mention in the papers. So successful was the boycott that it was claimed to be a major factor in scuppering Meade's later bid to become US President.

All the evidence is that correspondents were more fearful of their editors than of what the authorities might do to them if they broke the rules. The intense competition for readers between the many newspapers put reporters under great pressure to get exclusives, and to get them fast. The editor could sack reporters for failing to get the story, whereas the military often seemed to turn a blind eye when reporters inveigled their way to the front. And there was many a trick that reporters could use to sidestep the haphazard attempts at censorship.

George Smalley at Antietam was a case in point. It's highly unlikely that the officers alongside him didn't know that this 'aide-de-camp' was really a journalist. It's hard to escape the conclusion that they were just giving a nominal nod to the order banning correspondents, while in reality letting Smalley do his job as a reporter. Why? Perhaps because individual officers wanted to be given the badge of heroism in his reports. Or perhaps because they believed in press freedom, and Smalley had convinced them he could be trusted not to reveal sensitive information. Either way, it was a classic example of the confused way that government and the military tried to control the press.

And if soldiers were open to a reporter's flattery, civilian officials who were supposed to hinder their work could often be tempted by a bit of bribery. After the North's army was defeated at Fredericksburg in 1863, one of Smalley's colleagues on the *Tribune*, Henry Villard, was trying to get to a usable telegraph point, and he found himself banned from boarding a boat on the Potomac River. He gave the skipper $50, a large sum at the time, and got dropped off at Washington. He filed his story, and then was summoned to the White House to give the president his first detailed account of the defeat.

The most dramatic and perhaps ridiculous instance of the split between Lincoln and the military hierarchy – the president keen to co-operate where he could with the press, the army leaders worried about security leaks – was the case of the *New York Tribune* reporter, Henry Wing. Wing had witnessed the so-called Battle of the Wilderness in 1862, and Lincoln sent out a request for him to come to Washington so he and the Cabinet could be briefed. However, there was a problem. Secretary of War

Stanton had just given an order that Wing should be shot as a spy. So, there was the extraordinary situation of one part of the government cosying up to a reporter while another part wanted him executed for espionage. The president, of course, won the day, and got his briefing, but Lincoln went further. As a reward for Wing, the president ordered a special train with a protective escort to take him to Warrenton in Virginia so he could collect his horse!

***

On the other side of the battle lines, in the Confederacy to the south, newspapers wielded nothing like the influence of those in the North. There were few of them, they tended to be weeklies and often had circulations of only a few thousand. Though there was a system of censorship for the press, it was hardly necessary.

Almost without exception, Southern reporters and editors simply toed the official line. They saw their job as keeping up the morale of the Confederate troops and of the folks back home. Added to that, many of the correspondents in the South were rookies with no concept of accuracy or objectivity, with the result that all the South's papers turned out what amounted to little more than fantastical propaganda. Correspondents would exaggerate Northern casualties and make light of Southern ones. Reports of a Southern victory were likely to start, 'Glory to God in the highest!' The North was 'the cursed cowardly nation of swindlers and thieves'. Northern soldiers went into battle 'primed with whisky' or 'drunken with wine, blood and fury'.

***

It was, of course, inevitable during a bitter war between citizens of the same country that newspapers would be ardent flag wavers for their side's cause. Even George Smalley, one of the few correspondents to set himself high professional standards, when he wrote of 'a victory' meant a victory for the North. But many reporters in the North on the Union side, like their fellow journalists in the South, often crossed the line into bloodcurdling jingoism. In their dispatches, a Confederate soldier wasn't just killed in battle, but 'sacrificed to the devilish ambitions of his implacable masters'. And women in the South were reported to make necklaces out of Yankee eyes.

The need to get the maximum number of reporters into the field meant many a young man, better suited to office work, found himself having to file daily dispatches of events he'd either not seen or, if he had, not understood. To give the editor the scoops he wanted, reporters frequently exaggerated what they witnessed, or invented what they hadn't. In April 1862 at the Battle of Shiloh, near the Mississippi–Tennessee border, several members of the press corps got together to fabricate news of the battle. A number of them had been nowhere near the fighting, with some being as far away as Cairo, Illinois, more than 150 miles away.

Then, during the Seven Days Campaign, several Northern newspapers were spattered with made-up casualty figures. The *Boston Journal* reported that the Union suffered only 300 casualties during two days of fighting. It then had to publish a correction after General McClellan's official statement put the figure at 5,737 killed. The real number, revealed later, was 23,000.

Professor J. Cutler Andrews, in his history, *The North Reports the Civil War*, wrote, 'Sensationalism and exaggeration, outright lies, puffery, slander, faked eyewitness accounts, and conjectures built on pure imagination cheapened much that passed in the North for news'. And Edwin Godkin, who after the Crimean War had moved to America, wrote that the reports of the war written by his new colleagues were 'a series of wild ravings about the roaring of the guns and the whizzing of the shells and the superhuman valour of the men'.

William Russell was sent out by the London *Times* to cover the fighting. At Bull Run, he wrote of the inexperience of many Northern soldiers, and he described how members of Congress accompanied by their ladies had arrived with picnic baskets to watch the battle. When his report was then re-run back in the American press, there was outrage, and he was advised to seek safety within the British Embassy. After that, he found it hard to get accepted by any army units, and he gave up and went home.

***

War reporting – especially when your own country's future is at stake – has always been the toughest job for a reporter. There is, of course, the physical danger, and there can be the hostility of the soldiery who believe you're undermining their fight. Sometimes objectivity or even accuracy in correspondents' reports can get them branded 'unpatriotic'. Newspaper owners can regard this as bad for business and require editors to suppress any such reports.

So, the job of the media to hold the mighty to account for their mistakes becomes a challenge in war like no other in journalism. William Russell's accounts of how British soldiers suffered unnecessarily during the Crimean War and *The Times'* editorial support for what he wrote is then a great tribute to both that reporter and his editor, John Delane.

During the American Civil War, there was no victory of the media over the mighty, and none either of the mighty over the media. It was, instead, the triumph of profit and patriotism over all else. The newspaper industry on the Union side had acquired unprecedented influence. That was partly because new technology allowed it to make and distribute a product – exciting, morale-boosting news – that millions wanted to consume. And the power of the press also owed much to its protected status granted it by the Constitution, as well as to its ability to sway public opinion.

Newspapers themselves had become a power alongside the mighty. Lincoln recognised that, and took little or no part in trying to curb the press during the war. In practice, censorship was left to the generals and the War Department, and they – undermined by the president, and lacking the necessary bureaucracy – made a half-hearted and often cack-handed job of it. As a result, reporters were left to write whatever they wished, a freedom they often abused, with scant regard to accuracy, in order to beat the competition and give their readers what they wanted: upbeat news of the war.

* * *

In telling the story of Civil War reporting, we've spoken only of men. Unlike in our own time when women have taken their place as leading war correspondents, female reporters were rare in 1860s America. But there were at least three writing about the conflict. They were not present at any of the great battles, but they did see the enemy close up. They were the sisters, Lida and Lizzie Dutton, and their cousin, Sarah Steer, from Loudon in Virginia.

When Confederate troops came marauding through their town, the three women risked their lives hiding Union soldiers, feeding them and tending their wounds. They then published accounts in the local paper, *The Waterford News*, of what they'd seen:

> The next day or two the rebels again visited this district and appropriated to their own use several horses and two wagons loaded with corn, belonging of course to Union citizens. They also visited the tannery of Asa M. Bond and arrested [*sic*] thirty-five dollars' worth of leather.

It was a humble start to a tradition of women correspondents that would take a century to establish itself.

On both sides of the Atlantic in the 1860s, women were regarded as second-class citizens, and were not considered up to the job of reporting from a battlefront – either physically, mentally or ... because they were women. In Britain, war itself – the First World War – would play a major role in giving greater democratic rights to women.

But before that, there was to be a fight for women's rights – a fight, however, not between the media and the mighty. In fact, most newspapers lined up alongside the government to attack, mock and try to stifle the women's suffrage struggle. That's the story for the next stage of our journey.

9

SUFFRAGETTES

The Truth for a Penny

The suffragettes are a regrettable by-product of our civilisation, out with their hammers and their bags full of stones because of dreary empty lives and high-strung, over-excitable natures.

The Times, *March 1912*

We don't know exactly when Emmeline Goulden was born. Her birth certificate records it as 15 July 1858, but Emmeline always celebrated her birthday on the day before, Bastille Day. She felt a strong link with the moment in Paris which had marked the start of the French Revolution, and she said, 'I have always thought that the fact that I was born on that day had some kind of influence over my life'.

A more likely explanation for her later militant activities was family tradition. Though she was brought up in a modest middle-class home in Moss Side, Manchester, Emmeline's parents told her early on how she came from a line of radical political activists. One grandfather had been charged with civil unrest, the other had been present at the Peterloo Massacre, and her grandmother had campaigned against the Corn Laws. Emmeline's parents supported similar liberal causes in their own day, and expected their eleven children – five daughters and six sons – to join in. Emmeline later recalled helping as a child to collect money for the newly freed slaves in America.

Given this liberal-minded family background then, it comes as something of a shock to us today that the Goulden parents didn't think their daughters deserved the same benefits of schooling as their sons. The Gouldens believed the girls needed only to learn the art of 'making home attractive' to potential husbands. The parents supported the idea that women should be given the vote, while at the same time believing them incapable of matching men's achievements. Emmeline's father was once heard to say, 'What a pity she wasn't born a lad'. It was a graphic illustration of how deep rooted was the prejudice against women in Victorian society. And it wouldn't begin to change till the First World War.

Women's suffrage had become a hot issue in radical circles from around 1867. Though England had been the first country to spread parliamentary representation beyond the ranks of the nobility as early as 1297 – to two knights for each shire and two burgesses for each town – progress afterwards had then been agonisingly slow. So, by the start of the nineteenth century, only 2–3 per cent of the population – all men, of course – had the right to vote. In 1867, the second Reform Act for the first time gave the vote to some working-class men. Although two-thirds of men, as well as women of all social ranks, were still excluded from the ballot, the changes were enough to prompt liberal-leaning thinkers to hope that more democratic progress might soon be won, and the debate began in earnest about whether, when and how women too should be able to elect Members of Parliament. The suffrage campaigner Millicent Fawcett wrote that including women in government had entered 'the phase of practical politics'.

However, for the Liberal Party in Parliament, 'practical politics' was all about winning votes, or rather losing them. It was estimated that women were more likely to vote Conservative, so if millions of them were given the vote, the Liberals would be out of office, maybe permanently. When, in the 1880s, a new bill was being debated to give more men the vote and it was proposed that women might be added, the Liberal Prime Minster William Ewart Gladstone dismissed the idea, saying that 'women's suffrage would overweight the ship'. On the other side of the party divide, the Tories were dead set against enfranchising women on principle. For the Conservative Party, it was simple: women couldn't be trusted when it came to choosing an MP.

Emmeline Goulden first got drawn into the suffrage campaign at the age of 14. She came home from school one day to find her mother just leaving for a public meeting about women's voting rights. Emmeline decided she'd go along too, and after hearing an enthralling speech by Lydia Becker, editor of *The Women's Suffrage Journal*, she was hooked. 'I left the meeting,' she wrote, 'a conscious and confirmed suffragist.'

From then on, it was the issue that dominated her waking hours and when, at the age of 20, she began a romantic relationship, it was inevitably with a man who was a strong supporter of women's suffrage. He was a barrister, twelve years older than her – Richard Pankhurst. Emmeline suggested something so outrageous it was hardly mentionable in middle-class Victorian England: she proposed that they live together in a 'free union', in other words, without marrying. Richard pointed out that this would undermine her credibility in political life. She took the point, and so in 1879 she became Mrs Emmeline Pankhurst.

During the next ten years, she gave birth to five children. One died of diphtheria at the age of 6. Three of them, Christabel, Sylvia and Adela, would as adults join their mother's political campaign. Throughout these years of child rearing, Emmeline remained active for the cause. She and her husband agreed that she should not be 'a household machine', so they employed a servant to help with the children.

Emmeline Pankhurst (left) and her daughters Christabel (centre) and Sylvia (right).

Emmeline Pankhurst never believed that gentle persuasion won political battles. She resigned from the Women's Liberal Federation because it was too moderate, and in 1894 became excited by the newly founded Independent Labour Party (ILP). But when she applied to join her local branch in Manchester, it was again brought home to her the size of the obstacles women faced in political life. This new, forward-looking, radical organisation, the ILP, which was committed to bringing the working classes into Parliament, rejected her application on the grounds that she was not a man. After a struggle, she was accepted by the party's National Committee instead.

So, what did the press make of this new-sprouting movement to give women the vote? The answer is, up to 1905, not a lot. Most newspaper editors decided it was a cause for the lunatic extreme. The moderate campaigner Millicent Fawcett wrote that in 1900 it was usual for 'magnificent meetings ... to receive from the anti-Suffragist press either no notice at all or only a small paragraph tucked away in an inconspicuous corner'. The suffragists regarded it as a conspiracy by the newspapers in cahoots with the government. In Parliament during the later years of the century, various Private Members' Bills were introduced to extend the vote to women, but they got little attention from the majority of MPs. The truth was that in the country at large most women were apathetic, while many men – if they knew much about the women's suffrage campaign at all – were hostile.

***

In 1905, Emmeline Pankhurst's life entered a new, headline-grabbing stage. By now she was head of the family – her husband Richard had died seven years earlier – and her three daughters, Christabel, Sylvia and Adela, had joined her in running her own newly founded organisation to press for women's right to vote, the Women's Social and Political Union (WSPU). No one outside her few associates in Manchester had heard of the WSPU. There was no mention of it in any newspapers at the time. Even the *Labour Leader*, the official paper of the ILP, didn't report it. And this despite the fact that the paper supported votes for women and its editor, Keir Hardie, had become a friend of Pankhurst's. In 1904, she was on the fringes of a fringe movement. In 1905, all that changed.

Pankhurst now believed that all the years of moderate speeches, and promises of support from MPs, had been a waste of time. The motto of the new WSPU was 'Deeds not words', and she herself said, 'The condition of our sex is so deplorable that it is our duty to break the law in order to draw attention to the reasons why we do'.

From 1905 onwards, the
WSPU under the Pankhursts
became more and more
militant, while the press
gradually realised their actions
couldn't be ignored. In May,
a bill to enfranchise women
was rejected by the House of
Commons amid – according
to *The Times* – 'laughter'
and 'ministerial cheers'.
The Times did not report
the protest demonstration
outside Parliament organised
by Pankhurst.

Emmeline Pankhurst arrested outside
Buckingham Palace while trying to
present a petition to King George V. The
police officer seems to have lifted her
clear off the ground.

So, what could she do to get
publicity for the cause? Later
that year, on 13 October, she
came up with the answer. The
WSPU decided to send Christabel Pankhurst and a fellow campaigner, Annie Kenney, to a meeting in Manchester where the
leading Liberal politician, Sir Edward Grey, would be speaking. The
plan was for the women to get themselves arrested. They started
by shouting from the floor, 'Sir Edward, when will the Liberal
Government give women the vote?' When he refused to answer,
they started heckling him. The police were called in. There was a
scuffle, and the women were taken into custody.

The next day, they appeared at Manchester Police Court,
Christabel Pankhurst charged with assaulting the police and
Annie Kenney with obstruction. Both women were found
guilty. Pankhurst was fined 10 shillings or a jail sentence of one
week. Kenney was fined 5 shillings, with an alternative of three
days in prison. The women refused to pay and were sent to

Strangeways Prison. That evening almost 1,000 people attended a demonstration to protest at their treatment.

Now the press realised that the women's suffrage movement was a news story. The London *Evening Standard* reported the events, but dismissed the women's behaviour as better suited to 'children in the nursery'. Even *The Manchester Guardian*, founded in the aftermath of the Peterloo Massacre and which saw itself as the mouthpiece of informed liberal opinion, condemned the unladylike behaviour of Misses Pankhurst and Kenney. Their actions, it told its readers, were 'such as one might attribute to women from the slums'.

The *Daily Mail* told its readers that this kind of law breaking damaged the women's cause, and – seeking to belittle the campaigners – it invented the word 'suffragette', the ending '-ette' signifying something small and insignificant. However, the militants liked the idea of being separately identified from the more peaceful campaigners, and from that moment on they adopted the name with pride.

Even the moderate women's campaigner, Millicent Fawcett admitted there'd been a press 'sensation'. She added, 'Instead of the withering contempt of silence, the anti-suffrage papers came out day after day with columns of hysterical verbiage directed against our movement.'

The Times, in these early days, seemed to be flummoxed as to what to do. At first it remained silent about Christabel Pankhurst and Annie Kenney's protest and their arrest. But it was no longer the silence of 'this is not important'. It was a silence that seemed to recognise the danger of women's militancy, and the paper decided – for the moment at least – to avoid giving it any space in its pages. *Times* readers were given a detailed report of Sir Edward Grey's speech, but were told nothing at all of the disturbance by the two women, nor of their arrests. But the paper's editor, Charles Moberly Bell, was soon to change his mind.

It seems that a journalist's wish not to be beaten by competitors got the better of his distaste for the suffragists, and two days later he ran a report of the Police Court hearing. And to Moberly Bell's credit, he kept to *The Times*' reputation for balance and objectivity. The report read:

> At Manchester City Police Court on Saturday, Miss Pankhurst and Miss Kenney, two prominent upholders of women's rights, were summoned for obstructing South Street in the city ... An assault consisted of spitting in the face of a police superintendent and a police inspector and hitting the latter in the mouth.

And the paper even went so far as to quote the women's justification for their actions. They had told the court, '...as they were denied votes, making a disturbance was the only way they could put forward their claim to political justice'. And more surprising, *The Times* now even reported the demonstration in support of Pankhurst and Kenny, including, 'Mrs Pankhurst, mother of one of the defendants, said she was proud that her daughter had taken so courageous a stand'.

During the next few months, however, the paper fell back into near silence about the activities of the Pankhursts and the WSPU. It would report public meetings where leaders of the Liberal Government were speaking, without referring to the heckling and protests from the floor, other than to throw in the odd remark about a speech being 'disturbed only by the odd lady interrupter'.

By 1906, however, *The Times* was starting to fall in line with the rest of the press. The suffragette agitators were no longer 'ladies', they were 'women' (a more disparaging term in Edwardian England), who now 'harangued' the audience in a 'disorderly scene'.

By October of 1907, the paper's language had become much more subjective. A *Times* report of a protest at Parliament said,

'Several of the excited women shrieked hysterically', and in a leading article two days later, the paper made a virulent attack not only against the militant tactics of the Pankhursts and the WSPU, but against the whole idea that women should be given the vote. The protesters' behaviour was 'unseemly', 'disgraceful', 'outrageous'. When brought before the court, 'They appeared to have taken leave both of common sense and good manners … It is all excessively vulgar and silly, but it offers a very good object lesson upon the unfitness of women to enter political life.' And the editorial ended, 'The worst of mob rule is the rule of a feminine mob; and we trust that no minister will allow himself to be party to the utter debasement of political life that would be involved in yielding to the clamour of such a mob.'

The Times was the newspaper most read by members of the government, the opposition, bishops, leaders of industry and commerce – all those in positions of power – but the population at large was being treated to a similar tirade of belittling insults. The *Daily Express* in 1907 headlined an editorial, 'The supremacy of man' (they meant males, not mankind), condemning the militants – or 'malignants', as it called them – for their 'folly and fury'.

The power of the printed word was clear, and about the same time, the WSPU launched its own newspaper, *Votes for Women*. It was described as being 'designed to give the public that information which suffragists had looked for vainly in the press'. It started out as a monthly, selling 5,000 copies at 3 pence each. The take-up was so encouraging that after a year it was turned into a weekly and the price was slashed. WSPU activists stood on street corners with a pile of copies under their arm, and holding up a front page while they called out, 'The truth for a penny! The truth for a penny!' Edith Craig recorded how she sold the paper outside a fashionable London restaurant:

I offer it verbally to every soul that passes. If they refuse, I say something to them. Most of them reply, others come up, and we collect a little crowd until I'm told to let the people into the restaurant, and move on. Then I begin all over again.

At the height of its popularity, *Votes for Women* was selling 30,000 copies a week.

The mainstream press made an occasional attempt at balanced coverage. In 1907, the *Daily Chronicle* even commissioned Evelyn Sharp, a WSPU member, to write a regular column, but it lasted only a few months, until the paper's editor told her he was stopping it because it 'alienated so many readers'.

It was undoubtedly true that a majority of the population, including many women, were still against the vote being extended to women. And this provided a respectable fig leaf for the Liberal Government to cover its embarrassment at rejecting female franchise. The prime minister, Herbert Asquith, declared that the government would not allow any proposal before the House of Commons to give votes to women without first 'an overwhelming declaration in favour of the suffrage ... from the women of England'. The media and the mighty were at one in their opposition.

However, Emmeline Pankhurst now came to realise that any publicity was good publicity. As her daughter Christabel commented, 'We had certainly broken the press silence ... which by keeping women uninformed, had so largely smothered and strangled the movement.' And the proof of the effectiveness of the new militant tactics came on 21 June 1908, when half a million women and some men gathered in London's Hyde Park to demand women be given the vote. There may not have been a majority across the country in favour, but numbers were growing.

The year 1908 was the start of what the militants christened 'The Stone Age'. A few days after the mass rally in Hyde Park, two women protesters got through a police line guarding the prime minister's residence, and smashed windows in No. 10 Downing Street. Christabel Pankhurst said it was 'women's

On trial at Bow Street Magistrates Court in 1908. On the far left, in the dock, is Christabel Pankhurst. Her mother Emmeline is nearest to us. Between them is fellow suffragette, Flora Drummond. The inscription on the back of the original photo says 'For asking people to rush the House of Commons. During the trial for Sedition.' The three women look bored by the proceedings – it was one of many occasions when they faced charges.

first use of the political argument of the stone'. It was a time too when the militant wing became increasingly isolated from the rest of the women's movement. Some suffragettes felt so strongly that the peaceful tactics were damaging the cause that they even turned their campaign against the moderates. A group of them rushed into the Albert Hall and broke up a meeting of the Women's Liberal Federation (WLF). *The Observer* – a supporter of the WLF – told its readers, 'These shrieking women turned the event into a Bedlam … all sense of decency lost … it was a melancholy and disheartening spectacle; and the pity of it was that they were very often women who in saner moments would be treated with tender respect as gentle ladies.'

***

The next five years saw the Pankhurst wing of the women's movement stepping up the drama of their demonstrations. Window smashing and chaining themselves to railings became regular features of street protests. Then, when that failed to achieve anything, they turned to arson. They set fire to a café in Regent's Park, the Orchid House at Kew gardens, pillar boxes and a railway carriage.

A public lending library in Birmingham was burned to the ground. A piece of paper attached to its railings said, 'Give women the vote', and a parcel left nearby was found to contain one of Emmeline Pankhurst's books with another note saying, 'To start your new library'. Another suffragette threw an axe into a carriage carrying Prime Minister Asquith, and her co-protesters tried and failed to burn down the theatre in Dublin where he was due to speak. The militants even resorted to bombs, one at St Paul's Cathedral, though they all either failed to go off or caused minimal damage.

The most spectacular protest came in 1913, when WSPU member Emily Davison stepped in front of the king's horse on Derby Day and was killed. Five thousand women walked in procession behind her coffin. Davison was the sole casualty of the suffragettes' campaign. Most of their attacks were against property, not people, and at no stage was anyone hurt in their protests, other than the suffragettes themselves.

Nevertheless, the papers were unanimous in condemning the militants' actions. All of them attempted to marginalise the Pankhurst wing as extremists, while praising the peaceful suffragists, though without necessarily endorsing their claim to the vote. The *Daily Express*, for instance, argued that the Pankhursts and their supporters were insane, and included in its reports and editorials every word possible to convey that idea. The militants were 'crazy' and 'frenzied'. The paper asked, 'What should be done with the mad suffragists' who were 'fanatical' and 'wild'?

The paper also attacked them as 'criminals', 'inciters of crime' and 'hooligans', prosecuting a 'campaign against society', able to construct 'infernal machines', collect a 'secret arsenal' and 'plot a war'. They were 'anarchists', and the *Express* answered its own question as to what should be done with them. In an editorial on 8 May 1913, headlined 'The Last Straw. Suffragette Crime Goes Beyond All Bounds', it said they should be deported to the island of St Helena in the South Atlantic, where Britain's then most notorious enemy, Napoleon, had been imprisoned.

Other papers adopted the same line. *The Daily Sketch* declared, 'The name of a suffragette will stink throughout recorded history.' *The Times* could be just as strident. It categorised suffragette demonstrations as 'futile', 'riotous' and the product of 'hysteria'. It published a letter saying that suffragettes should be birched. The paper also attempted to persuade its more educated readership with what it saw as rational argument.

In 1912, it published another letter, by the eminent bacteriologist, Sir Almroth Wright, which stated, 'No doctor can ever lose sight of the fact that the mind of woman is always threatened with danger from the reverberations of her medical emergencies. It is with such thoughts that the doctor lets his eyes rest on the militant suffragist.'

Then *The Times* went further, not only using such thinking to attack the Pankhursts and the militants, but also to undermine the whole idea of giving women the vote. The paper laid before its readers ten 'logical' reasons against it. They ranged from 'Women's interests are already represented by men', and 'Female enfranchisement would lead to a wife neglecting her domestic duties' to 'Women could be unduly influenced by the clergy', and ending with, 'The real reason why women ought not to have the political franchise is the very simple reason that they are not men'.

The Manchester Guardian was one of the few papers to show any restraint. In November 1910, on what the suffragettes called 'Black Friday', Emmeline Pankhurst led 300 women on a protest march to Parliament Square. The Home Secretary, Winston Churchill, directed the police to break up the demonstration, and officers were seen punching the women, twisting their arms and even pinching their breasts. The *Guardian*'s editor, C.P. Scott, wrote that these protesters 'are citizens like the rest of us and they have a right to fair treatment and to the protection of the law', but the paper, although in a relatively restrained tone, did not approve of militant action. It regarded Emily Davison's Derby Day death as 'futility' and claimed that the 'horrible responsibility' for it lay on the shoulders of the militant movement. Women, said the editorial, should seek 'honourably and sanely the enfranchisement which is their right'.

***

In 1909, Emmeline Pankhurst's WSPU adopted a new tactic, one which was so successful that it even attracted the sympathy of the press and the public. And what's more, it forced the government to change tack. It was the prison hunger strike.

More than 1,300 suffragettes were arrested during protests for various offences, and approximately 1,000 refused to pay the fines and so were sent to jail. Some, like Emily Davison, were put behind bars as many as ten times. From 1909 onwards, jailed suffragettes began to highlight their cause by refusing to eat or drink. The prison authorities didn't want to be accused of allowing these women to kill themselves, so they began to force food and water into them. Government ministers approved, because they, in turn, wanted to stop the suffragettes rousing support for their cause by becoming martyrs. The government got it wrong.

In March 1912, Emmeline Pankhurst was sent to Holloway Prison for smashing windows, and went on hunger strike. She wrote later, 'Holloway became a place of horror and torment. Sickening scenes of violence took place almost every hour of the day, as doctors went from cell to cell performing their hideous office.'

For the press, there was a sensational grisliness about force-feeding and they reported details of the women's treatment for the shuddering curiosity of their readers. The *Illustrated London News* even employed artists to produce imaginary drawings of the painful treatment the women suffered. In March 1913, the *Guardian* printed an account by Sylvia Pankhurst of her own experience:

> I was trembling with agitation, feverish with fear and horror, determined to fight with all my strength and to prevent by some means this outrage of forcible feeding. ... when the door opened, six women officers appeared ... I struggled as hard as I could, but they were six and each one of them much bigger and stronger than I.
>
> They soon had me on the bed and firmly held down by the shoulders, the arms, the knees, and the ankles ... I felt a man's hands trying to force my mouth open. I set my teeth and tightened my lips over them with all my strength. I felt I should go mad. I heard them talking: 'Here is a gap.'
>
> Then I felt a steel instrument pressing against my gums, cutting into the flesh, forcing its way in. Then it gradually prised my jaws apart as they turned a screw. It felt like having my teeth drawn; but I resisted – I resisted. I held my poor bleeding gums down on the steel with all my strength. Soon they were trying to force the india-rubber tube down my throat.

She goes on to describe being left on the bed 'gasping for breath and sobbing convulsively'. She was subjected to the same procedure that evening, but she was now too tired to struggle, and the routine was repeated every morning and every evening. 'Infinitely worse than any pain,' she wrote, 'was the sense of degradation.'

The *Guardian* had come out against force-feeding from the start. Scott, the editor, had condemned it as 'torture' in 1909.

'We're strongly of the opinion,' he wrote, 'that so extreme a measure should not have been resorted to.' The Labour opposition in the House of Commons came to realise they now had an issue associated with votes for women which they felt they could exploit with some popular support, and in 1912, the leading Labour politician, George Lansbury, caused an uproar by striding across the floor of the house to confront Prime Minister Asquith face to face, and denouncing him as 'the man who tortures innocent women'. He added, 'You should be driven from public life!' *The Times*, although its editorial urged the Home Secretary to stay firm in his treatment of these 'window smashers', reported the encounter in full.

In April 1913, Asquith's Liberal Government changed its policy. It introduced what became known as the 'Cat and Mouse Act'. It was so called because of the way a cat plays with a mouse before finishing it off. Under the new law, the authorities would no longer force-feed suffragette prisoners. Instead, they would wait till the hunger striker was weak, then release her 'on licence'. Once outside, as soon as she regained her strength and started her political activism again, she'd be sent back to jail and the same sequence would start again.

The Times, too, had done a U-turn on force-feeding. The Home Secretary, it told its

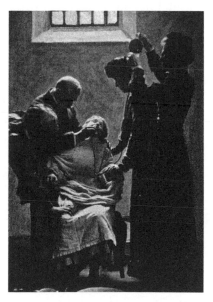

Many newspapers that had previously attacked and insulted the suffragettes gave their readers graphic reconstructions of them being force-fed in prison. The women were now presented as the victims of a cruel system.

readers with toe-curling hypocrisy, 'ought to have introduced the bill long ago', adding, 'Our own impression is that a hunger strike … will lose most of its charms, since it will neither offer a chance of martyrdom, nor make a picturesque appeal to sentiment'.

But the damage had been done to the anti-suffrage cause. As *The Times* itself confessed, 'Forcible feeding has become utterly repugnant to the public sentiment'. In other words, it made the suffragettes look like victims of a cruel system, rather than anarchists attacking society, as the press and the powerful had wanted.

***

With the outbreak of war in 1914, everything changed. Emmeline and Christabel Pankhurst decided that the survival of the country had to come before women's rights, and they persuaded their fellow WSPU members to halt all militant activity. Emmeline wrote, 'When the time comes we shall renew that fight, but for the present we must all do our best to fight a common foe.' It caused a split in the Pankhurst family. Sylvia and Adela rejected their mother and elder sister's stand, and declared themselves pacifists. Emmeline said she was ashamed of them. She now put the same energy she'd given to the women's movement into the war effort. She organised rallies and lobbied the government to help women enter the workforce while the men were away fighting.

The press also changed its tune – although slowly. That barometer of Establishment opinion, *The Times*, at first failed to catch the significance of what was happening. In an editorial dated 29 January 1915, titled 'Women and Farm Labour', it remarked, 'What farmers want right now is essentially man's work … little can be expected of women at the moment', and it went on to advocate that boys be trained up.

The balance was tipped the other way, however, in July. Emmeline and Christabel were organising a mass rally to publicise the desire of women to serve their country. They found support from an unexpected source: Lord Northcliffe, owner of *The Times* and the *Daily Mail*. In total, he controlled 40 per cent of the morning newspapers sold, plus 45 per cent of the evening papers and 15 per cent of the Sundays. He saw the sense of drawing women into the war effort and, what's more, he foresaw the logical conclusion of giving them that responsibility. Christabel wrote that Northcliffe:

> ...liked the brisk efficient ways and earnest spirit of the suffragettes, whom he now knew for the first time. It was the end of his opposition to votes for women. He promised his support and that of his newspapers when the time of the votes for women settlement should come.

Northcliffe kept his promise. During 1916, *The Times* listed the work of women in a vast range of occupations from sheep clippers and chimney sweeps to doctors, nurses and munitions workers and, in an article headed 'The New Woman', the paper was full of praise for 'this new and glorious creature, truly emancipated by the stern hand of war ... justifying her claim to an equal share of the nation's burden'. The paper was getting close to backing votes for women.

Exactly one year later, the shift came. By now, as well as the millions of women in the workplace for the first time, 80,000 others had enlisted in non-combat roles in the armed services. *The Times* now informed its readers:

> The real case for their enfranchisement in these days rests with the palpable injustice of leaving women, who have become for the first time an essential factor in the national effort, without the vote ... We doubt very much whether there is any great hostility left in this country to the principle of Woman Suffrage. Its advocates are almost forcing an open door.

And so, with the end of the war in 1918, a law was passed giving women the vote – but it was not all women. It only included the 8.9 million women over the age of 30 who owned a certain amount of property or who were university graduates. Equality eventually came in 1928, when, like men, all women over the age of 21 were granted the right to cast their vote.

***

When the 1918 Act came in, both *The Manchester Guardian* and the *Observer*, the two main liberal newspapers, told their readers that women's suffrage had been won by the 'statesmanship' of the moderate wing of the suffragist movement, rather than by the impassioned leadership of Emmeline Pankhurst and the militant suffragettes.

Is that true? Or does the stance of the *Guardian* and the *Observer* reflect something else – a very English attachment to political stability, and an abhorrence of revolutionary methods. Would women have won the vote after the First World War, if Emmeline Pankhurst and her daughters hadn't set fire to buildings and chained themselves to railings in order to force the issue onto the front pages of the nation's newspapers?

Women's struggle for voting rights had been a different kind of media battle from what we've been used to on our journey through the centuries so far. From the invention of the printing press in the fifteenth century onwards, governments had been wary, often frightened, of writers and publishers using the printed word to reach large sections of the population and to stir up discontent and even rebellion.

The media and the mighty have always been natural enemies. That's what we've seen over the centuries, from the war between Henry VIII and the pro-papal pamphleteers, through to *The Times*' Crimean War attacks on ministers over the unhealthy conditions for front-line British soldiers. There have certainly been times when newspapers were split in their loyalties, some defending, some attacking, those in power. And it's true that the media and the mighty have sometimes been united against an outside enemy, as they were both in the North and the South during the American Civil War. But with the suffragette struggle, we've seen a very different battle line drawn up. It was the first time the mighty and the whole of the media united in such strength against a group of their own citizen readers.

Why? The answer is simple. The press, as we've seen, had become big business. Profits were driven by selling newspapers and you didn't sell papers by adopting deeply unpopular causes. This meant that – far from being revolutionary, which the press had been in the early days – newspapers now tended to be conservative (with a small 'c'), avoiding anything extreme or marginal which might frighten readers away. That coincided with the views of those in government, who saw women's suffrage as a threat to their own powerbase. So, in the militant days of the women's suffrage movement, between 1905 and 1914, the media and the mighty lined up together to oppose it. But in the end, real power lay with the media, not with the mighty.

What set Emmeline Pankhurst apart was that – unlike the moderate suffragists – she understood this. She realised she could use the press – hostile as it was – to further her cause. She wrote later:

> Never lose your temper with the press or the public – is a major rule of political life … Even exaggerated or distorted reports, which made us seem more terrible than we really were, told the world this much: that we wanted the vote and were resolved to get it.

Although the media and the mighty joined together to try and defeat the suffragettes, Pankhurst hijacked the media. The press couldn't resist a 'good story' and headlines about the militant women's latest escapade – no matter how insulting or belittling

– forced people to think about an issue they were barely aware of before. And when Emmeline Pankhurst came out as a stalwart patriot on the outbreak of war, many in the country started to ask themselves whether this now-admirable woman might have been right about votes for women as well.

***

During the four years that Britain and her allies were at war with Germany, there was, in fact, little coverage of the suffrage question either in newspaper reports or editorials. Inevitably it was the fighting that filled the columns of the popular and the more serious press. For the first time, there was an effective system of censorship. But that apart, war correspondents, even when the opportunity came up, failed in their job of accurately reporting the facts or holding the mighty to account for their failings. The First World War was the all-time low for the media. So, let's go now to the trenches in Belgium to find out more.

10

THE FIRST WORLD WAR

A Few Writing Chappies

The first casualty, when war comes, is truth.

US Senator Hiram Johnson (1866–1945)

In the early months of 1915, Philip Gibbs, special war correspondent for the London *Daily Chronicle*, was told that if he
returned to France again he'd be put up against a wall and shot.
The threat was not to be taken lightly. It came from the British
Secretary of State for War, Lord Kitchener.

On the face of it, Gibbs didn't seem the man to take such
risks. He was described as physically small and by temperament
emotional. At the age of 22, in 1899 he had written a book
on the British Empire – he saw himself as a historian and a
literary figure. His first step into journalism had been far from
the dangers of war. He'd taken a job as literary editor of the
Daily Mail, and by the time hostilities broke out in 1914, he was
36 years old and seemed settled in the gentle world of writing
and literary criticism.

So, how did this bookish man, now on the verge of middle
age, suddenly get himself into such a scrape, with a Cabinet
minister threatening to execute him, just a year later? There was
something inside Philip Gibbs that wasn't satisfied, and – as he

saw younger men going off to fight – he decided he wanted to be a war correspondent, which was, he said, 'the crown of journalistic ambition, the heart of its adventure and romance'.

And Gibbs was not alone. He wrote later, 'There was a procession of literary adventurers' arriving at newspaper offices in Fleet Street, '… scores of new men of sporting instincts and jaunty confidence, eager to be "in the middle of things", willing to go out on any terms so long as they could see a "bit of fun"'. Newspaper proprietors didn't have a much better idea of the challenges of reporting the mass slaughter that lay ahead, and the common view in editorial offices was that war correspondent was a job for a hunting man, someone who knew about horses and could get along with cavalry officers.

Gibbs' first assignment was not exactly what he'd yearned for. He got a job with the *Daily Graphic* as a sketch artist. He travelled to Serbia, which had just been invaded by the Austro-Hungarian Army, and sent back to London drawings of the troops there, which the *Graphic* then worked up into more professional illustrations for publication. But it gave him a taste for action, and in the autumn of 1914, he joined the *Daily Chronicle* and was sent to write about the fighting in northern France and Belgium. He confessed to 'an immeasurable ignorance of the meaning of warfare' and said he had thought it would be 'remote, picturesque and romantic'. This eye-fluttering, poetic vision is evident in his account, published by the *Chronicle*, of the aftermath of the First Battle of the Marne in September 1914. He accompanied a grave digger disposing of the corpses of German soldiers left on the battlefield, and wrote:

My guide grasped my arm and pointed to a dip in the ground beyond the abandoned village of Levignen. 'See there,' he said, 'they take some time to burn.' He spoke in a matter of fact way, like a gardener pointing to a bonfire of autumn leaves … and I knew that those leaves yonder had fallen from the great tree of human life, and that this bonfire was made from an unnatural harvesting.

For all his romantic writing style, Gibbs showed a practical talent in getting his reports back to the *Chronicle* newsroom. At one point, he even persuaded a War Office messenger to carry them to London, where they were then rushed across to the *Chronicle* offices by some obliging officials in the War Office itself. But this kind of helpfulness to the press in the early months of the war soon stopped when Lord Kitchener found out what was going on.

Kitchener had hated war correspondents ever since he'd come across them during the Sudan Campaign of 1898. They were 'drunken swabs' who got in his way. In 1914, what Gibbs and his fellow reporters wrote was already subject to censorship. The freedom with which Russell and other correspondents had operated during the Crimean War sixty years earlier was not to be repeated this time, and just four days after the outbreak of war the government pushed through the Defence of the Realm Act. Its terms were simple: 'No person shall by word of mouth or in writing spread reports likely to cause disaffection or alarm among any of His Majesty's forces or among the civilian population.' In other words, the generals and government ministers could stop the press publishing anything they didn't like.

Kitchener went further than that. He ordered that any correspondent found in the field should be arrested, expelled and his passport confiscated. At first, the order was loosely applied, so allowing Gibbs, for instance, the freedom to wander the battlefield at the Marne. But by early 1915, Kitchener got tougher. He ordered the arrest in France of a number of named correspondents. One of them was Gibbs, and he again now showed his determination and resourcefulness. He returned to Britain, where he persuaded the Red Cross to appoint him as an inspector of field hospitals in France.

Philip Gibbs.

With these official papers in his pocket, he set off again for the front. However, he didn't get far. When his boat docked at Le Havre, military police came on board and arrested him. He was held for ten days, and it was at this point, before he was sent packing, that he was informed that Lord Kitchener was very angry with him, and that if he ever came back, he'd be shot.

***

But even Kitchener couldn't ignore the needs of the British public for some news of the war on the Western Front where their menfolk were fighting. But the information to be circulated had to be positive about the progress of the war, reassuring about the well-being of the men, and certainly must contain nothing of use to the enemy. He couldn't trust journalists to do that.

So, Kitchener appointed Colonel Sir Ernest Swinton to the commander-in-chief's staff with the job of writing up reports to be sent to the newspapers. Kitchener insisted that even these dispatches by a trusted senior insider should not be released till he'd personally vetted them. They were issued under the byline 'Eye-witness'. 'Eye-wash', more likely, said Fleet Street editors.

A taste of Swinton's style is clear from his account of trench warfare in the Aisne sector:

Where our men are holding the forward edges of the high ground on the north side they are now strongly entrenched. They are well fed and in spite of the wet weather of the past week are cheerful and confident.

However, the government also realised that it had to do more than put out occasional fact-less, mildly encouraging communiques from the front. If the war was to be won, then the wholehearted support of the nation must be harnessed. Propaganda was the answer. The enemy must be painted as a merciless aggressor.

A government Press Bureau was set up, which expanded into a Ministry of Information, to be headed by the owner of the *Daily Express*, Lord Beaverbrook. Reuters news agency – which, ever since its founding in 1851 had taken pride in its fast and objective reporting of overseas news – was brought under the direct control of the Foreign Office, which bought a controlling interest in the company. Some of the great writers of the day were roped in, including Rudyard Kipling, who declared, 'There are only two divisions in the world today: human beings and Germans'.

As it soon turned out, the press were willing accomplices in spreading the word. The *Daily Mail* told its readers that the Kaiser was a 'lunatic', a 'barbarian', a 'monster' and a 'criminal'. But we shouldn't get the idea that the government's system for controlling news ran like a faultless machine. In the early stages, it was sometimes chaotic. Take the way that the War Office tried to manipulate news about the Battle of Mons in August 1914. At Mons, the British Army was defeated in its first encounter with the Germans – historians later called it the start of 'The Great Retreat'. However, to judge by the government's initial communique, it was nothing of the sort:

The British forces have reached their new position. Fighting has gone on more or less continuously, but the enemy has not effectively harassed our operations … The casualties cannot be estimated exactly, but are not heavy.

The government might have got away with this cover-up, except that two correspondents, Arthur Moore of *The Times* and Hamilton Fyfe of the *Daily Mail*, had seen the real story. At the *Times* office, the acting editor, George Freeman, was shocked to read Moore's dispatch:

> Since Monday morning the German advance has been one of almost incredible rapidity … Naumer fell, and General Joffre was forced to order a retreat along the whole line. Our losses are very great. I have seen the broken bits of many regiments.

Freeman was certain it had no chance of getting through the censor, so he picked up his pen and crossed bits out that he thought were too near the truth to be passed, and off it went to the Chief Censor, F.E. Smith. To Freeman's immense surprise, Moore's report came back, not only with the bits about the retreat and the defeat restored, but Smith had also added his own paragraph at the end:

> To sum up, the first great German effort has succeeded. We have to face the fact that the British Expeditionary Force, which bore the great weight of the blow, has suffered terrible losses and required immediate and immense reinforcement. The British Expeditionary Force has won indeed imperishable glory, but it needs men, men, and yet more men.

Moore's dispatch, complete with Smith's addition, was published in full in a special Sunday edition of *The Times* on 30 August, and on the same day the *Weekly Dispatch* published Hamilton Fyfe's report – with a similar conclusion by Smith – under the headline 'Our soldiers overwhelmed by numbers'.

So, what was F.E. Smith up to? He was using his authority as censor to push his own agenda that the army needed more recruits, and when there was widespread alarm in the country at the news that the war was apparently being lost almost as soon as it had begun, he lied, blaming the newspapers for the defeatist talk and claiming he'd been too busy to look at their reports.

Smith was forced to resign soon afterwards, but it had been a sharp lesson for the government. A more effective mechanism of press control was needed. At the same time, some members of the Cabinet were also beginning to realise that the press might not be quite the irresponsible and disloyal enemy that Kitchener claimed. Yes, correspondents kept flouting army regulations in order to get the story that their editors demanded, but at the same time, there was considerable evidence that reporters, editors and newspaper proprietors were happy to strike a patriotic note, too. Not only were they repeating the propaganda about the Kaiser being a 'monster', for example, but most dispatches from the front were also careful to be upbeat about the soldiers' morale. Even Arthur Moore's revelations for *The Times* about the bloody retreat at Mons had included, 'Let me repeat that there is no failure in discipline, no panic, no throwing up of the sponge. Every one's temper is sweet, and nerves do not show. The men are … steady and cheerful.'

It seemed to show that perhaps the press could be trusted after all – up to a point anyway.

* * *

So, in June 1915, a new system for correspondents was introduced. It would allow what one member of the headquarters staff described as 'a few writing chappies' up to the front, but their movements, as well as what they wrote, would be strictly policed.

One of these privileged 'chappies' was Philip Gibbs, who was to file stories for the *Daily Telegraph* as well as the *Daily Chronicle*.

There were six of these official correspondents in all; most, like Gibbs, representing Britain's main daily papers. Gibbs' first act in his new role was to put on an officer's uniform – khaki jacket and tie with trousers tucked into puttees, regulation boots and a peaked cap which could be swapped for a tin helmet when danger dictated. He was told he had the honorary rank of captain, and was distinguished from a real officer by a green armband.

He and his fellow correspondents arrived at General Headquarters at St Omer, 20 miles inland from Calais, where they were greeted by the commander-in-chief himself, Sir John French. The general made a short speech, saying that he trusted their honour and loyalty, then they were taken to an old house in the nearby village of Tatinghem, which was to be their lodgings and their office. There were orderlies to run errands for them and to keep the place clean, there were lorries and cars with drivers to take them around, there was a group of officers who would escort them to the front, and – living, eating and sleeping with them – there were the censors.

Despite all these gestures of an official embrace, Gibbs and his fellows soon found they weren't always quite so welcome. Junior officers they met complained that they 'were prying around' and 'giving the whole show away'. The escort officers had been ordered to waste the correspondents' time as much as they could, and the censors assigned to Gibbs and the others were officers close to retirement, often yearning for the good old days of adventure in the British Empire, and resentful of now having to nursemaid this bunch of civilian intruders.

There was Colonel John Faunthorpe, a big game hunter who boasted of bagging more than 300 tigers, and who openly ridiculed Gibbs and the others. There was Hesketh Hesketh-Pritchard, ace sniper, explorer and first-class cricketer; Colonel the Hon. Neville Lytton, who annoyed the others by playing Bach on an eighteenth-century ivory flute and imitating the sound of a duck lapping weeds; and finally came Colonel Hutton Wilson, who insisted that all war correspondents were Bolsheviks.

The six correspondents settled into a set pattern of working. On days when it was expected there'd be some newsworthy action, they'd sit down and carve up between them the various sectors of the front. Then, each would set off in a chauffeur-driven car, notebook at the ready, and accompanied, of course, by an escort officer. Gibbs and the others then did their job as best they could, observing the fighting from as close as was safe, and interviewing anyone who'd talk to them.

By late afternoon, they'd be back at their house in Tatinghem and sitting around together, taking it in turns to share with the others what they'd seen, then each man went to his room to write his report. The deal was that they could hold back any personal impressions for use only in their own dispatches. The censors were on standby, ready to cross out anything they thought might be of use to the enemy, or – since they were, in practice, an unsupervised law unto themselves – anything they thought unpatriotic or just didn't like. Dispatch riders then rushed the censored reports to GHQ at St Omer, where staff secretaries dictated them by telephone to other secretaries in the War Office in London, so they could be typed out and hand-delivered to the various newspaper offices. Editors were required to publish their man's report in full, without any deletions or additions.

The results of this closely controlled system were hardly Pulitzer-Prize-winning journalism. On the eve of an attack, Gibbs wrote, 'It would be good to see the real business again and to thrill once more to the awful music of the guns'. And one of Gibbs' colleagues at the Tatinghem house, William Beach Thomas, on 4 August 1915, gave readers of the *Daily Mirror* a jaunty picture of life for the brave lads in the trenches:

As the chicken roasted and the frying potatoes sizzled, an occasional bullet 'pinged' over the trenches ... I might be saying that it was about the finest, proudest old regiment in the British army, which would be invidious in view of all the other finest, proudest old regiments in the British army.

And a few weeks later, he wrote:

There cannot be the least doubt about the goodwill prevailing between officers and men; the cheerful confidence as to the final result of the war which was characteristic of all ranks; whatever there may have been in the past, there seems to be splendid organisation today.

War correspondents examining a dud shell. William Beach Thomas of the *Daily Mail* is second from right, while far right is Perry Robinson of *The Times*. By their uniforms – and sometimes in their thinking – they were indistinguishable from army officers.

Ministers could see that the new system was working. Correspondents, so long as they were kept on a tight leash, weren't such a bad lot after all. They seemed as keen as Cabinet ministers to sustain the morale of the country. And thus it was that the mighty and the media – so often in the past at each other's throats – teamed up.

* * *

The stage was set for the First World War's most notorious cover-up conspiracy between the press on one side and the government and the generals on the other – the Battle of the Somme. It began on 1 July 1916 and would last for four and a half months. Three million men fought and a million were wounded or killed. On the first day alone, 19,240 British soldiers were killed, and another 38,230 were wounded.

During the opening hours of the fighting, the correspondents stayed in their quarters, as instructed by the chief of intelligence, General Charteris. Regular updates – carefully vetted, of course – were delivered to them on the progress of the fighting. This is what newspaper readers were told.

In the *Daily Chronicle*, Gibbs wrote:

It is on balance a good day for England and France. It is a day of promise in this war.

The Manchester Guardian reproduced the Press Association report, under the headline 'Our casualties not heavy':

The first day of the offensive is therefore very satisfactory ... It is no longer a question here of attempts to pierce as with a knife. It is rather a slow, continuous, and methodical push, **sparing in lives** [my emphasis].

And most papers used the Reuters report written by Herbert Russell:

> Good progress into enemy territory. British troops were said to
> have fought most gallantly and we have taken many prisoners.
> So far the day is going well for Great Britain and France.

This was all rehashed official communiques, but when, over
the next weeks, the correspondents were allowed out to see
the fighting for themselves, they kept up the pretence, even
though by now they could see that many tens of thousands of
men were being killed or wounded. Two weeks into the battle,
William Beach Thomas even told *Daily Mirror* readers that, for
one Lancashire regiment, climbing out of the trenches into a
hail of enemy bullets was like a jolly stroll in the countryside
with a few pals:

> Officers and men all speak with excitement and delight of 'going
> over'... As one officer put it, 'Going over means a dash into open
> air and freedom after the tedious, cramping life of the trenches'...
> Off they started and they ran straight into a storm of machine
> gun fire. But they went on in little groups of five or six, with ciga-
> rettes between their lips and Lancashire jokes in their mouths.
> Of course, they had casualties, but not a man faltered.

Compare this with an account by one volunteer officer in the
Sussex Yeomanry of what he came across, 'going over':

> The place was rotten with dead; green clumsy legs
> High booted, sprawled and grovelled along the saps
> And trunks, face downward, in the sucking mud,
> Wallowed like trodden sand-bags loosely filled;
> And naked sodden buttocks, mats of hair,
> Bulged, clotted heads slept in the plastering slime,
> And then the rain began, – the jolly old rain!

This is from Siegfried Sassoon's poem *Counter-Attack*. Sassoon was awarded the Military Cross for gallantry in action, and was wounded in 1917. He then became disillusioned with the aims and conduct of the war, and he detailed his reasons in a statement which was read out in Parliament. 'The war upon which I entered, as a war of defence and liberation,' he wrote, 'has now become a war of aggression and conquest.'

* * *

By 1917, it was clear to many back home in Britain that they were being sold a pack of lies by the papers. Their reports were now seen to be at odds with what they knew. There was barely a family without a husband, son, brother, uncle or nephew killed or wounded. At the Somme, some entire divisions – recruited from one county – had been almost wiped out. And yet Gibbs was still telling *Telegraph* readers – on 21 September, for instance – about wounded men 'in grand spirits' and that 'there was no moan among them whatever they'd suffered'.

Many of those in the fight, month after month, year after year, knew different. They blamed the press. G.H. Mair of the *Sunday Chronicle* wrote that the ordinary soldier came to have a much greater 'detestation for the institution of war correspondent than he had even for the Staff', which also tells us a lot about the falling morale of men who, by now, didn't trust their commanding officers either.

The government's answer was to step up propaganda, and the papers fell in with it. There was a glut of stories about the inhumanity of the enemy. So, when the *Daily Mail* demanded its man in Belgium, F.W. Wilson, come up with something suitably shocking, he – as he later admitted – invented a heart-rending story about 'a baby being rescued from the Hun in the light of burning homesteads'. *Mail* readers were so moved that thousands of them wrote in offering to adopt the infant. When the *Mail* instructed Wilson to send the baby to London, he announced that it had 'died of some very contagious disease so it couldn't even have a public burial'.

The most oft-repeated inhumanity story claimed that the Germans had set up a factory to boil down the corpses of their dead troops in order to make nitroglycerine for explosives, as well as boot polish. It first came to light in a *Times* report on 16 April 1917, which attributed it to a US Consul who'd visited Germany. And when the tale caught public attention, the paper published an account by its German correspondent verifying the factory's existence. *Punch* even published a cartoon showing a German scientist pouring his brother's boiled remains into a shell case.

It was all fake news. The Germans pointed out that the factory was actually processing the corpses of horses, not men. The British press ignored the denial, and it was not until 1925 that the UK Government of the day admitted that it had been a hoax, although whether started by the Head of Military Intelligence or by *The Times* itself has never been clear.

* * *

Today we are well aware of the suffering and the mass slaughter that was the First World War. From the population served by Britain's newspapers, 744,000 young men were killed or missing in combat, another 44,000 died from diseases contracted at the front. The wounded numbered 1,675,000.

Behind every one of these deaths or injuries there was a story of suffering on the battlefield, in hospitals, or back in Britain. We've come to learn about it through the writings of the war poets, books, films, TV documentaries, school lessons and exhibits in places such as the Imperial War Museum, and through annual armistice day commemorations. It is difficult, then, for us to imagine today that during the war itself, people knew next to nothing about the scale of the carnage.

Phillip Knightley, in *The First Casualty*, his excellent, comprehensive account of the war correspondent through the ages, points out that throughout the First World War, 'casualty figures became debased and lost their real meaning'. There's evidence, however, that at least some of the correspondents were only too aware of the magnitude of the killing. In 1923, Gibbs wrote that he and his fellow reporters had seen 'the whole organisation of that great machine of slaughter'.

Correspondents obviously couldn't know exact numbers, but they were aware that the deaths and injuries were on a vast scale, and Gibbs admits that he was deeply affected by what he witnessed. 'The effect of such a vision, year in, year out,' he wrote, 'can hardly be calculated in psychological effect.' As Knightley asks, why then did Gibbs not at the time make some effort to do his job as a journalist and report this gigantic, shocking story?

Historians are always careful to not judge the actions of our ancestors by the standards of our own day. We have to remember that during the First World War there was a real fear that Britain would be invaded, conquered, ruled by and absorbed into the German Empire. That could be stopped only by recruiting millions of men to form an armed human barrier against the potential invaders, and that, in turn, required steadfast support and enthusiasm back home from the wives, girlfriends, siblings, parents and friends of those men. We have to ask ourselves, if – for example – TV news cameras had been around in 1916, in the trenches shooting pictures for all to see of the kind of brutal and bloody scenes we now know were commonplace, what then would have happened to the war effort? As Prime Minister David Lloyd George said to *The Manchester Guardian*'s editor, C.P. Scott, in 1917, 'If the people really knew [the truth], the war would be stopped tomorrow. But of course, they don't know and can't know.'

It's undoubtedly true that the government had national security in mind when it introduced tight controls over the correspondents and what they wrote. By the standards of the day, and given the unprecedented scale of the fighting, that might be thought an honourable motive, but censorship and corralling journalists had other benefits for those in power, too. Wouldn't an unfettered press start to ask awkward questions? They might suggest that the high casualty numbers, for instance, were the result of incompetence by the generals. They might start to complain about the lack of government funding for armaments, or tell the public about any one of a thousand other blunders and oversights. So, it was an old story: gagging and blindfolding the correspondents was a way of letting those in power off the hook.

And what about the journalists? Why did they cave in, stick within the government's rules and fail to tell the truth? The system of control was, of course, heavily weighted against them, but then that's what reporters are always up against, and it's their job to be resourceful and find ways around such obstacles. Most correspondents were, without doubt, sucked into the need to be patriotic, and not – by revealing the discomfort and suffering of soldiers or the scale of defeats – to undermine national morale and so damage the war effort. And some correspondents so identified themselves with the men and officers around them that they went native. Some even took this a step further and pretended they were heroic warriors rather than objective reporters. Consider this dispatch, which appeared in *The People*, two weeks into the Battle of the Somme:

A thunderous crash is right in our ears; the shrapnel splinters ring on our steel helmets. A young Scot says 'I'm for the dressing station.'

'You're going the wrong way,' I answer. 'Come with me, I'll show you.' I help him over the rising ground and point down toward the road.

'Are we going over?' he pants out.

'Yes, my boy,' I answer and add unveraciously [i.e. lying], 'but the road's safe enough. Now boys, mind the wire, come on' ...we are over the parapet – through the barbed wire – we are under the bank – the machine gun is still at its work.

But is the journalists' own failure to challenge the authorities when things went wrong, and their compliance and co-operation in suppressing the truth, justifiable in any way, given the threat to the nation between 1914 and 1918? Here's what Beach Thomas, who'd reported for the *Mirror*, wrote seven years after the war ended:

A great part of the information supplied to us by British Army Intelligence was utterly wrong and misleading. The dispatches were largely untrue so far as they deal with concrete results. For myself, on the next day and yet more on the day after that, I was thoroughly and deeply ashamed of what I had written, for the very good reason that it was untrue.

Gibbs himself, writing in 1923, went even further:

We identified ourselves absolutely with the armies in the field. We wiped out of our minds all thought of personal scoops and all temptation to write one word which would make the task of officers and men more difficult or dangerous. There was no need of censorship of our dispatches. We were our own censors.

So it's hard to escape the conclusion that, during what came to be known as the Great War, journalists – in the other war, the centuries old conflict between the media and the mighty – threw in the towel, almost from the start. The press, with very few exceptions, conspired with the most powerful in the land to ignore uncomfortable truths, cover up blunders, and to lie and lie and lie again to the British public.

In 1920, Philip Gibbs was knighted for his services during the war as an official correspondent.

***

What makes the press' surrender even more surprising is that it didn't come at a time when the newspaper industry was weak – the reverse, in fact. The two main newspaper proprietors of the day, Lord Northcliffe and Lord Beaverbrook, controlled vast business and communications empires, and felt they had a right to instruct their editors what and how to report and what line to take in their leader columns. The power of the press barons was unprecedented. There was a joke doing the rounds during the war that in time of crisis 'Lord Northcliffe sent for the king'.

So, next we're going to find out more about the great newspaper emperors, and to see – once peace came – what impact they had on the balance of power between the media and the mighty.

11

THE PRESS BARONS

Mad, Bad and Dangerous

What the proprietorship of these papers is aiming at is power, but power without responsibility, the prerogative of the harlot throughout the ages.

Prime Minister Stanley Baldwin (1867–1947)

On the evening of 19 December 1934, Viscount Rothermere, owner of the *Daily Mail* and the *London Evening News*, climbed the steps to the columned entrance of the Reich Chancellery in Berlin, and a few minutes later amid its marble halls was shaking hands with Adolf Hitler. It was the German leader's first major formal reception for a foreign visitor at his official residence since he had taken power in January the year before. The line-up to greet Rothermere was worthy of a head of state. There was Hitler's right-hand man and the creator of the Gestapo, Herman Göring, the Minister of Propaganda Joseph Goebbels, as well as the Führer's close ally and foreign policy advisor, Joachim von Ribbentrop. Rothermere had brought with him his son, Esmond, and the *Mail*'s senior correspondent, George Ward Price, as well as the leading British banker and founder of the Anglo-German Fellowship, Ernest Tennant.

As the evening's banquet progressed, Hitler heaped praise on his guest of honour. At one point he even referred to Germany's defeat during the Great War, saying, 'Lloyd George and your brother won the war for Britain'. Rothermere was the younger brother of Lord Northcliffe (whom we met earlier supporting the Pankhursts and the suffragettes), and during 1915 Northcliffe had led a campaign through the pages of his newspapers to ensure enough shells and other ammunition reached the front line. Northcliffe's actions had forced the government to create a Ministry of Munitions headed by David Lloyd George, and the criticism voiced in Northcliffe's papers also helped bring down the government of Herbert Asquith. Hitler's remark about the role in the war played by Northcliffe and his newspapers was perceptive. It was an open recognition of the power wielded in Britain by wealthy newspaper owners.

The banquet was such a success that Rothermere formally invited the Führer to a return of his hospitality at Berlin's Adlon Hotel. Again, there was a similar list of attendees from Germany's topmost political rank with the addition, this time, of several women, including Frau Magda Goebbels, and an actress named Emmy

Sonnemann, who came with Göring. Partnering Rothermere was Princess Stephanie von Hohenlohe. It was Princess Stephanie who'd made all the arrangements over the previous days for the dinner party at the Adlon Hotel. She was, however, far more than Rothermere's fixer of catering. She was his mistress, his European ambassador, and – as we shall discover – a German spy.

Viscount Rothermere.

The two grand events of that December 1934 cemented a warm relationship between Rothermere and Hitler which would continue until the outbreak of war in 1939. The press baron's admiration of the Führer was not some sudden overnight happening. It had been building up over the previous four years.

* * *

Viscount Rothermere had started out as plain Harold Harmsworth. Unlike his brother, Alfred Lord Northcliffe, Harold did not see himself as a journalist. Not at this stage anyway. He was an accountant. The two men had founded the *Daily Mail* in 1896. Its slogan was 'A Penny Newspaper for One Halfpenny' and it broke new ground. It was the first paper in Britain to abandon the boring-looking mass of dense type on the front page which marked the other dailies. Instead, the *Mail* shouted out the news of the day with attention-grabbing banner headlines, and its news stories and articles were simple and short, designed to attract large numbers of working-class readers. The *Mail* was also the first paper to include a women's section with features on fashion and cookery.

Harold Harmsworth's career was typical of how the press barons developed their power, both in the UK and the USA. First would come a link-up between government and newspaper proprietor. The government needed favourable publicity, and in return for providing it, the man who controlled the newspapers would be rewarded, not only with public recognition, but sometimes with cash, and in Britain always with a peerage or some other ennoblement. Then, having once established himself, the typical press baron would assert his independence of government, no longer the servant, but now trying to be the master – the power behind the throne. Underpinning every step along the way was the baron's ability to influence the opinion of millions of people who read his newspapers each day.

During the war, Harmsworth, despite personal sadness – two of his sons were killed in action – made sure that the newspapers he controlled backed the government in the war effort. In 1917, the Liberal Prime Minister Lloyd George decided that such a loyal, talented and influential man needed to be drawn into the Cabinet itself, and he made Harmsworth Air Minister. Then, when the war ended, Lloyd George rewarded him with the title 1st Viscount Rothermere of Hemsted in the County of Kent.

However, by 1922 it became clear that the new Viscount Rothermere had his own agenda. After his brother's death that year, Rothermere was now in full control of the *Daily Mail*. The next two years saw the government change three times, with no party commanding an overall majority in the House of Commons. The Liberals, Conservatives and then the Labour Party all attempted to govern, and Rothermere was an influence one way or the other on the fate of all three. First, he reversed the *Daily Mail*'s previous support of Lloyd George and the Liberals – he was hoping to earn himself an even higher aristocratic title by backing instead a particular faction of the Tory Party. Then, when this Conservative grouping failed to form an effective coalition, it was the turn of the Labour Party, under Ramsay MacDonald. This was the first time that Britain had had a Labour prime minister, and Rothermere – like many in the Establishment – was appalled at the idea of a socialist ruling the country. So now he turned the *Mail* against Labour.

Matters came to a head in October 1924 when MacDonald, like his two predecessors, found himself without enough support on the floor of the House of Commons and had to declare yet another general election – the third in two years. And with four days to go before the people went to the polls, Rothermere was handed a powerful weapon to wield against the detested socialists.

A month before, MI5 had intercepted a letter signed by Grigory Zinoviev, chairman of the Soviet Union's Communist

International, whose declared aim was 'the overthrow of the international bourgeoisie and the creation of an international Soviet republic'. In the letter, Zinoviev urged British communists to promote revolution in the country through acts of sedition. The head of MI5 and the head of the Police Special Branch showed the letter to Prime Minister MacDonald, and the three men agreed to keep it secret. But someone leaked the text of the letter to the *Mail* and *The Times*. It was a godsend to Rothermere, and he published it. A *Mail* editorial set out to terrify its readers into voting Tory:

> Everything is to be made ready for a great outbreak of the abominable 'class war' which is civil war of the most savage kind. Meantime, the British people, as they do not mean to have their throats cut by Zinoviev's mercenaries, must bestir themselves ... For the safety of the nation, every sane man and woman must vote on Wednesday, and must vote for a Conservative government which will know how to deal with treason.

It did the trick. The Labour Party was trounced, and the Tories were elected by a landslide. MacDonald believed he was the victim of a conspiracy, and in a speech on 24 October, he declared:

> It is a most suspicious circumstance that a certain newspaper and the headquarters of the Conservative Association seem to have had copies of it at the same time as the Foreign Office, and if that is true how can I avoid the suspicion – I will not say the conclusion – that the whole thing is a political plot?

Rumours soon spread that the Zinoviev letter was a forgery, and it was claimed that it was leaked to the *Daily Mail* by a certain Major George Joseph Ball, who subsequently went to work for Conservative Central Office.

Rothermere was now firmly established at the final stage of the classic press baron's career. Using the power of his papers, he now saw himself as the grand puppet-master controlling who would and who wouldn't be in political office. And he was doing it to further his own personal views and prejudices, in particular, his loathing of left-wing politicians, whom he saw as crypto-communists.

The new Conservative prime minister, with a whopping 209-seat majority behind him, was Stanley Baldwin. We might think that his comfortable position in the House of Commons would put him well out of range of any press baron's heavy guns. But it did not. By 1926, the *Daily Mail* was selling over 2 million copies a day. Rothermere himself was reckoned to be the third richest man in Britain, and he was about to take on a new challenge worthy of his towering stature.

In 1929, he and Lord Beaverbrook, owner of the *Daily Express*, set aside their commercial rivalry, and together they mounted a campaign to persuade the government to turn the British Empire into a single trading bloc without barriers between its member nations. This set the two barons on a collision course with Prime Minister Baldwin, who favoured protecting British commerce with trade tariffs. The *Mail* and the *Express*, now reaching a combined readership of around 6 million, even ran their own Empire candidates in by-elections.

Rothermere's self-belief and ambition was now puffed up to demi-god proportions and, in 1930, in advance of the general election, he informed the prime minister that the *Daily Mail* would only support him if he revealed the names of at least eight out of ten members of his future Cabinet. Baldwin stood his ground and replied, 'A more preposterous and insolent demand was never made on a leader of any political party. I repudiate it with contempt and I will fight that attempt at domination to the end.' Then on 17 March 1931, at the Queen's Hall in

London, Baldwin made what was to become a famous speech attacking Rothermere and Beaverbrook:

> Their newspapers are not newspapers in the ordinary acceptance of the term, they are engines of propaganda for the constantly changing policies, desires, personal wishes, personal likes and personal dislikes of two men. What the proprietorship of these papers is aiming at is power, but power without responsibility, the prerogative of the harlot throughout the ages.

Today we've become used to a US President daily accusing the media of being liars, it's hard to appreciate the force of Baldwin's one-off attack against the press. Back in 1931, 'harlot' was a shocking insult to throw at men of such celebrity and power. Rothermere and Beaverbrook were unapologetic, but the anti-government vitriol of their pro-Empire campaign did begin to calm down.

* * *

Rothermere, however, was about to set his sights on an arena usually reserved for only the mightiest on the planet. It was now that he stepped onto the world stage and attempted not only to steer the direction of British foreign policy, but to be a driving force behind the great decisions over war and peace that would guide the future of Europe.

The new phase in his career began in the most unlikely of places: the casinos of Monte Carlo. When away from the heady challenges of running a newspaper empire and influencing governments, Rothermere loved gambling, and it was by the roulette tables of the Riviera in 1927 that he'd met Princess Stephanie von Hohenlohe. The FBI, who would later investigate allegations that the princess was a German spy, stated that it was no accidental meeting. They believed that she deliberately targeted the British press baron.

The FBI file described her as 'reputedly immoral, and capable of resorting to any means, even bribery, to get her ends'. She persuaded Rothermere that Germany and the other nations defeated in the First World War had been unnecessarily punished in the treaty after the fighting had finished. He was so impressed by her and her argument that he wrote in the *Mail* that the discontent among the defeated countries could be 'the starting point of another conflagration'.

The relationship between the viscount and the princess blossomed. It was probably sexual, and certainly political. And when, following the German elections in 1930, Adolf Hitler became leader of the second largest party in the Reichstag, she promoted the idea with Rothermere that the Nazis were Europe's most effective bulwark against communism. He responded by telling *Daily Mail* readers that they should celebrate Hitler's rise 'as the rebirth of Germany as a nation'.

In 1933, Princess Stephanie moved to London – to a sixth-floor apartment at the Dorchester Hotel – to be close to Rothermere. He was now paying her £5,000 a year to act as his emissary in Europe. At the same time, according to the French Secret Service, she'd been promised £300,000 (the equivalent of several million in today's money) from German sources if she could persuade Rothermere to campaign for the return to Germany of territory ceded to Poland at the end of First World War. She earned her money easily, and a suitable argument duly appeared in the *Mail*.

By now, Hitler had become Chancellor of Germany and the Nazis were in power, and Rothermere, in another *Mail* article, dismissed suggestions that this was a brutal dictatorship:

Nazi atrocities ... as anyone who visits Germany quickly discovers for himself, consist of a few isolated acts of violence ...

which have been generalised, multiplied, and exaggerated to give the impression that Nazi rule is a bloodthirsty tyranny.

And he even defended Nazi anti-Semitism. Germany, said his editorial, 'has been rapidly falling under the control of its alien elements ... Israelites of international attachments were insinuating themselves into key positions in the German administrative machine.'

* * *

The year 1934 also saw Rothermere turn the attention of *Daily Mail* readers to events nearer to home. He now tried to promote a British version of the Nazi regime. Oswald Mosley's National Union of Fascists (NUF) was growing in strength. It had between 35,000 and 40,000 paid-up supporters, known as the 'blackshirts', and the Conservative Party was getting worried that it was losing members to the NUF. Rothermere threw his support behind Mosley, and on 22 January the *Daily Mail* came out with a notorious front-page headline, 'Hurrah for the Blackshirts!', over pictures of Mosley and his supporters standing to attention. The accompanying report proclaimed in large type that it had been written 'By Viscount Rothermere'. It read:

> Timid alarmists all this week have been whimpering that the rapid growth in numbers of the British Blackshirts is preparing the way for a system of rulership by means of steel whips and concentration camps. Very few of these panic-mongers have any personal knowledge of the countries that are already under Blackshirt government ... As a purely British organisation ... they have no prejudice either of class or race.

And it ended with instructions on how young *Daily Mail* readers could join up.

But over the next six months, Rothermere came to the conclusion that Mosley didn't have the talents he recognised in Hitler
and when, in July, Mosley went to a meeting with Rothermere
in a hotel room, he found the viscount not standing to greet
him, but instead sprawled on the bed. And if the blackshirt leader
didn't get that message, a moment later he could be in no doubt
that the viscount had grown tired of him. When Mosely asked
the baron for his continued support, Rothermere replied, 'I'll let
you know. I'll let you know.' He never did. But there were no
more blackshirt hurrahs in the *Mail*.

✳ ✳ ✳

Meanwhile, Rothermere had given Princess Stephanie the job
of setting up a meeting with Hitler. So off she went to Berlin,
and there her title soon gave her an introduction to Hitler's personal adjutant, Captain Fritz Wiedemann, who she then lured
into her bed. Wiedemann reported back to Hitler that she was
Viscount Rothermere's mistress. The Führer gave Wiedemann
20,000 Reichsmarks to pay for her hotel suite, restaurant bills
and all her travel expenses, as well as to buy her expensive
clothes and gifts. Soon she was in Hitler's presence and receiving
a letter for Rothermere which thanked him for his support. She,
in turn, presented the Führer with a gift from the British press
baron. It was a framed reprint of the page from the *Daily Mail*,
which hailed Hitler's initial success in the German elections.

This, then, was the chain of events that now led to the grand
banquet in the Reich Chancellery in December 1934, with
Rothermere as guest of honour surrounded by the highest-
placed figures in the Nazi hierarchy. It was the first of several
meetings between the two men over the next months and
years. Several of the joint sessions were informal, all described
with great warmth by Rothermere in the columns of his paper.
There was the one 'beside a glowing log fire as the short winter

Hurrah for the Blackshirts!

BECAUSE Fascism comes from Italy, shortsighted people in this country think they show a sturdy national spirit by deriding it.

If their ancestors had been equally stupid, Britain would have had no banking system, no Roman law, nor even any football, since all of these are of Italian invention.

THE Socialists, especially, who jeer at the principles and uniform of the Blackshirts as being of foreign origin, forget that the founder and High Priest of their own creed was the German Jew Karl Marx.

Though the name and form of Fascism originated in Italy, that movement is not now peculiar to any nation. **It stands in every country for the Party of Youth.**

It represents the effort of the young generation to put new life into out-of-dats political systems.

That alone is enough to make it a factor of immense value in our national affairs.

Youth is a force that for generations has been allowed to run to waste in Britain. This country has been governed since far back in Victorian times by men in the middle sixties. When prosperity was general and the international horizon calm, that mattered little, but to cope with the grim problems of the present day the energy and vigour of younger men are needed.

Being myself in the middle sixties, I know how stealthily and steadily that seventh decade saps one's powers and stiffens one's prejudices.

By VISCOUNT ROTHERMERE

and disgusted by the incompetence of their elders in dealing with the depression that has followed on it. The other is made up of men too young to remember the war but ready to put all their ardour and energy at the service of a cause which offers them a vigorous constructive policy in place of the drift and indecision of the old political parties.

Blackshirts proclaim a fact which politicians dating from pre-war days will never face—that the new age requires new methods and new men. They base their contention on the simple truth that parliamentary government is conducted on the same lines as it was in the eighteenth century, though the conditions with which it

views" were an effective substitute in human affairs for action, the National Government would be the best that Britain has ever had. But the experience of the past two years has proved that these futile and time-wasting devices are no more than a screen for inertia and indecision.

THE huge majority obtained by the present Government at the general election of 1931 was the last vote of confidence that the nation will ever give to Old Gang politician. Two years from now another general election will be almost due. The whole future of Britain will depend upon its issue.

A prolongation of the present régime may be regarded, in the country's present mood, as out of the question. There will be a pronounced swing either to Right or Left.

If the inflated, impulsive, and largely ignorant electorate which Old Gang statesmen have brought into existence were to return the Rump of extreme

BRITISH BLACKSHIRTS MARCHING IN LONDON.

Daily Mail, 15 January 1934. Viscount Rothermere's notorious endorsement of British fascism.

afternoon faded into darkness'. And there was the one in Hitler's 'spacious but simple' rooms 'decorated to his own quiet taste, where he entertained myself and some of his more intimate collaborators to an after dinner concert which is his only relaxation'. Rothermere added:

> What magic has restored hope to the German hearts, given to German eyes the flash of self-confidence, and magnetised this mighty nation until one feels in its midst as if one were in a gigantic power house? Hitler. That is the whole answer.... His eyes have remarkable powers of magnetism.

It was as though the great newspaper magnate had been bewitched by the Führer.

Over the next three years, the *Daily Mail* became the British mouthpiece for the Nazis and their leader. Rothermere himself wrote editorials and sometimes, on his visits to Germany, news reports too. They all painted Hitler and his regime in sympathetic colours, while attempting to raise support in Britain for an alliance with Germany.

In July 1936, *Mail* readers were told, 'The close association in international affairs of two such mighty states would create a force that no aggressor would dare to challenge.'

In May 1938, following the violence of Kristallnacht, when Jewish businesses and synagogues were smashed and 30,000 Jews became the first of 6 million to be shipped off to concentration camps, Rothermere published a bizarre defence of the man responsible:

> Herr Hitler is proud to call himself a man of the people, but, notwithstanding, the impression that has remained with me after every meeting with him is that of a great gentleman ... He is a man of rare culture. His knowledge of music, painting and architecture is profound.

Outlandish as Rothermere's opinions seem to us today, we have to remember that he was not a lone voice in 1930s Britain. There were many in the country's top political and other influential circles who held similar views. So, for instance, even the former Liberal Prime Minister David Lloyd George, who met Hitler in 1936, described him as 'the greatest living German'. And in 1938, the British Government negotiated peace – if not an alliance – with Hitler's Germany. Prime Minister Neville Chamberlain, after flying back from Munich where he'd agreed a non-aggression pact with Hitler, was surrounded by jubilant crowds at the airport, as he held high a piece of paper and declared it 'peace in our time'. That didn't make Chamberlain and his Cabinet Hitlerphiles, but it did show that they regarded the Führer as an honourable man they could do a deal with. Rothermere was the public voice of this movement, and by the time of the Munich pact, it was a voice that was getting hysterical. He sent Hitler a telegram to congratulate him, 'Frederick the Great was a great popular figure, may not Adolf the Great become an equally popular figure? I salute your excellency's star which rises higher and higher.'

And even the following year, just four months before the outbreak of war, Rothermere was still worshipping the German Chancellor, endorsing his Aryan racism and pressing for an Anglo-German alliance. Hitler, he wrote in the *Daily Mail*:

> ... believes that Germany has a divine mission and that the German people are destined to save Europe from the designs of revolutionary communism ... Herr Hitler has a great liking for the English people. He regards the English and the Germans as being of one race.

It was to be the press baron's last hurrah. A month later, he relinquished ownership of the *Daily Mail* to his son, Esmond. So what caused this U-turn? Rothermere had suddenly found himself on the wrong side of history, and – what was more damaging – on the wrong side of Princess Stephanie. He'd ended his relationship with her in January and tried to pay her off. She sued him for breach of contract. That triggered the British security services to take an interest and they seized documents that turned out to be copies of letters between Rothermere and Hitler. MI5 warned the government that if the papers were made public, not only Rothermere but other members of the British aristocracy would be embarrassed too, so they were suppressed, but enough was revealed in the princess' court case to show that Rothermere had negotiated in secret with Hitler.

The viscount was now worried that he could be arrested and charged with treason. So, he paid the princess a large, undisclosed sum to keep quiet and to leave the country. He also fled and went to live in Bermuda.

On the morning of the outbreak of war, 4 September 1939, the *Daily Mail*, now controlled by Rothermere's son, ran a front-page editorial, as though the word 'hypocrisy' had never been invented:

> No statesman, no man with any decency could think of sitting at the same table with Hitler or his henchman the trickster von Ribbentrop, or any other of the gang. We fight against the blackest tyranny that has ever held men in bondage. We fight to defend and to restore freedom and justice on earth.

If not an apology, it was at least a wise commercial decision to reflect a changing mood in the nation.

Fourteen months later, Harold Harmsworth, 1st Viscount Rothermere of Hemsted in the County of Kent, former press baron, died in luxurious exile.

***

'Mad, bad and dangerous to know', the words used by Lady Caroline Lamb to describe her lover, Lord Byron, could just as well be applied to the press barons and to their successors, the 'media magnates' who, in our own day, have come to own TV news channels as well. Rothermere was one in a line of them.

One of the first of the breed, James Gordon Bennett Senior, who owned the *New York Herald* in the mid-nineteenth century, declared, 'Nothing can prevent success but God Almighty, and he happens to be entirely on my side'. The power to mould the minds of millions of ordinary citizens was such a heady drug that it often bent the brains of the men who fed on that power.

A press baron amid the mighty: Churchill's coalition government, May 1940. Lord Beaverbrook, owner of the *Daily Express*, seated second from left, had just been appointed Minister of Aircraft Production.

Then there was Joseph Pulitzer who, three decades later, founded the *St Louis Post Dispatch* and the *New York World*. Pulitzer pioneered what became known as 'yellow journalism', badly researched stories, more thrilling or shocking than relevant to readers' lives. He used the news and opinion pages of his New York paper to get himself elected as congressman, and – without a whiff of irony – to crusade against the influence of big business.

Megalomania, for Pulitzer, brought real madness. He became so terrified of any noise that he had constructed a completely soundproof annex to his mansion on New York's East 73rd Street. It had padded doors, cork floors, double walls and a ventilation chimney hung with thousands of silken threads to absorb the faintest whisper.

One of Pulitzer's most renowned contemporaries, Edward Wyllis Scripps, was, in the end, hardly more rational.

Scripps founded thirty-two newspapers, which he microman-
aged from his desert mansion in California. His editors would
be summoned there and find this bearded figure in a skullcap
– he was terrified of catching cold – rawhide boots and dressed
like a hobo. He reputedly smoked forty cigars and drank a gallon
of whisky a day.

Lloyd George, who found himself at times both the benefi-
ciary and the victim of press barons' power, coined a phrase for it.
In 1919, he told the House of Commons that Lord Northcliffe
was suffering from 'diseased vanity', and he tapped his own head
to make the point. It was true that newspaper proprietors –
despite the fact that their power came from an ability to influence
popular opinion – often cared little what others thought of them
personally. *Daily Express* night editors, for example, would get a
phone call at 3 a.m. from Lord Beaverbrook and hear in the background the silly giggles of a mistress.

Whether the madness of these magnates was manifest in
certifiable dementia or extreme eccentricity, it almost always
involved a blind – almost religious – belief in themselves and
their ability to change the world. The late twentieth-century
owner of the London *Daily Mirror* and the *New York Daily News*,
Robert Maxwell – described as a 'great brute who liked to act
as God on five telephones' – reportedly once installed himself
in a penthouse suite organising world peace via phone calls
to Mother Teresa. He became increasingly paranoid about his
employees and had the offices of those he suspected of disloy-
alty wired to hear their conversations. He eventually fell to his
death off the back of his yacht. It was then discovered that he'd
propped up his empire by diverting hundreds of millions of
pounds from pension funds and other sources. Maxwell's empire
was dissolved and sold off in the following years.

The highest accolade for being 'bad and dangerous to
know', however, must go to William Randolf Hearst. At its
height, his empire consisted of thirty newspapers, including

the *San Francisco Examiner* and the *New York Journal*, plus many magazines. He paid gangs of hoodlums to terrorise striking journalists on the *Chicago Examiner*, as well as to beat up news vendors – about thirty were murdered – in order to dissuade them from selling his rivals' newspapers. He was twice elected to Congress, and in 1904 he even ran for the Democratic nomination for President of the United States. He was defeated by the party's conservative wing, who didn't like his advocacy of working men's rights – they were the ones who bought his papers.

In the 1930s, however, he switched politics dramatically to the far right, and became a vocal advocate of fascism. Like Rothermere, he struck up a relationship with Hitler. When the two men met, the Führer asked him why he was so unpopular back home. The press magnate replied, 'Because Americans believe in democracy, and are averse to dictatorship.' Hearst's newspapers started to run unchallenged accounts of speeches by the Nazi leader, Hermann Göring, and by Hitler himself, as well as Mussolini and various dictators in Latin America. Hearst was the model for Orson Welles' 1941 film *Citizen Kane*, and was so enraged by it that he banned any advertising, reviews or mention of it in his papers.

✳ ✳ ✳

On our journey through the first 400 years of the relationship between the media and the mighty, we've often seen governments hijacking the press by one means or another – bribery, bullying, censorship, cronyism, or however. The result has been few out-and-out fist fights between the two blocs. But that's exactly what the press barons engineered. They accumulated so much power that they were able to assert the independence of their newspapers from government, but it wasn't the independence of a press committed to attacking the mighty with the power of truth, nor even of a press representing popular opposition to a government, it was an independence summed up in the words of that early newspaper owner, James Gordon Bennett Senior, 'Get out of my way, ye drivelling editors and drivelling politicians!' Note the words '*my* way'. The press became the personal tool of men like Northcliffe, Rothermere, Hearst and all the others, who sooner or later became obsessed to the point of mania by their own importance.

The clue to how the press barons managed to accumulate such power can be put in two simple words: market and machines. The market for news in the nineteenth century grew and spread like a forest fire in a drought. The press has always been about much more than disseminating facts and opinions. It's been about making money, because people are, and always have been, willing to pay to find out what's going on in the world and what others think about it. With the spread of education to the masses in the nineteenth century, the demand for news sky-rocketed.

At the same time, the machinery had arrived to meet that demand. The technology – the steam-powered rotary press – had been invented and was, decade by decade, improved until millions of newspapers could be printed in just a few hours overnight. The result was that the press became big business. But the business leaders who built those commercial press empires found themselves in a different position from other great entrepreneurs: oil magnates, car manufacturers, high financiers, and the rest. Press barons not only acquired wealth, but they also controlled a mechanism which could sway public opinion, and they used both. That was real power.

Lord Beaverbrook was a past master at combining the two – money and publicity – to get his own way. He enjoyed using his papers to attack his opponents and promote his friends, and it was said that he believed he could buy anyone and anything. His defenders would say that he didn't go quite as mad and bad as some of his fellow press barons. Like Hearst, he used his newspapers to get into politics, and became a Cabinet minister during both world wars. In 1941, when he was Minister of Aircraft Production, he was credited with increasing the output of fighter planes and bombers by 15 per cent. That was an undoubted service to his country. But, like the other great newspaper proprietors, he turned the press into a weapon of personal power, ready to shoot down anyone who disagreed with him. And he used his *Daily Express* to plug his own pet scheme, the Empire crusade, which – as we saw – earned him, alongside Rothermere, a prime minister's damnation as the 'harlot' yearning for 'power without responsibility'.

So, back in the interwar years, was any part of the press clean of megalomaniac owners? C.P. Scott, of *The Manchester Guardian*, perhaps. He made no secret of his liberal views nor that his was a liberal paper, but his famous credo that 'comment is free, but facts are sacred' underpinned a clear definition of a newspaper's function, one which any student of the craft could subscribe to today. He argued that a journalist's job is accurate news reporting. Even editorial comment, he claimed, has its responsibilities, 'It is well to be frank; it is even better to be fair'. And with an eye, no doubt, on the press barons, he added, 'Although the business side of a newspaper must be competent; if it becomes dominant, the paper will face distressing consequences'.

There was also part of the newspaper industry that the barons, busy with their national titles commanding millions of readers, often didn't bother with. That was the British regional press. When, just before the war, some of Viscount Rothermere's dealings with Hitler were becoming known, the *Yorkshire Post* published a sober, rather dull editorial, but one which seems a breath of respectable fresh air amid all the mad, bad, dangerous doings:

> Discussions with heads of foreign governments are best left to persons whose status is on both sides clearly understood. A newspaper owner has great responsibilities towards the public

of his own country; he should be particularly chary of placing himself in situations liable to misinterpretation, or abuse abroad.

***

The outbreak of the Second World War in September 1939 brought questions on both sides of the media–mighty divide. For the government, the issue was – would the press do their patriotic duty? Would ministers and generals be able to manage and control reporting of hostilities as they had during the Great War? And, for reporters, editors and newspaper proprietors, the worry was – would censorship stop them writing what they wanted?

Which side would be calling the shots? That's the question we're going to answer next.

12

THE SECOND WORLD WAR

Bloody Marvellous!

The two most important American war correspondents are the two men who sit in Washington and prepare the army and navy communiques.

Newsweek *magazine, 20 July 1942*

In early August 1943, General George S. Patton Jr, commander of the United States Seventh Army, was visiting troops in a military hospital evacuation tent in Sicily, when he noticed a soldier slouched on a stool who didn't seem to have much wrong with him. Those who witnessed what happened next were shocked.

Patton was a controversial figure. Dwight D. Eisenhower, at the time supreme commander of the Allied forces in Africa and southern Europe, and later America's 34th President, pronounced him 'the most brilliant commander of an army in the open field that our or any other service produced'. Patton's nickname was 'Old blood and guts'. He deliberately cultivated a flashy image, with his pearl-handled, silver-plated revolvers in cowboy holsters, his highly polished helmet, riding breeches and high cavalry boots. He often assumed a threatening scowl which he called his 'war face', and regarded glory as the legitimate ambition for every military man.

General Patton, left, with Brigadier General Theodore Roosevelt Jr., during the invasion of Sicily, at about the time of the slapping incidents.

The soldier who'd come to Patton's attention in the hospital tent was Private Charles Kuhl, who'd been diagnosed by doctors as suffering from 'exhaustion' and 'psychoneurosis anxiety'. Patton went over and asked him where he was wounded. Kuhl shrugged, and said he felt 'nervous', adding, 'I guess I can't take it'. The general was incensed, and he slapped Kuhl across the chin with his gloves, then he grabbed the man by the collar and dragged him to the tent entrance, shoved him out and kicked him in the butt, yelling, 'Don't admit this son of a bitch!' He ordered the medical staff to send Kuhl back to the front, then screamed, 'You hear me, you gutless bastard? You're going back to the front!' Patton continued to rage for the rest of his tour of the hospital, and the *Daily Mail* correspondent, Noel Monks, overheard him shouting, 'There's no such thing as shell shock. It's an invention of the Jews'. Kuhl was picked up and brought back inside, where it was discovered that he had a fever and soon after was diagnosed with malaria.

A week later, General Patton was visiting another evacuation hospital, and this time spotted a soldier who was huddled and shivering, and asked him what the trouble was.

The man replied, 'It's my nerves. I can't stand the shelling anymore.'

Patton again lost his temper, slapped him across the face, and began yelling, 'Your nerves, hell, you're just a goddamned coward. Shut up that goddamned crying. I won't have these brave men who have been shot at seeing this yellow bastard sitting here crying!' Then he slapped him again, and shouted: 'You're going back to the front lines and you may get shot and killed, but you're going to fight. If you don't, I'll stand you up against a wall and have a firing squad kill you on purpose. In fact, I ought to shoot you myself, you goddamned whimpering coward!'

And with that, he pulled out his pistol. The hospital commander intervened, Patton left the tent and was heard to declare, 'I won't have those cowardly bastards hanging around our hospitals. We'll probably have to shoot them some time anyway, or we'll raise a breed of morons.'

This time, however, he'd picked on the wrong man. The soldier he'd assaulted and threatened was Private Paul Bennett, a four-year veteran at the age of 21, with an excellent fighting record throughout the Sicilian and Tunisian campaigns. He'd been brought in to the hospital with symptoms of dehydration, fatigue and confusion, and hadn't been able to sleep since his friend had been wounded. Nevertheless, he'd told doctors he wanted to get back to the front line, and had to be ordered to stay in bed.

Reporters based at the local press camp were aware of the two incidents, and they interviewed medical staff to fill in the details. The doctors and nurses had been particularly upset by the sight of the general waving his gun at the sick soldier. The twenty or so journalists based there then held a meeting to decide what to do next. They all agreed not to file the story. They felt that for it to be widely known that a four-star general like Patton had assaulted and abused sick soldiers would depress morale both in the armed forces and back home. So, instead of publishing the facts, they chose three of their number – Demaree Bess of the *Saturday Evening Post*, Merrill Mueller of *NBC News* and Quentin Reynolds of *Collier's Magazine* – to fly to Army Headquarters in Algiers and give a summary of the incidents to Patton's superior, General Eisenhower himself.

Eisenhower told the correspondents they were free to write the story if they wished, but he made his own view clear: it would be a powerful propaganda weapon for the enemy and would embarrass the US Army command. The reporters tried to do a deal. They'd withhold publishing an account of Patton's behaviour if Eisenhower, in return, would fire him. That would have made the supreme commander of Allied forces in Africa and southern Europe the puppet of the press, and there was no way he could even consider it. He refused. The journalists thought about it, and decided to suppress the story anyway. And that's the way it stayed for the next three months.

During that time, however, the slapping incidents became common knowledge throughout the US Army ranks. Eisenhower was sufficiently concerned to hold his own investigation, found the story to be true and wrote to Patton. The language of the letter was uncompromising, and spoke of the general's 'brutality' and 'abuse of the sick' with an 'exhibition of uncontrollable temper in front of subordinates'. And it suggested Patton apologise not only to the two men he'd hit, but to all the medical staff as well. An Associated Press correspondent, Edward Kennedy, went to see Eisenhower and warned him this would mean the story would get out anyway, and why not let the correspondents write it so there was an accurate account? Eisenhower again refused.

Patton kept his dissatisfaction to himself, writing in his diary, 'It is rather a commentary on justice when an Army commander has to soft-soap a skulker to placate the timidity of those above'. Nevertheless, he regarded his commander's letter as an order, and he summoned the two privates to his office to say sorry. Next, he visited the hospitals to do the same in front of the doctors and nurses. Then finally, he drove to each division under his command and gave a fifteen-minute address in which he apologised for any instances where he had been too harsh on soldiers. He didn't refer specifically to the slapping incidents, but by now everyone knew what it was all about. At his final speech, when the moment came for him to say sorry, he was interrupted. The men knew what was coming and before him began a chant of 'No, general, no, no!' Their show of support left Patton close to tears.

The embargo on publishing any account of the slapping incidents was broken, not by correspondents attached to Patton's forces, but back in Washington. Drew Pearson, a journalist and radio broadcaster, got to hear of it through a friend who was a staffer in a government office. Pearson decided he'd tell the story on his radio show, and submitted the script for censorship. However, because he was on home soil, he wasn't subject to the same censorship as correspondents in the field. The internal censor's office in Washington seemed out of its depth, didn't think it could stop a story on the grounds that it might damage morale, and let it through.

And so, on 21 November, Pearson revealed Patton's misconduct to his listeners. Or rather, he recited a garbled version. He somehow mixed details of the two assaults into one, then declared that the soldier in hospital was 'out of his head' and had screamed at Patton, 'Duck down or the shells'll hit you!', before the general struck him. Pearson twice announced in the broadcast, with no evidence, that Patton's career was over – he'd never command a combat unit again.

At Eisenhower's HQ, there was confusion. At first, in a knee-jerk reaction, a blanket ban was thrown over anything to do with the story. Then a staff officer issued a statement setting out the bare facts, and told correspondents they could use that and nothing else. Finally, another officer announced they could write whatever they knew was true. Although now three months old, the Patton slappings, in all their disreputable detail, made front-page news and led radio news broadcasts across the United States and much of the rest of the world.

The Times in London was not so sure. Its correspondent in Algiers, Philip Ure, was still worried about possible damage to the war effort. The editor agreed. So, the paper ran a small down-page item beneath the headline 'An unfortunate incident' (note the singular), in which Ure wrote that the whole thing had now been put into perspective by the US Army statement, and he concluded, 'General Patton is too great a commander to be anywhere but in the field of active service'.

***

The way both the media and the mighty handled the Patton slapping incidents tells us a lot about relations between the two during the Second World War. The media had become steadily more powerful. This was partly because of the continuing influence of the press barons, but it was also the result of improved technology. The telegraph, the telephone and wireless transmission – though they might seem primitive to us today – were delivering correspondents' reports back to newsrooms in Britain and America ever faster. At the same time, more efficient presses could now churn out millions of newspaper copies in a few hours. And there was a new means of distributing news. All-day radio had arrived in America, and – via the BBC – in Britain. So, the reading and listening public on both sides of the Atlantic were now used to getting the news, in full, every day. They expected their favourite newspaper or radio station to keep them informed. Governments couldn't ignore that.

So, if the media had become stronger, why had they caved in and not even attempted to defy the government and publish the Patton story? The answer is that, in the way journalists saw their wartime role, not too much had changed since the Great War. In fact, governments and generals had soon found with the outbreak of war that the media – by and large – was on their side. Many war reporters again identified with the officers around them, and correspondents and editors felt a strong obligation to support the war effort. So Eisenhower knew he wasn't taking much of a risk when he appealed to their sense of patriotic duty not to give details of a high-ranking general's misconduct and so undermine morale in the army and back home.

When the story did break, three months later, there was something of a difference between the way the two lots of journalists, the Americans and the British, handled it. Unlike the American papers and radio, who'd pounced on the story as soon as they saw they couldn't be blamed for revealing it, the London *Times* had buried it. The paper couldn't ignore the story, but felt it had to make clear to its readers that no real harm had been done by the general's behaviour. Throughout the war, although both the British and American media tended to identify themselves with government policy, that was more marked among British reporters and editors. Why was that? The most likely explanation is that the constant threat of an enemy invasion of Britain was more immediate than that faced by Americans. Therefore, the need to do everything possible to support the war effort was that much greater in Britain. And that meant the press and the BBC were expected to get behind the war effort.

✳ ✳ ✳

On the outbreak of war in 1939, the British Government and the military hierarchy had decided the best way to protect national security was to control the press just as they had in the Great War. An Emergency Powers (Defence) Act was immediately approved by Parliament, which meant everyone, including newspaper editors, were banned from 'obtaining, recording, communicating to any other person or publishing information which might be useful to the enemy'. A Ministry of Information was set up to put out official statements (its staff numbered 999), and Allied generals got their adjutants to dust off the old 1914–18 files on press relations. There would be an official 'correspondent' to be called 'Eyewitness', just like before, and a limited number of reporters, shepherded by conducting officers, would be installed at GHQ in northern France to report on the British Expeditionary Force. They'd be allowed to send back tightly censored reports which didn't damage morale.

Even the GHQ conducting officers seemed a throwback to the old-school eccentrics who'd done the job last time. Many were upper-class pre-First World War cavalry officers, who may once have had their gallantry recognised, but were now surplus to combat requirements. Typical was Captain Charles Tremayne, former chairman of the Beaufort Hunt and captain of the England polo team, who drank gin for breakfast, and – it was said – could get through six bottles in two days.

The thirty-two privileged newsmen who now found themselves under the supervision of Tremayne and the other escort officers soon found it a ludicrous arrangement. One of them, O.D. Gallagher of the London *Daily Express*, who'd cut his teeth as a war correspondent in the Spanish Civil War, got so frustrated that he wrote a tongue-in-cheek dispatch which suggested getting rid of newspaper correspondents at the front entirely. 'Why not do like the Germans,' he asked, 'and instead rely on official propaganda? At least that would be more honest.' The censors told him they didn't like his attitude, and he found himself on a boat back to London. There, the *Express* editor told Gallagher that he saw the truth of what he'd written, but didn't feel able to publish it, because 'we can't fight the army in wartime'.

The *Express* did make one complaint. It wasn't a demand for the freedom to report whatever it wanted, it was a demand for a better standard of propaganda. When the Germans invaded Poland at the end of September 1939, the communiques put out by the Ministry of Information were so useless that the paper told its readers, 'Soon Britain will need leaflet raids on itself to tell its own people how the war is going'.

* * *

During these early months, there was little action for the correspondents at GHQ in northern France to report, and they called it the 'Bore War'. All that changed in May 1940, when the German Army rapidly advanced through Belgium, Holland, Luxembourg and into France.

Over a period of eight days, 338,000 British soldiers were rescued from the beaches around Dunkirk by a hastily assembled fleet of 800 small private boats which ferried them back to the Kent coast. Overnight 'Operation Dynamo', as it was known, became a legend of British never-say-die, all-pulling-together spirit. It was the newspapers who, following the government's lead, created that legend. And they did it without having a single correspondent there to witness the event at first hand.

As the Germans advanced, GHQ had decamped with its staff, and that included the correspondents and photographers based there. By the time of the evacuation of Dunkirk, they were all back across the Channel in England. So, the papers had to rely solely on interviews with the troops coming ashore, who were overjoyed at being safe now. They told of dauntless discipline, dispatch riders entertaining crowds of soldiers with a display of acrobatics, while overhead Nazi Stuka dive-bombers threatened, and men played cricket on the sand to pass the time.

The other big angle on the story was Prime Minister Winston Churchill's speech to the House of Commons on 4 June. Taken overall, it was a balanced assessment. He gave a detailed account of the fighting which had preceded Dunkirk and described it as 'a colossal military disaster'. Of Dunkirk itself, he reminded the country, 'We must be very careful not to assign to this deliverance the attributes of a victory. Wars are not won by evacuations.'

However, it was the inspiring rhetoric of Churchill's conclusion that has remained in the public mind ever since, and that was what the papers seized on:

We shall go on to the end, we shall fight in France, we shall fight
on the seas and oceans, we shall fight with growing confidence
and growing strength in the air, we shall defend our Island, whatever the cost may be, we shall fight on the beaches, we shall fight
on the landing grounds, we shall fight in the fields and in the
streets, we shall fight in the hills; we shall never surrender.

The *Daily Mirror*'s banner headline over its Dunkirk story was
'BLOODY MARVELLOUS!'. The word 'bloody' in 1940 was
far more risqué than today. So, the *Mirror*'s headline was the language of the ordinary soldier. It might have shocked, but it was
from the mouths of heroes. The *Sunday Dispatch* suggested that
God had been responsible for saving so many lives:

> The English Channel, that notoriously rough stretch of water,
> which has brought distress to so many holidaymakers in hap-
> pier times, became as calm and smooth as a pond ... and while
> the smooth sea was aiding our ships, a fog was shielding our
> troops from devastating attack.

Even the *New York Times* was infected by the enthusiasm, 'So
long as the English tongue survives, the word "Dunkirk" will be
spoken with reverence'.

Twenty years later, when the war was long over, historical
research revealed that, while undoubtedly there had been much
calm courage on the beaches of Dunkirk, that wasn't the whole
story. There'd been less heroic incidents too: troops hiding in a
cellar screaming drunk, savage gangs of soldiers – deserted by
their officers – looting the town, a corporal of a Guards regiment who'd had to threaten to shoot anyone on his boat who
disobeyed him, and more.

Even if reporters had been there to witness such incidents, the
question is whether any British newspaper would have published
them knowing that it would bring shame to a nation desperate

for reassurance. We can't know for sure, but it would have been out of character at the time for papers to print anything which might puncture the rising balloon of euphoria that was Dunkirk.

Looked at purely from the point of view of what was best for national security, and even survival, we can admit it's fortunate the full picture didn't emerge at the time. But looked at against the ebb and flow of power between the media and the mighty, Dunkirk is a graphic illustration of how, during the Second World War, the press was happy to drop journalistic objectivity and accuracy, and instead join hands with the government and the generals in a vigorous bout of morale-boosting propaganda.

Newspapers reacted like this partly out of patriotic duty, and correspondents sometimes – as in the Great War – saw themselves as soldiers armed with pens not guns, but editors and newspaper owners also wanted to please their readers. The British people were in the mood to be cheered up and so that's what they got.

***

There was another way in which the Second World War dealt the advantage to government in the information battle for the minds of the country's newspaper readers and radio listeners. The 1939–45 conflict was truly a world war, fought across four continents, with its effects felt even in the remotest spots on the planet. When battles were fought and armies advanced and retreated, it often happened at such speed and over such a vast area that it was impossible for even the most assiduous war correspondent to do anything but report a microcosm of events. Journalists were almost always dependent on the authorities for any overall picture of who was winning and who was losing. The days of the war reporter sitting on horseback next to the generals atop a hill to watch the cavalry charge in the valley below were long gone.

For a start, much of the conflict now was up in the clouds. In the days after Dunkirk, the Luftwaffe began to attack convoys of ships in the Straits of Dover and then targets in south-east England. RAF fighter planes took to the air, day after day, to bring them down. The British people could be forgiven for thinking this was a part of the war that they could see and understand for themselves, but that was far from being so.

The Battle of Britain could be seen, day after day, by the people of Kent, while the rest of the country was treated to commentaries on the radio. Here's the BBC correspondent Charles Gardner. It's the summer of 1940:

> There's one coming down in flames – there, somebody's hit a German – and he's coming down completely out of control – ah, the man's bailed out by parachute – he's going to slap into the sea and there he goes – SMASH – Oh boy, I've never seen anything so good as this – the RAF fighters have really got these boys taped.

A bit of *Boys' Own* adventure was one thing; however, what it meant was quite another. Was this picture of 'flames' and 'SMASH' part of a victory, or was it an exception? As the *Express* man, O.D. Gallagher, wrote later, 'You watched a dogfight. You saw a spurt of smoke … How could you hope to know where it came down?' But readers and listeners had to be given a bigger picture. And they got it, albeit dressed up like a cricket match. 'Biggest raid ever. Score 78 to 26. England still batting', proclaimed the newspaper sellers' street billboards of East London.

The number of losses came from the only source that could possibly know, the Air Ministry. On 15 September it put out a press release announcing that 185 German planes had been shot down on the 'greatest day' in the battle. However, later evidence showed that the government was not in the business of factual reporting. The real number of German planes lost that day was not 185, as announced, but just sixty.

During most of the fighting, in most of the theatres of war, the authorities were the ones in control of the key information that tracked whether the enemy was in retreat or triumphant, or whether the Allies were. And ministers and generals didn't pause before massaging the figures, if that was what it took to keep the people on side. Even when conditions for reporters were as good as they got, it still wasn't easy to build up an overall picture. The North African desert – where, for three years, Allied and German forces did battle – was described as 'a correspondent's paradise'. There were no towns or cities, no civilians to get in the way of attacks, just a vast, flat plain where two sets of enemy tanks could slug it out. Alan Moorhead of the *Express* called it a 'knight's tournament in empty space'. Correspondents were free to go where they wanted, censorship was thought to be reasonable. It all sounds straightforward, but Moorhead later described the reality:

> From the first to the last, we never 'saw' a battle in the desert. We were simply conscious of a great deal of dust, noise and confusion. The only way we could gather a coherent picture was by driving hard from one headquarters to another and by picking up reports from the most forward units.

The complexities of war technology and the vastness of battle-fields had, by the 1940s, skewed the information battle between the media and mighty in favour of the mighty. And there was not much the media could do about it.

* * *

The US authorities may have been more liberal than the British in the way they applied their censorship, but at the worst of times the Americans didn't hesitate to put the First Amendment right to a free press on one side and suppress even the most momentous news.

On 7 December 1941, Japanese bombers headed for Honolulu, and then dived to bomb and strafe the main base of the US Pacific Fleet at Pearl Harbor. By the time the last Japanese war plane disappeared in the eastern sky, five American battleships had been sunk and three others, along with three cruisers and three destroyers, had been badly damaged. Some 200 US aircraft were left burning wrecks, and 2,344 American forces personnel were dead. The Pacific Fleet was almost crippled.

The US service chiefs decided that the American people couldn't stomach such catastrophic news, and they immediately took steps to stop it getting out. Reporters in the Honolulu office of the United Press news agency had begun phoning over the

The battleship USS *Arizona* burning after the Japanese attack on Pearl Harbor. The *Arizona* was bombed four times before it sank, and among the 1,177 crewmen killed were 23 sets of brothers. Pictures like this, and the full details of the casualties, were withheld at the time.

first dramatic accounts of the attack when suddenly they found all lines cut. Then, an official communique was issued. It stated that only one old battleship and a destroyer had been sunk, while the Japanese 'had suffered heavy casualties'. The Secretary of the Navy, Colonel Frank Knox toured the wreckage of Pearl Harbor, then back in New York announced at a press conference that the entire balance of the Pacific Fleet 'with its aircraft carriers, heavy cruisers, light cruisers, destroyers and submarines is uninjured and is all at sea seeking contact with the enemy'.

It was hard to conceal the scale of such a huge disaster which had taken place alongside a large American city, but because the American press didn't challenge the official version, the news clampdown held. In London, *The Times* even gushed praise on the Americans for their openness:

> The full disclosure of losses made by the Secretary of the Navy has had a wholly steadying effect. Americans are no more afraid of the truth than Britons, and as free men they have the right to know it, secure in the confidence that they are not to be stampeded either by triumph or disaster. It is only tyrants who must keep their people in the dark.

Really? *The Times* was either as naïve as an 8-year-old, or was guilty of one of the most blatant pieces of pro-government propaganda ever pedalled by a respected member of the Western media.

The Pearl Harbor information blackout went on for a year, then, once the Americans had joined the war, its top admirals and the government decided to move official statements a little closer to the true scale of the losses. On the first anniversary of the attack, it was announced that five battleships had been 'sunk or damaged'. The facts were five sunk, three damaged. The full story of the losses didn't come out until several years after the war was over.

* * *

Were there any examples, throughout the six years of war, of correspondents or their newspapers or radio stations, either British or American, fighting against the system? Very few. And the usual outcome was to change nothing, as correspondents in southern Italy discovered in January 1944. Allied forces had begun the campaign to retake Italy from the enemy by establishing a bridgehead on the coast near Rome at Anzio. Then came a heavy German counter-attack. When it started to look like the Allies might be driven out, Churchill ordered the commander, General Alexander, to shut down the radio transmitter that correspondents used to file their stories. The general told them this was because journalists had been sending 'alarmist' reports suggesting there would soon have to be an evacuation on the scale of Dunkirk.

Both British and American correspondents managed to bypass the transmission blackout to send protest cables to their editors, the War Office in London and the Office of War Information in Washington. Newspapers in both countries now ran editorials protesting that the truth about the Anzio Campaign was being suppressed. The issue was raised in the House of Commons, and in the US, the Secretary of War faced questions about it from reporters in Washington. But neither government would shift.

The correspondents' radio transmissions weren't restored till there was more positive news to report – that the Allies were on top again and advancing. At the same time, the censors made sure that this was all that was reported. At this point, Winston Churchill made a statement about the matter in Parliament. It tells us a lot about who'd been on top throughout the war, the media or the mighty. Churchill declared, 'Such words as "desperate" ought not to be used about the position in a battle of this kind when they are false. Still less should they be used if they are true.' There were cheers from the surrounding benches, reported *The Times*.

***

Was there much difference in the balance of power between the media and the mighty compared with the Great War?

Very little. Most of the time, the media – whether it was correspondents in the field or editors in the newsroom – could be relied on to toe the line, publish nothing which might shake morale, and even to go along with fictions for the sake of the war effort. And just in case there was any deviation – through the inexperience of a reporter, or some (misplaced) belief in a free press – then there was always censorship to make sure nothing damaging got through. And the whole job was made easier for governments, generals, admirals and air marshals by the fact that war now was so complicated that the press probably couldn't find out what was really happening anyway.

Should reporters and editors have protested more and fought for the right to tell people what was going on, or at least more of what the reporters themselves knew? Here's the answer given by Charles Lynch, an American-born correspondent for Reuters news agency, who covered the D-Day landings. Thirty years after the war, his resigned weariness was undiminished:

> It's humiliating to look back at what we wrote during the war. It was crap ... We were a propaganda arm of our governments. At the start the censors enforced that, but by the end we were our own censors. We were cheerleaders. I suppose there wasn't an alternative at the time. It was total war.

* * *

With the arrival of peace, the pressure on journalists to favour patriotism over accuracy was released on both sides of the Atlantic. There was a chance now for editors and reporters on newspapers and in radio stations to take stock and move back towards their role as the consciences of their respective nations.

But it wasn't to be a simple return to the old pre-war days. Technology – as ever, on our long journey – had thrown up a new competitor for the attention of ordinary citizens. Television had arrived before the war, although very few households then had a TV set in their living rooms to take advantage of it. In Britain, the BBC's television service had been suspended during hostilities. Now, it was started up again, and soon a commercial TV channel was given a licence to broadcast as well. As post-war austerity eased up, the television set became the must-have item.

TV news was different from what anyone at home had known before. It showed you pictures of what was happening. Moving pictures, not a description in words by some – possibly biased – reporter. So, would television shift the balance of power between the media and the mighty? Would governments, generals, and anyone else in power, now be quaking at the thought that there could be no more cover-ups? Or would it be the same old story? We're going next to a small TV studio in central London, in 1958, to find out.

13

TV NEWS

The Idiot's Lantern

It's a terrible thing to appear on television, because people think you actually know what you're talking about.

Sir David Attenborough (1926–)

On Sunday, 23 February 1958, seven floors above a Kardomah coffee bar in a dull stone corner building overlooking London's Kingsway, the British Prime Minister, the Rt Hon. Harold Macmillan, took his seat in a small television studio opposite a little-known journalist called Robin Day. In the next fifteen minutes, history would be made.

It didn't need a keen-eyed observer to pick up the clues. The prime minister had come to the TV offices, rather than the interviewer and camera crew going to Downing Street. Winston Churchill or Anthony Eden would never had done such a thing. And then there was the banter between the nation's leader and the TV man as they took their places. The prime minister smiled, and in the dry, urbane way he had, complained that he'd been given a hard, upright seat, whereas the journalist on the other side of a table was 'enthroned' in a comfortable swivel chair. 'I feel I have been left on the mat,' said the prime minister, half joking. Day grinned and offered to swap seats.

'No, no,' replied Macmillan, 'I know my place.' And just in case there was any doubt about the significance of the event, he added, 'This seems to symbolise the new relationship between politician and TV interviewer'.

The occasion was a weekly programme broadcast on Sunday evenings by ITN, the news service of Britain's fledgling commercial television network. Prime Minister Macmillan, too, was new to the job. It was just a year since he had taken over from Sir Anthony Eden following Britain's humiliating retreat during the Suez Crisis.

The interview that Sunday lasted just thirteen minutes. Day wrote later that it was 'historic and unprecedented'. No one, he added, 'had previously interrogated a Prime Minister in this way outside Parliament.' The editor of the *Daily Express*, Derek Marks, agreed, and said it was 'the most vigorous cross-examination a Prime Minister has been subjected to in public'. However, if we go back and watch it now, words like 'interrogated' and 'vigorous cross-examination' can seem way over the top. In an age when we've got used to politicians facing the BBC's Jeremy Paxman, CNN's Christiane Amanpour or any of today's TV interrogators, Robin Day's interview with Harold Macmillan back in 1958 looks like a gentle game of pat-ball.

In the hours before the interview, Day had sat down with ITN's editor-in-chief, Geoffrey Cox, and together they'd agonised about it. The two men had been working together for a year, and were of the same mind that television was on the verge of revolutionising the way British people received their news, and this interview with the prime minister was going to be a milestone on that journey.

The question burning everyone's lips at Westminster that week was would Macmillan fire his Foreign Secretary, Selwyn Lloyd, who was coming under widespread criticism for his poor performance at home and abroad? Day and Cox felt that ITN's reputation for independence and integrity depended on that question not being ducked. The problem was how to phrase it so the prime minister had to answer, without asking him outright whether he was going to sack Selwyn Lloyd. It's a measure of the deference that was at the time expected of the news media towards politicians, that the two ITN journalists' main worry was that what Day might say would seem – in his words – 'grossly impertinent'.

When the camera was lined up and the director gave the signal, the interview began. At first, Day questioned Macmillan about a range of topics, nothing to do with the Foreign Secretary – the past week's by-election result, Britain's H-bomb, a recent Commonwealth trip. Then, towards the end, came the moment to put the crucial point. The wording had been agreed by the editor, Geoffrey Cox:

> What do you say, Prime Minister, to the criticism which has been made, especially in Conservative newspapers, about MrSelwyn Lloyd, the Foreign Secretary?

Macmillan's response was calm. He clearly took no offence:

> Well, I think Mr Selwyn Lloyd is a very good Foreign Secretary and has done his work extremely well. If I didn't think so I would have made a change, but I do not intend to make a change simply as a result of pressure. I don't believe that that is wise. It is not in accordance with my idea of loyalty.

Day followed up:

> Is it correct, as reported in one paper, that he would like, in fact, to give up the job of Foreign Secretary?

Macmillan:

> Not at all, except in the sense that everyone would like to give up these appalling burdens which we try and carry.

Day:

> Would you like to give up yours?

Macmillan:

> In a sense, yes, because they are very heavy burdens, but, of
> course, nobody can pretend that they aren't. We've gone into
> this game, we try and do our best, and it's both in a sense our
> pleasure and, certainly, I hope, our duty.

All very mild and courteous, we might think today. But – if the
national newspapers were to be believed over the next few days
– it shocked the nation. A *Daily Telegraph* editorial asked:

> Should the Prime Minister have been asked what he thought of
> his own Foreign Secretary, before a camera that showed every
> flicker of the eyelid? Some say Yes; some say No. Who is to
> draw the line at which the effort to entertain stops?

Bill Connor, who wrote as 'Cassandra' in the *Daily Mirror*, gave
full vent to his outrage:

> If anybody wants a demonstration of the power of television
> let him refer to the interview which Mr Robin Day had with the
> Prime Minister on ITV on Sunday night … So here you have
> the ridiculous situation of how the British Prime Minister can
> suddenly be put on a Morton's Fork which forces him into
> defending and maintaining a colleague who is obviously a
> disaster to British foreign policy. Mr Robin Day by his skill as
> an examiner has been responsible for prolonging in office a
> man who probably doesn't want the job and is demonstrably
> incapable of doing it.
> The Idiot's Lantern is getting too big for its ugly gleam.

The *Observer* thought democracy itself was threatened, 'Will the television screen begin to bypass the House of Commons, or even (dread thought) the Press?'

The last few words here in the *Observer* were telling. Behind the press' outrage at the temerity of this upstart member of the media family in thinking it had the right to harass the nation's elected leaders, there was worry too about newspapers' own place in this brash new world. Would people start to rely on TV for their news? Would they stop buying newspapers. Indeed, was television itself now making the news? Newspaper editors were getting nervous. They were having to report on their front pages what their TV competitors were broadcasting. The lead story in the *Daily Mail* on the day after the interview, was headlined, 'PREMIER BACKS LLOYD – Does he want to go? Not at all':

> The Prime Minister last night made a public defence of Mr Selwyn Lloyd, much criticised Foreign Secretary who flopped badly in his foreign affairs debate speech last week. Mr Macmillan was being interviewed on an ITV programme.

* * *

For such an inoffensive (to our senses) conversation as that between Mr Day and Mr Macmillan to cause such an uproar tells us a great deal about what had gone before, about what television viewers expected to see and hear on the sets in the corner of their living rooms. ITV – and its news provider, ITN – had only begun broadcasting three years before. It was the BBC which had established the pattern for television news.

The radio service of the British Broadcasting Company had been set up in 1922, partly in reaction against the domination of the press by a few newspaper owners and the power that gave them to influence popular opinion. The government of the day wanted a means of conveying unbiased news to the nation, and the new wireless radio technology was the perfect way to do that. The television service of the BBC – now the British Broadcasting Corporation – briefly came on air before the outbreak of war, but was then suspended during the hostilities. When it was relaunched in 1946, those in charge were so worried about the news appearing to be opinionated or slanted that they kept newsreaders out of vision. Most of the time, all that viewers saw on their screens were still photographs and maps. It was like radio with a few captions.

Moving pictures were considered a risky innovation, and were relegated to a brief package of film at the end of the news programme, illustrating predictable and safe events – a royal visit, or a flower show. The BBC's first post-war director general, Sir William Haley, declared solemnly that moving pictures 'could give rise to the need to subordinate the primary functions of news to the needs of visual presentation'. In other words, a snappy bit of film might elbow out serious reporting. And when eventually 'Auntie' – as the BBC was nicknamed, for its staid reliability – decided it might send a reporter and film camera to speak to a government minister, the impression given was

often one of almost sycophantic politeness.

Not everyone thought this a satisfactory way to present politics, and *The Manchester Guardian* ran a parody of the typical BBC airport interview:

'Sir, would you say that your visit to Timbuktu was worthwhile?'

Geoffrey Cox, 1953. (by kind permission of Ros Gallant)

'Oh, yes, I would definitely say my visit had been worthwhile. Yes definitely.'

'Ah, good. Could you say what topics you discussed, sir?'

'No, I'm afraid I couldn't do that.'

'Well, thank you very much, sir.'

The closest the BBC got to any kind of informative interview with politicians came in 1952 when a weekly programme called *Press Conference* began. In this, three or four journalists sat behind a desk and asked questions of someone in the public eye. One of the newsmen who took part was the *News Chronicle*'s political correspondent at the time, Geoffrey Cox, the man who would soon be in charge of ITN, the BBC's rival commercial TV news service. For Cox, the experience in front of the BBC's cameras was an eye-opener. He wrote later, 'As journalism, the programme was scrappy and inadequate. We seemed to get in each other's way, to press none of our points home, to bring out no really new information.' It was a lesson he wouldn't forget, when soon he was playing the lead role in revolutionising TV news in Britain.

***

It was into Auntie's placid little backwater in 1955, then, that the brash upstart dived. ITN came on air – the news service of Britain's second television channel, supported not by taxpayers, but indirectly by advertisements.

ITN was governed by the same fairness and balance restrictions as the BBC. With the Television Act, Parliament decreed that the new commercial service, like the BBC, must present the news 'with due accuracy and impartiality'. ITN's first editor, Aidan Crawley, however, didn't see this as the kind of straightjacket that the BBC had chosen to wear. Yes, its news bulletins would be accurate and impartial, but they would also be lively and personable.

Crawley had been impressed by what he'd seen on American TV, where the news was delivered by journalists who could be seen sitting in the studio and talking to the viewers. He now brought that way of presenting the news to ITN, and a new word entered Britain's dictionaries – 'newscaster'. He even put a woman in front of the camera to present the news, Barbara Mandell – an unprecedented move at the time. Crawley lasted only fourteen months before he resigned when the independent television programme companies who funded ITN tried to slash his news budget. The man who replaced him was Geoffrey Cox, the *News Chronicle* journalist who'd been so dissatisfied with the BBC's political interview programme.

Cox had had what he called 'a varied apprenticeship'. He was a New Zealander who came to Oxford as a student in 1932, and then joined the *News Chronicle*. Eighteen months later, he got his lucky break. Spain was in the throes of civil war, and General Franco was advancing on Madrid. Franco loathed the *Chronicle* for its liberal views, and he'd even thrown one of its reporters into jail for a few months. So, the newspaper's editor now looked around the newsroom to see who should go out there next. He couldn't afford to lose any of his best men, so his eyes lighted on young Cox. He was expendable.

And so, Geoffrey Cox found himself in Madrid alongside republican and communist fighters, one of only two British journalists there. But the city did not fall to Franco, even though he bombed its streets from the air. Cox's reports from Madrid were front-page news on the *Chronicle*, day after day. When he returned to London, it was as a newsman with a reputation, and he was poached by the *Daily Express*, first as their Vienna correspondent before being moved to Paris. From there he covered the outbreak of war in 1939.

A year later, he decided he'd had enough of writing about wars, and it was time to start fighting them instead. He joined a New Zealand infantry brigade and saw action in Greece and Libya, and was twice mentioned in dispatches. Two years later, his career switched to yet another route. He was recruited by New Zealand's diplomatic service and, as first secretary of the legation in Washington, he found himself sitting around the same conference table as President Roosevelt and Winston Churchill. When the war was over, he decided to go back to the *News Chronicle*, first as political correspondent then as assistant editor.

In 1953, Cox witnessed something which, he wrote later, 'convinced me that television could revolutionise news coverage'. He was working for the *Chronicle* over the summer in Washington, and morning after morning, he sat in his bedroom at the Mayflower Hotel watching the little TV set. The networks were covering the proceedings of the Senate Investigations Sub-Committee, chaired by Senator Joseph McCarthy. The whole American nation was gripped to see McCarthy probe, harass and bully those he suspected of communist sympathies. Anyone in government service could be called before him and be made to account for actions, friendships – thoughts, even – going back a decade or more which might indicate any contact with communists. Cox wrote:

> I watched the cameras depict the hunched, swarthy figure of McCarthy, with deep set eyes and thinning hair, now in whispered consultations with his young counsel ..., now swinging round to put a question to the witness in either deceptively soft tones, or with a whip crack of hostility.

This was the time of the Cold War, when Soviet communism was the monster intent on destroying the American way of life, and it was also when American soldiers were battling the communists in the mountains of Korea. People with sons or husbands out there fighting watched and listened to McCarthy and urged him on. Cox continued:

Relentlessly the cameras swung from the intent, sneering, gri-
macing face of the senator to the tense, sad faces of the accused,
who, by their very appearance on this stand, were also his victims
… It was drama at once garish and ghoulish.

What Cox recognised was that no newspaper account of the
McCarthy hearings could compete with these pictures. No press
reporter could, in words, convey the subtleties of the confronta-
tions. Only television would enable the public to make up their
own minds about the rights and wrongs of what came to be
called the 'McCarthy witch-hunt'.

Truth, for Cox, was a religion, and he saw television as a unique
way to spread the gospel. He felt that his time with the New
Zealand Army during the Second World War had been his own
light on the road to Damascus. He wrote later about his work as
a wartime intelligence officer, briefing commanders in the field:

The keen faces around me, drawn with weariness and strain,
were of men who were going to base their actions, at least in
part on what I told them. The lives of the men they commanded
and indeed their own would depend upon the accuracy of the
information I imparted. It was a chastening discipline but a stim-
ulating one. It developed in me a relish for establishing the truth,
which is an end in itself. Television, properly used, provides an
invaluable new means of achieving that end.

***

On our journey through the centuries, we've seen how developments in technology have always brought new threats to the
mighty. The invention of the printing press over 500 years ago
had meant that, for the first time, individuals or small groups
could supplant the government in telling people what to think,
and could stir up discontent or even rebellion. The arrival of ever

better versions of the steam-powered rotary press in the nineteenth century could deliver copies of newspapers to millions of people overnight. These papers may not have called for revolution, but they could, and did, inform democratic opposition to the mighty, and eventually placed great power in the hands of a few individuals who controlled the newspaper empires.

Television was an even bigger leap forward. Newspaper buyers could always decide that what they read over their breakfast table was mistaken, one-sided or just plain wrong, and could refuse to believe it, but if you watched on your TV, with the prime minister actually saying 'X', or you saw for yourself the striking workers being beaten by the police or witnessed your nation's soldiers running away under enemy fire, it was much harder to deny such things had happened. This simple phenomenon was what Cox recognised. There was no intermediary writer telling you what he or she had seen, or thought they'd seen, with all their own prejudices. Now, with television, you could see it for yourself. When Cox wrote his memoirs, he called the book *See it Happen*. That was the truth-telling capacity of TV news in three words.

When Cox took over from Aidan Crawley at ITN, he saw his predecessor's lively style of presenting the news, and he liked it, and in Robin Day, who'd trained as a barrister and worked as a BBC Radio producer before Crawley took him on at ITN, Cox recognised someone with 'the makings of a very considerable journalist' and their partnership was formed.

Television technology, in the hands of men like Cox and Day, posed a new kind of threat to those in power. It wasn't the threat of political opponents or revolutionaries spreading their dangerous opinions among the populace, and it wasn't the threat of powerful newspaper proprietors using the press to amass their own private wealth and influence. It was the simpler, but more dangerous threat of showing people the government's own blunders and lies, right there, in black and white (or soon full colour), in a way that was hard to dispute. Nigel Ryan, who worked as a reporter under Cox and eventually succeeded him as editor of ITN, said that Cox taught his staff 'to think of the viewer as a voter, and the first function of news to provide the objective information on which the electorate could make up its own mind'.

When Cox, in his account of briefing army commanders, spoke of the truth as an end in itself, he'd added, 'Television, *properly used*, provides an invaluable new means of achieving that end'. Properly used. These words are significant. As well as recognising the immense power of this new technology, Cox also saw its limitations. Watching TV pictures in your living room is *not* like being there. The camera operator, or the editor back at base, can be selective. The final edited report can focus on a single incident of police beating up a striking worker and ignore the countless examples of good humour with strikers and policemen joking together. A politician's apology for a mistake can be edited out, while the part where he or she seems to insult an opponent is left in. Pictures of 'retreating troops' may be all that the camera crew managed to see while, a few miles away, the main army could be advancing. And, of course, television news isn't just pictures, it's millions of words spoken by reporters and newscasters.

Ryan observed that Cox 'was a stickler for political balance' and added, 'He saw television as a force for good, and opposed censorship in all its forms'. So attached was he to this principle, so keen that those in power should not be assisted by the media, that he introduced a new rule for his reporters when they came to interview politicians. The minister or opposition spokesman should not be given a list of questions in advance so that they could prepare their defence. This practice produced a more confrontational style of political interview, not unlike a cross-examination in a court of law. And Robin Day, of course, had trained as a barrister.

So, how did the mighty react to this new threat from the media?

From the time of Thomas Cromwell in the reign of Henry VIII, the mighty had fought back in three ways. Sometimes they'd used the press themselves to promote the government's policies, either by printing and distributing their own propaganda sheets or later by persuading some newspapers to back the government's position. At other times, the mighty simply blackened the name of those in the press who opposed them, by calling them cheats, liars and idiots. And at other times – especially when the nation was in crisis, during wars for instance – the mighty attempted, often successfully, to control and censor what was published.

Now, with this new technology in the hands of men like Cox, none of these strategies was quite so easy. In the UK at least, ITN and the BBC could not be persuaded to take a pro-government, pro-Establishment line – it was against their founding charters. And anyway, viewers were getting so used to a diet of more balanced opinion that they would have been highly sceptical of a government-run TV channel, even if it had been feasible to set one up. The mighty could have a go at accusing the BBC and ITN of being untruthful – or, as we'll see later on our journey, of being unpatriotic – but now this too had become harder to carry off, when TV pictures seemed to tell the truth. Censorship was an option, but not in peacetime. A government which tried to gag TV news when the safety of the nation was not at stake would be an easy target for parliamentary opponents. They'd have a field day.

So, the mighty now had to be more subtle in their centuries-long battle with the media.

* * *

One of the most extraordinary things about Robin Day's interview with Prime Minister Harold Macmillan in 1958 was not just that it showed TV as a powerful new weapon in the arsenal of the media. Behind the images of the nation's leader being grilled by a journalist, and the outraged headlines in the news-papers, something else was going on. The mightiest man in the country was learning how to turn the new medium to his advantage. And it was Robin Day himself who spotted this.

In the moments before he and Macmillan took their seats in the studio that Sunday, the two men, plus Geoffrey Cox and the prime minister's press secretary, Harold Evans, had assembled in Cox's office. Evans had taken Day on one side and said, 'I suppose you're going to ask him about Selwyn Lloyd?'

Day had replied, 'No comment', and they both laughed. And it dawned on Day that Macmillan was not going to be caught unawares by a question about his Foreign Secretary. Day wrote later:

> Those who criticised me for asking the question about Selwyn Lloyd were unaware that Macmillan was expecting such a question and was ready to answer it. It was not putting the Prime Minister on a Morton's Fork. This was not because I had forewarned him. On the contrary, he was told nothing about the questions except the main areas to be covered.

When it came to the key questions about the future of Selwyn Lloyd, Macmillan was not in the least phased. He answered quickly and calmly, and afterwards he didn't express the slightest annoyance, either to Cox or Day. Not only did he expect the question, but as Day came to realise, he got his press secretary to prompt the ITN man just in case he hadn't thought of raising it. So, in fact, instead of being put on the spot by an impertinent TV journalist – as the newspapers alleged – it was the prime minister who was engineering an opportunity to clarify to the nation his position on whether the minister should be sacked or not.

And what's more, throughout the interview, Macmillan looked at ease. As Day himself put it, 'He might be Edwardian in style and appearance, but on the twentieth-century box that Sunday evening he showed himself to be more than an accomplished parliamentary performer.'

Macmillan himself referred to this interview as the first time he had really mastered television. He'd become a 'TV personality'. And this, he realised, was the way to beat this new news medium at its own game. Martin Harrison, Professor of Political Science at Keele University, watched the interview, and noted:

> Macmillan first grasped that television was neither a meretricious toy nor the instrument of torture he once termed it, but the means by which political leaders must henceforth reach the electorate, and through which they must now as a matter of course account for themselves.

The battle between the media and the mighty had changed for ever. Figures for where British people got their news tell of the rise of television. In 1957, 24 per cent said TV was their main news source. Five years later, the number had more than doubled to 52 per cent. Radio dived during the same period, from 46 per cent to just 17 percent. The popularity of newspapers – for all the fretting after the Day–Macmillan encounter – held steady, hovering around 30 per cent. The papers had found themselves in a different world and they'd had to adapt. They couldn't now just report yesterday's news – the nation would already have seen that on last night's TV. To keep selling newspapers, they'd had to find new angles on the big stories of the day. No more dismissing the TV set as 'the idiot's lantern'. It was the people's window on the world, and newspaper editors had better get used to it.

***

Later in their careers, both Geoffrey Cox and Robin Day were knighted. Not – like the newspaper magnates of old – for their services to the nation – for which read 'government' – but for what they did to promote accurate and balanced journalism, a necessity in a democracy. And where Cox and Day had led the way, the BBC now shed its old straightjacket and followed. Both its TV and its radio news services, which had been criticised for their undue deference towards politicians, now adopted a more penetrative style of political reporting. Robin Day himself was recruited by the BBC and brought his techniques to both radio and TV there. He became known as 'The Grand Inquisitor'. He, in turn, described Geoffrey Cox as 'the finest journalist in British broadcast history'.

In the decades following the 1958 Macmillan interview, politicians and others in power have found that TV and radio interviews have become more and more vigorous and aggressive. The mighty can no longer do as Macmillan did, be relaxed and feel in control facing the cameras. It's not enough. For a government minister now, an interview is like dodging daggers thrown at you by an expert marksman. So, how have the mighty coped with this new world? It's been tough for them, no doubt about that. The very nature of politics has changed over the past sixty years, with – as Harold Macmillan saw himself – television becoming the main route for politicians to reach voters.

One shield the mighty have picked up to protect themselves from the attacks of interviewers has turned out to be no better than a limp rag. Yet they keep on using it. In the twenty-first century, ministers, MPs, local government officers, anyone in power, have all learned a technique to frustrate the TV – and the radio – interviewer. It involves ignoring the question and simply making whatever announcement you want to get over to the viewing public about your latest policy. Repeating the question simply provokes a repeated failure to answer it. The result has become a frustrated TV audience of voters who, more and more, see their elected leaders as shifty and dishonest. Not something Cox or Day could have anticipated.

***

In our investigation into the subtleties of powershifts between the media and the mighty in Western democracies, it's easy for us to forget the places where journalists who try to tell the truth about those in power can face punishments as harsh as anything in Henry VIII's England. And where, unlike in Tudor times, the state operates with a bureaucratic efficiency that makes it much harder for journalists to hide what they're doing.

While whole nations of TV viewers in Britain and America, by the 1960s, had started to take it for granted that they could put their feet up of an evening to watch the events of the day unfold, people in the Soviet Union had no such luxury. In a land where the government and the party told you what to believe, there was nowhere else to go to check out what they said.

Or was there? To find out, we're going next to Moscow in 1969.

14

THE SOVIET UNION

Scruffy, Dog-Eared and Undaunted

I write it myself, edit it myself, censor it myself,
publish it myself, distribute it myself,
and spend jail time for it myself.

Vladimir Bukovsky, Soviet dissident (1942–)

On 24 December 1969, Natalya Yevgenyevna Gorbanevskaya and a couple of her friends had gathered in her Moscow apartment. Natalya was hard at work on her typewriter when she was interrupted by a heavy hammering on the door and shouts to open up. She knew it was bound to happen sooner or later. She guessed it was a KGB raid.

Even owning a typewriter was enough to make her a person of interest in the eyes of the Soviet state's security agency. She'd bought the machine in the backstreets of Moscow on the 'grey market' – not an illegal act in itself, but likely to attract the suspicion of the authorities if they got to know about it. But Natalya Gorbanevskaya was doing something far more dangerous, that day in her apartment, than simple typing. She was compiling and editing Issue No. 11 of the underground newspaper, *A Chronicle of Current Events.*

Gorbanevskaya had been on the KGB's watch list for the past decade. In her student days, she'd been expelled from Moscow State University for 'political activism'. She then worked as a librarian and translator, while in secret she was a member of a growing circle of Moscow intellectuals who met to discuss their dissatisfaction with the Communist regime.

By the mid-60s, the group was receiving more and more letters smuggled out of prison camps in Siberia and elsewhere

Natalya Gorbanevskaya. (© Dmitry Kuzmin)

that made it clear that the number of political prisoners was far greater than had previously been thought. The group also passed among themselves other documents, many handwritten, that detailed how prisoners were starved and worked to death. Gorbanevskaya and her fellow dissidents wanted to get this information out to as wide a readership as possible.

Since the death of Stalin in 1953, there'd been a steady spread of underground, unofficial publications attacking the actions of the Soviet authorities. We can't call it the 'underground press' because – perhaps for the first time since the invention of the printing press, 500 years earlier – here was a group of rebel writers who only rarely had access to any such refinement as a press. Their word for what they were doing was 'samizdat', which means 'self-publish'.

The usual means of circulating a dangerous document was for one person either to write it out in longhand, or to type it with a few carbon copies underneath. These would then be given to other trusted like-believers who would, in turn, write out or type a few more copies and pass them on, and so on, and so on, like a chain letter. This was the only way of evading official Soviet censorship, and it was risky for those taking part. Anyone caught possessing or copying material attacking the actions of the state could find themselves spending years in a prison camp themselves.

One result of the crude system of copying and recopying, perhaps thousands of times, was that samizdat publications often had dog-eared, blurry, wrinkled pages with lots of scrawled corrections and typographical errors. The scruffy appearance of samizdat documents became a source of pride among dissidents. It was a symbol of the resourceful and rebellious spirit of those who produced samizdat, in contrast to the clinical, automated uniformity of official state newspapers.

Most samizdat publications were one-offs, a piece of dissident poetry, for example, or an account of a single instance of political oppression, such as a trial or an arrest. And even whole books were laboriously typed out time after time – *One Day in the Life of Ivan Denisovich* by Aleksandr Solzhenitsyn was circulated in this way. But Gorbanevskaya and her group decided there was a need for something different, something closer to a newspaper. It would come out at regular intervals – or as regular as dodging the KGB would allow – and would report a range of news relevant to the dissident movement. So that was the birth of *A Chronicle of Current Events*, and Gorbanevskaya was its first editor – and typist.

Issue No.1 began to circulate around April 1968. Its front page quoted, as did each of the subsequent sixty-four issues, Article 19 of the 1948 Universal Declaration of Human Rights:

Everyone has the right to freedom of opinion and expression; this right includes freedom to hold opinions without interference and to seek, receive and impart information and ideas through any media and regardless of frontiers.

The first issue gave an account of the trial of Yuri Galanskova, Alexander Ginzberg and others for producing a literary samizdat magazine, and the *Chronicle* highlighted the repressive measures taken by the authorities against those who'd protested at the subsequent convictions and prison sentences meted out to the two men.

The second issue, which came out two months later, gave a first-hand account of how political prisoners were treated in the labour camps:

> The most powerful means of influencing the prisoners is hunger. The usual rations are such as to make a person feel perpetual want of food, perpetual malnutrition. The daily camp ration contains 2,400 calories (enough for a 7–11-year-old child), and has to suffice for an adult doing physical work, day after day for many years, sometimes for as many as fifteen or twenty-five years! Those calories are supplied mainly by black rye bread. The convicts never even set eyes on fresh vegetables, butter, and many other indispensable products.

While Issue No. 3 was being prepared, Natalya Gorbanevskaya found herself in trouble. On 21 August, Red Army tanks rolled into Czechoslovakia to crush the so-called 'Prague Spring' when the Czech Communist leader, Alexander Dubček, had begun to introduce a more liberal system of government in the country. The invading Soviet forces arrested Dubček and brought him back to Moscow in handcuffs. Four days later, a group of seven protesters marched into Red Square. In the lead was Natalya, pushing a pram carrying her 3-month-old son. On the stroke of noon, she reached down and pulled out from beside the baby a Czechoslovak flag as well as banners proclaiming, 'For Your Freedom and Ours' and 'Hands Off Czechoslovakia'.

Almost immediately, a whistle blew and plainclothes KGB men rushed in from all corners of the square. Gorbanevskaya would write a full account of what happened in the next issue of the *Chronicle*:

> They ran up shouting, 'They're all Jews!', 'Beat the anti-Soviet-ists!' We sat quietly and did not resist. They tore the banners from our hands. They beat Victor Fainberg in the face until he bled, and knocked his teeth out. They hit Pavel Litvinov about the face with a heavy bag, and they snatched away from me a Czechoslovak flag and smashed it. They shouted at us, 'Disperse, you scum!' But we remained sitting.

A few minutes later, cars arrived, and all the protesters were bundled in, including Gorbanevskaya and her baby. Passers-by who expressed their sympathy were also arrested. Gorbanevskaya was beaten while in the car. After questioning, she was declared to be 'of unsound mind' – a charge that would be used against her later – and, for the moment, was released. In a letter addressed, via the *Chronicle*, to Western newspapers, she declared:

> My comrades and I are happy that we were able to take part in this demonstration, that we were able, if only briefly, to interrupt the sludge of barefaced lies and the cowardly silence, to show that not all the citizens of our country are in agreement with the violence which is being used in the name of the Soviet people.

By December 1969, the KGB had a clearer picture of the threat this woman posed to the stability of the state. She'd now overseen production of nine more issues of the *Chronicle*. It was at this point – in December 1969 – that the security agents hammered on the door of her apartment, and shouted for her to open up. She knew they wouldn't be so lenient this time. Her first thought was to protect the identities of those who'd contacted her with their accounts of arrests and descriptions of life in the prison camps. She stuffed their handwritten letters

СУД НАД НАТАЛЬЕЙ ГОРБАНЕВСКОЙ.

7 июля 1970 года состоялось заседание судейской коллегии по уголовным делам Мосгорсуда по делу ГОРБАНЕВСКОЙ Н.Е.

Председатель Богданов В.В.

Народные заседатели Андреев, Заславская.

Прокурор Праздникова

Адвокат Каллистратова С.В.

Эксперт проф. Лунц

Начало судебного заседания 10.30

Окончание 00.40

Председательствующий, открыв заседание, опрашивает стороны о заявлении ходатайств. Защита ходатайствует об отложении дела в связи с тем, что на изучение материалов дела в четырех томах было предоставлено лишь два дня. Одновременно были заявлены ходатайства защиты : I. о направлении дела для дополнительного расследования, 2. о проведении повторной судебно-психиатрической и дополнительной комплексной экспертизы, об истребовании документов для приобщения к делу и о вызове свидетелей в судебное заседание.

В ходатайстве о направлении дела для дополнительного расследования указывается, что в нарушение ст. II4 УПК РСФСР в постановлении о привлечении Н.Горбаневской в качестве обвиняемой от 25 декабря 1969 г. не содержится никаких конкретных данных о том, какие именно деяния ей вменялись и когда они совершены. Постановление не содержит ничего, кроме почти дословного текста ст. 190¹ УК РСФСР, т.е. по существу обвинение предъявлено не было. Это грубейшее нарушение права на защиту, поскольку, адвокат, изучая дело, не знал и не мог знать, какие действия Горбаневской следствие считает подпавшими по ст. 190¹ УК.

Во втором ходатайстве адвокат Каллистратова С.В. заявила о необходимости проведения повторной судебно-психиатрической экспертизы, поскольку Горбаневская 19 ноября 1969 г. была представлена на медицинскую комиссию под председательством психиатра Лукьянского Н.К., и эта комиссия на основании изучения которая болезни и катамнестического анализа более чем за 10 лет, а также данных освидетельствования, пришла к выводу, что Горбаневская

Issue No.15 of *A Chronicle of Current Events*, featuring an account of Natalya Gorbanevskaya's trial.

into the back of a drawer in her desk, and she managed to conceal other incriminating documents inside her coat, before the KGB men burst in. What's extraordinary is that although they searched her apartment they found only two of the documents she'd hastily hidden.

Gorbanevskaya and her friends were all taken away for questioning. The others were released, but this time, not Natalya. Meanwhile, Issue No. 11, which she'd been typing when the raid interrupted her, was duly published by her colleagues, who added a report about her detention.

In July the following year she was put on trial and found guilty of various crimes under the Soviet criminal code 'committed while of unsound mind'. She was sent to the Serbsky Institute, a psychiatric institution which was notorious for identifying what it called 'continuous sluggish schizophrenia', whose symptoms – 'stubbornness and inflexibility of convictions' and 'reformist delusions' – sounded suspiciously more political than medical. Anyone thought to suffer from this strange complaint could then, conveniently, be condemned to indefinite incarceration in a mental asylum. After diagnosis, Gorbanevskaya was transferred to Butyrskaya Prison psychiatric hospital. There's no record of what happened to her two children, boys aged 2 and 9 – we can only assume they were looked after by relatives and friends. Over the next two years, she was dosed with psychotropic drugs with the aim of 'curing' her. They failed, and when she was released in 1972, she went straight back to help her friends on the *Chronicle*.

***

The Soviet Communist Party leaders in charge during the period when *A Chronicle of Current Events* was published regarded themselves as a liberal regime. Liberal, that is, relative to what had gone before. Under Joseph Stalin, any writing of any kind which didn't originate from the Communist Party itself had risked the author being stood up against a prison wall and shot.

In the long history of the media versus the mighty, the Stalin era is the age of total victory for those in power. Stalinist bureaucracy would have been the envy of Thomas Cromwell in the reign of Henry VIII. Cromwell had lacked the governmental machinery to have unchallenged control over his rebellious press. Stalin had no such problem. The terrifying efficiency of his security agency, the NKVD, saw to that.

After Stalin died in 1953, Nikita Khrushchev brought in a limited 'thaw' that saw his predecessor's most extreme mechanisms of repression dismantled. Unofficial writing, for instance, no longer carried the death sentence. It was now that the dissident movement was born and samizdat publishing began. But, as we've seen with the treatment of Natalya Gorbanevskaya, it was still a dangerous time for underground journalists. Those who produced the *Chronicle* were careful never to advocate the overthrow of the Communist regime in the USSR, and confined themselves to revealing human rights abuses. Nevertheless, the *Chronicle*'s editors had to be constantly looking over their shoulders.

At least ten people held that position during the *Chronicle*'s fifteen-year life – we don't know the exact number because of the necessary secrecy around their activities, and we don't know what happened to them all. However, as well as Gorbanevskaya's spell in a prison mental hospital, at least four other *Chronicle* editors were sentenced to between three and seven years in a labour camp, plus up to five years after that of 'internal exile', which meant being freed from prison but confined to some wild and remote district, usually in Siberia.

Crushing freedom of expression in the Soviet Union was more than just a convenient way of wiping out political opponents. Just as a free press is seen in Western democracies as a basic right (though, as we've seen, sometimes watered down in practice), so in the USSR the opposite was regarded as a fundamental principle of good government. Early Marxists had held it to be an inviolable truth that the media should be in the hands of the people, not of a few capitalists. But since it wasn't practicable for millions of people to have a say in what went into thousands of newspapers, 'the people' were taken to be those who represented them, i.e. the Communist Party. Newspapers, and all other media outlets, needed to be controlled by the party leaders in order that the people could understand the objectives of their society, and do what was necessary to implement those aims. Blanket censorship was for the benefit of the people.

In the Soviet Union, the result was a state-owned media empire which made the businesses of Hearst, Rothermere and Beaverbrook look, by comparison, like a few village newsletters. At its height, the Soviet Union published more than 8,000 daily newspapers with a combined circulation of about 170 million. Nearly 3,000 of those papers, as well as being in Russian, were also simultaneously translated into almost sixty languages, to reach all of the East European satellite states, as well as the dozens of ethnic races across northern Asia. The national papers were distributed across the entire Soviet Union – over 5,000 miles, east to west, and 2,000, north to south – in one morning, a feat achieved twenty-five years before the *New York Times* managed anything similar in the USA.

Broadcasting in the USSR presented special problems. Gostelradio's programmes had to cater for listeners and viewers scattered over eleven time zones, and its transmitters had to broadcast across countless mountain ranges, vast desert steppes, Arctic wastes and offshore islands. In addition, of course, foreign radio – such as Voice of America and the BBC – had to be kept out, so 1,700 jamming stations were built and continuously operated.

Over decades, the two major national newspapers, *Pravda*, which meant 'truth', and *Izvestiya*, which was 'news' (hence the joke in the West that the only truth was that neither contained any news), became more than propaganda tools. They developed into the chief mechanisms for delivering orders from the Central Committee to local party officials and activists. The media, in other words, became the vital frameworks propping up the whole of the communist state's control apparatus. So, to be a reporter or an editor was a prestigious job. Three out of every four journalists were party apparatchiks.

***

A Chronicle of Current Events and all the other samizdat publications were no more than a handful of minnows among thousands of killer whales. So, did they have much impact? Were the Soviet mighty worried by the attacks of the samizdat guerrilla media?

Limited to such slow, primitive methods of duplicating each new issue, samizdat editors could never hope to reach more than a few thousand readers at most. We do know however that the *Chronicle* was read by Soviet dissidents far from Moscow, who were inspired to follow its example. Similar newspapers were set up, for example, in Ukraine, Lithuania and among the Crimean Tartars.

And there's one delicious irony. The forbidden samizdat writing in fact reached many thousands of Soviet citizens for whom it was never intended. And what's more, they were among the most influential members of Soviet society. They were the armies of censors who were employed across the USSR. Of course, they were the party faithful, but we can never know how many of them had their faith shaken by the constant, day after day exposure to accounts of arbitrary beatings, harassment and varied sufferings in labour camps, which they had to read before deciding whether to ban them or not.

One of the most famous dissidents, Andrei Sakharov, who in 1975 was awarded the Nobel Peace Prize for his work revealing human rights abuses (the authorities didn't allow him to leave to collect his award), was in no doubt about the influence of the *Chronicle* in particular. He described it as 'an expression of the spirit and moral strength of the human rights movement in the USSR. The authorities' hatred of the *Chronicle*, manifested in innumerable acts of persecution, only confirms that evaluation.'

But the biggest impact of the underground newspapers came outside the Soviet Union. Every issue of the *Chronicle*, for instance, was translated into English by Amnesty International and published throughout the West. The sixties and seventies were the Cold War years, when governments in the US and Europe were hungry for information that blackened the reputation of their arch enemy. They got it from samizdat, and that, in turn, was publicised by the few Soviet dissidents who'd managed to leave the country. Natalya Gorbanevskaya herself, for instance, was allowed to settle in France in 1975. There, she edited a journal devoted to the dissidents' cause and broadcast for Radio Free Europe's Russian service. She and other émigré Soviet rebels were reliant in their campaigns on the continual stream of underground papers smuggled out of the USSR.

Did any of this put pressure on the Soviet Union to become less repressive? The answer has to be: No. At least, not in the short term.

And another question: did the underground publications, which kept Soviet dissidents informed and made them feel part of a larger movement, play any part in bringing about the ultimate collapse of the USSR? It's difficult to see any direct cause and effect, but it's also hard to escape the notion that there was some connection between samizdat and the reforms brought in by Mikhail Gorbachev, the last Soviet leader, when he came to power in 1985. A major plank of his policy was 'glasnost', meaning openness.

Gorbachev's vision was not one of total democratic freedom, but he did want Communist Party leaders to be freely elected, and that needed more objective information available, in order that the people could make up their own minds when they voted. And so he loosened central party control of the press.

However, the result was not what he intended. All the long-suppressed criticism of the Communist system – from its corruption to its harsh and arbitrary punishments – for the first time could burst out into the open. And in 1991, Soviet rule came to an end. Samizdat was needed no more.

Or was it? In 2015, a Russian website appeared, calling itself *A New Chronicle of Current Events*. It published a list of 217 political prisoners held in Vladimir Putin's Russia at that date. Depressing? At least the underground media is still alive in Russia and kicking out at the mighty.

***

During the Cold War years, the Soviet Union's underground journalists could never in their most ambitious dreams aspire to competing with the state on the TV or radio airwaves. The typewriter was the limit of samizdat technology.

Meanwhile, television news in the West was facing its biggest challenge yet. It was being used to report a war. We've seen that, ever since the Crimean War, armed conflict between nations is when the greatest strain has been placed on relations between the media and the mighty. Governments and the military have had a good excuse to impose censorship and other ways of controlling what journalists report. Editors and correspondents, on their side, have felt under pressure to be patriotic, not to be the bearers of bad news, and have often backed off from their duties as truth-tellers. So, what would happen now there was a powerful new way of reporting from the battle-front? How would TV crews and editors report war to their viewers, if they were allowed to at all? And would TV pictures of the horrors of combat undermine a nation's will to fight? What about the inevitable blunders – atrocities even – in the chaos of war? Would TV show them in all their bloody brutality? To answer, we're going next to Vietnam. It was called 'the first TV war'.

15

VIETNAM

Bang-Bang and Body Bags

Television brought the brutality of war into the comfort of the living room. Vietnam was lost in the living rooms of America, not on the battlefields of Vietnam.

Marshall McLuhan (1911–80)

On 8 June 1972, in the South Vietnamese village of Trảng Bàng, a group of terrified South Vietnamese men, women and children were hiding inside the local Cao Dai Temple. They'd been driven from their homes by North Vietnamese fighters who'd advanced into the village and set up a sniper base there. The villagers thought they'd be safe in the temple, but when they heard bomber aircraft circling overhead, they became frightened and decided to leave and try to reach the protection of friendly South Vietnamese troops who were positioned not far away.

What came next would cause outrage across the world. It wasn't some massive catastrophe, such as the humiliating defeat of a whole army, or a large-scale civilian massacre, though some of the Trảng Bàng villagers would be killed. Instead, it was what happened to one 9-year-old girl that would soon be watched by many millions far from this conflict in the comfort of their living rooms or from the counter of their local bar.

A few hundred yards down the road where the escaping villagers were heading, five men happened to be waiting. They were journalists: a photographer from the US news agency, Associated Press, and an NBC cameraman, as well as a reporter and his two-man film crew from the British TV network, ITN. The ITN reporter, Chris Wain recalled later what they saw, 'That morning we'd arrived at the village of Trảng Bàng, which had been infiltrated by the North Vietnamese two days earlier. They were dug in, awaiting a counter-attack. In the late morning, two vintage Vietnamese bombers started to circle overhead.'

Then suddenly, the journalists saw a flash and an explosion 400m up the road. Out of the smoke and debris, running towards them, came half a dozen children. Here's Wain again, 'There was a blast of heat which felt like someone had opened the door of an oven. Then we saw the children. None of them were making any sound at all – until they saw the adults. Then they started to scream.'

One of the children, a girl, was naked. She was Kim Phúc, 9 years old. She was crying out, '*Nóng quá! nóng quá*! [Too hot! Too hot!]'. Later, she said, 'I heard the noise of the bombs, then suddenly I saw the fire everywhere around me. I was terrified, and I ran out of the fire. I saw my brother and my cousin. We just kept running. My clothes were burnt off by the fire.'

Wain and his cameraman, Alan Downes, then hesitated for a moment, undecided whether to film it. It was a strong story, of course, but would the programme editor in London run such harrowing pictures of a small naked girl in agony? In the back of their minds was another worry. In the days before digital video cameras, which can shoot hours of moving picture, the old 16mm film cameras had less than twelve minutes of run time for each roll of film, and it would all have to be developed in a laboratory before it could be edited together. Shoot too much, and you could miss your deadline. So, a camera crew always had to consider carefully every sequence they filmed, and

The iconic image captured by Nick Ut of the Associated Press. (© Associated Press)

ask themselves, 'Is it necessary?' After deliberating for a second or two, they decided to risk it, and as the screaming little girl got closer, Downes and his sound recordist, Tom Phillips, started filming. Meanwhile, the NBC cameraman, Le Phuc Dinh, did the same, and photographer Nick Ut shot still pictures for the Associated Press.

Wain stopped the girl and tried to help in the only way he could. He poured water over her. As she turned, Downes' film recorded how the skin had been stripped from the top of her left arm, and when she moved further round, a large area of her back could be seen scorched red raw. The next shot showed a crying woman running in the opposite direction holding her badly burned baby. The explosion had been from four napalm bombs. Napalm is a flammable liquid, which – once it catches fire – sticks to the skin.

Ut took Kim and the other injured children to the nearest medical unit, the British-run First Children's Hospital in Saigon.

When Wain and his crew had finished their work, they went to find out how Kim was, and a nurse told them, 'She will die tomorrow'. Wain then arranged for her to be moved to a specialist plastic surgery hospital. There, over the next fourteen months, Kim underwent seventeen operations.

But back when it all happened, the American public almost didn't get to see those scenes on the Trảng Bàng road. The NBC film was immediately flown to Hong Kong, where the film editor – aware that the network had a ban on nudity – removed the pictures of Kim from the final edited report, before transmitting it to New York. And when the *New York Times* editors first saw Ut's still photographs, they too – for the same reason – thought them unsuitable for their readers. But the next day, there was a rethink at the *NY Times*, and what was to become one of the iconic pictures of the Vietnam War, of Kim naked, running and screaming, appeared on its front page.

For the Nixon administration in Washington, it was deeply embarrassing. The napalm had been dropped from a plane operated by America's South Vietnamese allies. But even more damaging, it was a US military commander who'd given the order to bomb the fleeing group of children. They'd been mistaken for enemy fighters. As well as Kim's appalling injuries, four others from the village were killed, including two of her cousins. Thirty years after the incident, audio tapes from the Oval Office of the White House were released – as part of the Watergate investigations – and a worried President Nixon can be heard, suggesting that anti-war elements may have faked the pictures. 'I'm wondering if that was fixed,' he's recorded saying to his chief of staff, H.R. Haldeman.

'Could have been,' Haldeman replies, 'Because they got that picture of the little girl without any clothes. It made a hell of a bounce. But, it was North Viet ...' He stops to correct himself. 'South Vietnamese bombing South Vietnamese by accident. They thought they were hitting the enemy, but they got their own refugees, apparently. Haldeman then adds: 'Napalm bothers people when you get a picture of a little girl with her clothes burnt off.'

'I wondered about that,' says Nixon.

However, any allegations that Kim's injuries were false news were soon overturned, when Alan Downes' ITN film – with no upsetting scenes cut out – was broadcast on American TV news shows. An American officer had blundered, and viewers could see the result for themselves – the might of the United States had been responsible for inflicting horrific suffering on a 9-year-old girl.

Kim's own story – despite the pain she's suffered ever since – has had a happier sequel. She now lives in Canada, where she and her Vietnamese husband raised two sons. She founded the Kim Foundation, which provides medical and psychological assistance to child victims of war.

***

What happened that day near Trảng Bàng in 1972 was terrible for Kim and the other villagers, but in the greater picture of a war that lasted sixteen years, it was just one incident in a conflict marked every day by scores of bombings, minor battles and the uncountable deaths of civilians in remote spots of the Vietnamese jungle. What made the Trảng Bàng bombing different was that, at that place, at that moment, photo journalists happened to be there to record it and then show it to the world.

The American President – the mightiest of the mighty – recognised that the pictures of one little girl's injuries could help turn a nation against the war, and he wondered – hoped, maybe – that the still photographs could have been faked. TV film, which back in 1972 could not be falsified as it could now, proved the incident had really happened. And, what's more, on the nightly news, America's families could hear for themselves Kim screaming and see the agony on her face.

Vietnam was the first televised war. It was also the longest war in America's history, lasting from 1959 to 1975. It was overseen by three different commanders-in-chief. First, President John F. Kennedy, then President Lyndon B. Johnson, and finally President Richard M. Nixon. At its height, under Johnson, there were over half a million GIs and other American military personnel on the ground, at sea and in the air fighting alongside the South Vietnamese Army in a war against communist North Vietnam and the Vietcong guerrillas.

As the years rolled on, the American public lost their appetite for the fight, and troop numbers were scaled down till finally TV was showing pictures of the last Americans in Vietnam scrambling on board helicopters to try and escape the overwhelming barrage of Communist firepower. The mightiest nation on earth would be defeated by one of the poorest, and the attempt to stem the tide of communism in South East Asia failed. Vietnam – like its neighbours in Cambodia and Laos – were in Communist hands. Most Americans agreed with Henry Kissinger, the American diplomat who negotiated the Paris peace deal that sealed the end of the conflict, when he said, 'The Vietnam War was a great tragedy for our country'.

The big question was, where did the blame lie for this humiliating defeat?

It was – and in many quarters, still is – widely believed that nightly TV news coverage was the culprit. By the mid-1960s, there were 100 million TV sets in America, and polls showed that 60 per cent of all American adults relied on television for news about the war. The theory is that, night after night, on the six o'clock news of all the major TV networks, images of shot and shell, blood and death stirred in Americans a repeated sense of dismay, disgust and horror, all of which fed a desire to stop the war. William Small, director of news at CBS summed it up, 'When television covered its first war in Vietnam it showed a terrible truth of war in a manner new to mass audiences. A case can be made … that this was cardinal to the disillusionment of Americans with this war.'

As Sir Robin Day put it, 'Blood looks very red on the colour television screen.' General William Westmoreland, who commanded US forces in Vietnam from 1964 to 1968, was in no doubt about the dangerous influence of TV news on American public opinion. 'Television,' he said, 'is an instrument which can paralyse this country.'

And American generals in command of the battle troops had another fear about having TV cameras around. Just like their predecessors in every war since the Crimea, they were concerned that the presence of the media exposed them to too much scrutiny, and that if ordinary people knew about some of the bad things and blunders that are inevitable during the chaos of war, they wouldn't understand and they'd want it all to stop. But, of course, that worry was intensified now because accounts of the bad things and blunders weren't just words in a newspaper, they were now there in full-colour moving images, with soundtracks of shooting and screaming, in the living rooms of the nation, night after night.

And the threat from TV crews was all made much worse for the military because the government had decided that this war would be fought without infringing the First Amendment of the Constitution. There would be 'freedom of the press', which now of course included TV as well. There would be no censorship, except where there was a danger of giving away military secrets. That was another wartime first.

Nor were there any official restrictions on where correspondents, photographers or TV news crews could go. They could hitch a lift on a military helicopter if the local commander agreed, or they could tag along with a jungle patrol. There were no escort officers to say where they could and couldn't travel, what they could and couldn't see or film. TV crews, like their print colleagues, could move around where they liked, within the limits of what they felt was less likely to get themselves killed. That was a very real restriction. Vietnam was the most lethal of wars for journalists: sixty-three of them never made it back.

Competition to get the best story, the most dramatic pictures, was fiercer than it had ever been. John Mecklin, the chief American press officer in Saigon, spoke for the generals when he said, 'In Vietnam, a major American policy was wrecked, in part, by unadorned reporting of what was going on.'

There were two strands, then, to the theory that TV coverage of the war sapped the morale of the American public: nightly television news broadcasts brought home to people just how horrific war can be, and TV news highlighted American defeats and mistakes in all their depressing detail. Let's have a look at each of them in turn.

***

First, did TV news really convey to viewers the full, brutal horror of war?

Many of the television correspondents who spent time in Vietnam didn't think so. Richard Lindley, who covered the war for British TV's ITN, discovered that shocking images filmed by his cameraman were often removed back in London by the programme editors before his reports were broadcast. 'When they get a film which shows what a mortar does to a man,' says Lindley, 'really shows the flesh torn and the blood flowing, they get squeamish. They want it to be just so. They want television to be cinema.'

American TV journalists found the same thing happened to their reports. When an NBC cameraman filmed a South Vietnamese general shooting a Vietcong suspect in cold blood during the 1968 Tet Offensive, the programme producers in New York broadcast it up to the moment that the dead man hit the ground, then they blacked out the screen for three seconds. It was thought advertisers might desert the channel if their products were associated with a twisted corpse. And, of course, the suffering of Kim Phúc almost didn't make it onto the screens when the ITN crew debated whether the horror and nakedness would be edited out later, as did in fact happen with the NBC pictures.

And there was another – more subtle – reason why many correspondents felt that TV reports could never reflect the true horror of war. There was something in the very nature of television itself that somehow diluted and filtered out the sometimes sickening, sometimes terrifying truth that the reporter and cameraman had experienced in the field. Sandy Gall, another of ITN's correspondents in Vietnam, puts it like this:

> I think you lose one dimension on television's small screen and things look smaller than life; the sound of battle, for example, never coming across. I am always let down when I eventually see my footage, and think, 'Is that all?'. The sense of danger never comes across on television.

Gall's view was confirmed in an opinion poll conducted in 1972 by *Newsweek* magazine. It suggested the American public were becoming tolerant of violent images from Vietnam. People were apparently so inured to the doctored pictures of the 'horrors of war' that they just washed over them.

So, there's strong evidence that night-after-night images of the war did not disgust and horrify the American public and turn them against the war.

***

But what about TV reports that revealed the more exceptional events, the defeats, the blunders and the misconduct – the atrocities even – in a graphic, colourful way that was not possible in the old days when newspapers were the only source of news? Did TV news regularly reveal such embarrassments?

The napalming of Kim Phúc and her fellow villagers is one example which showed that an American mistake could have consequences for innocent people, children even, whose pain and suffering the viewer could sympathise with. President Nixon and his chief of staff saw the problem this gave them. And there are other examples.

In August 1965, CBS correspondent, Morley Safer, and his film crew were with a troop of US Marines when they entered the South Vietnamese village of Cam Ne. Viewers back in the States were shown soldiers using their cigarette lighters to set fire to the roofs of small houses. Safer appears in front of camera and tells the viewer, 'This is what Vietnam is all about'. An elderly couple are then seen raking out the smouldering ashes, trying to save something from their home, while a group of women and children are crying, and Safer explains that an officer had told him that he was under orders to torch the 150 houses here in retaliation for the village being used by Vietcong snipers. He adds, 'If there were any Vietcong in these hamlets they are long gone.' The report then switches to images of four prisoners, blindfolded, their hands behind their heads. 'They are,' says Safer, 'four old men who don't speak English.' And he ends his report in front of the camera, speaking directly to viewers:

> There is little doubt that American firepower can win a military victory here. But to a Vietnamese peasant whose home is the result of a lifetime of back-breaking labour, it will take more than presidential promises to convince him that we are on his side.

And there is at least one example of a major American set-back being captured by TV news cameras. In 1968, during the Tet Offensive, when the Vietcong and the North Vietnamese

February 1968. Walter Cronkite of CBS News, the most respected journalist on American TV during Vietnam, would forsake his seat in the studio for a frontline reporter's role at critical times in the war. He's seen here interviewing a Marine commander during the Battle of Hue City.

had launched a widespread attack against the South, a squad of Vietcong guerrillas managed to occupy the grounds of the American Embassy in Saigon. This was big news by any standards, and it astounded and upset people back home in the USA – even the hard-bitten staff in TV newsrooms. At CBS News, Walter Cronkite, the doyen of US television journalists, watched the pictures coming in, and said, 'What the hell is going on? I thought we were winning the war.'

Across at the NBC office, a report by correspondent Howard Tuckner was edited and broadcast that evening. Over pictures of US soldiers running to take up shooting positions, Tuckner's commentary spoke of 'Vietcong snipers and suicide commandos holed up inside the embassy compound and firing from surrounding buildings'. 'The Americans,' he said, 'had to move cautiously.' And as a man is seen being stretchered into an ambulance, viewers were told that two US Marines had been shot dead by automatic weapons fire. There was the constant sound of gunfire in the background, as Tuckner revealed, 'The Americans used tear gas but there were not enough gasmasks for the troops who needed them.' He ended his report:

> Of all the Vietcong terrorist attacks on Saigon in the last three years, this was the boldest. Not only had a Vietcong unit managed to get inside the US Embassy compound, but the terrorists successfully held off the American forces for seven hours.

It looked like the Americans were being trounced. And these pictures – of America, the great power, being held to ransom by a few dozen irregular fighters – was interpreted by TV and newspapers alike as evidence that the whole Tet Offensive was being lost to the enemy. The most respected of commentators on American television, Walter Cronkite, told NBC's viewers:

> It seems now more certain than ever that the bloody experience of Vietnam is to end in a stalemate. This summer's almost certain standoff will either end in real give-and-take negotiations or terrible escalation; and for every means we have to escalate, the enemy can match us, and that applies to invasion of the North, the use of nuclear weapons, or the mere commitment of one hundred, or two hundred, or three hundred thousand more American troops to the battle. And with each escalation, the world comes closer to the brink of cosmic disaster.

President Johnson said, 'If I've lost Cronkite on Vietnam, I've lost Middle America.' TV had the pictures and it was telling Americans what to think: it was time to end the war.

In fact, Cronkite had got it wrong. Subsequent analysis showed that the Tet Offensive was not a defeat for the Americans and their South Vietnamese allies. Historians now see that it was the Vietcong who were driven back and that they never recovered.

But, in 1968, many in the US who'd seen the TV news and heard the words of Walter Cronkite believed otherwise.

Clearly then, there were times when TV did push general opinion in the United States towards ending the war.

***

However, as always in Vietnam, the story was not that simple. It's significant that TV images of the 1968 Vietcong occupation of the Saigon Embassy in reality told nothing about who was losing or winning the war. The plain fact was that no TV camera could ever answer that big question. The reason lay in the very nature of the fighting in Vietnam.

Correspondents in Vietnam faced the same problem that their predecessors had in the Second World War, except that in Vietnam, it was even worse. In the Second World War, journalists discovered that the theatres of war were so vast that they could only ever get a flavour of which way the war itself was going. In Vietnam, much of the fighting took the form of guerrilla warfare, with the communist Vietcong staging small-scale hit-and-run attacks on American troops on remote jungle paths. Vietnam was rarely, if ever, one great battle. It was thousands of minor – although bloody – skirmishes.

Brief vision bites of fighting, then, were soon the staple diet of the TV news machine. 'What bang-bang have you got for us today?' became the routine question when foreign editors in New York telexed their teams in Saigon. If the foreign editor liked what he was told, then a cumbersome process began. There was no way of sending pictures from Vietnam directly to New York. They first had to be flown to Hong Kong, where the film editor would assemble the story, usually cutting around thirty minutes of raw footage down to three or four. The finished package could then be transmitted by satellite to the US, but this was expensive, so unless the report was of outstanding news value, it would be flown back, often on a series of commercial flights. The result was that viewers in America didn't then see it until at least forty-eight hours after it was shot.

The vast majority of TV reports from Vietnam were therefore used as background information, to give a general flavour of the war, after viewers had first been told the day's latest developments. And the TV networks were, of course, dependent for the big picture on official statements, either on the wires from the American mission in Saigon or from the government spokesman in Washington. Those statements would inevitably give an optimistic slant to the day's big news out of Vietnam.

So scattered and fragmented was the fighting in Vietnam that it was often hard even for the American military themselves to understand which way the war was going. With no great battle lines marked out by trenches being pushed back and forth, winning or losing in Vietnam came to be measured in terms of the dead. How many of ours, and how many of theirs were killed today? This gave rise to a special language devised by the military spokesmen to shield people from the horror of what was being talked about. Innocent civilians slaughtered and maimed by accident were 'collateral damage' or – even more abstruse – the result of 'circular error probability'.

And in considering whether TV undermined the war effort, we also need to remember that there were times when the military press officers found television correspondents – far from unearthing battlefield scandals – were instead 'on the team'.

In 1970, CBS correspondent Richard Threlkeld and crew accompanied US Army Alpha Group 1/9 on a routine patrol through the jungle near the Cambodian border. He starts his report:

American soldiers are hiking their way through the sweaty jungles of South Vietnam searching for an elusive enemy. The temperature is almost 100 degrees.

Threlkeld then tells us what several of the men 'are thinking about'. One is 'thinking how he's going to meet his fiancée in Honolulu in two weeks and he'll show her the silver star the general pinned on him yesterday'. Dubaye, the medic on the team, is 'scared of getting killed picking up a wounded buddy'. Jordan would rather be where the action is – he's already been wounded three times and awarded three purple hearts, so the others call him 'Hero'. But today this is 'just a peaceful walk in the sun'.

Suddenly, there's a prolonged burst of automatic gunfire and the soldiers are seen running and crouching. One of them is hit. Dubaye, the medic, runs forward and helps him to safety. 'Hero' has been shot. Once his wounds have been quickly bandaged, and the shooting has stopped, Threlkeld asks him what happened. 'I opened up on him. He opened up on me,' says Hero. 'I got hit in both legs. That's about it.' Then he adds, 'I got three purple hearts' and he laughs, 'I don't need a fourth'. Threlkeld ends his report kneeling in front of the camera and tells us:

You've seen how it really was. Heroism, danger, fear, all rolled into one. Words don't describe it.

So, with a few exceptions, far from being subjected to a nightly barrage of negative images about American policy and actions in Vietnam, TV viewers were instead often watching unrealistic pictures of a tiny part of the war with the gory parts left out, while being told what the government wanted them to know about the latest American achievements in the war. Most nightly TV images were of insignificant 'bang-bang', good for a couple of minutes of air time and then to be forgotten. It was only by an occasional accident of being in the right place at the right time, that TV got the stories that might influence Americans back home to decide the war should end.

***

In fact, the three news events that may have done most to discredit the authorities during the Vietnam War were none of them filmed by a TV crew. All three were such major events in American twentieth-century history that you only have to say 'My Lai', 'Kent State' or 'the Pentagon Papers' for the most shameful memories of the Vietnam War to come flooding back.

The first reports of the My Lai Massacre began to leak out in 1969. It would be seen as the most notorious atrocity committed by American troops during the whole conflict. On 16 March 1968, a US Infantry company led by Lieutenant William Calley Jr had entered the village of My Lai, gathered the people there into groups, then mowed them down with automatic weapons fire. Any who survived were then picked off. This included a small child holding the hand of one of the dead. A GI 30m away dropped to one knee and killed him with a single shot.

The actual number killed was never established, but it was officially put at no less than 175, while it could have been as high as 504. The men responsible for the massacre tried to keep it secret, and managed to do so for a year. But even when, in November 1969, pictures of the dead and wounded taken by an army photographer became public, the story still got little attention in the American media. It was only when those images of the slaughter began to appear elsewhere in the world that it became big news in the USA.

There was outcry and confusion. *Time* called My Lai 'an American tragedy'. *Newsweek*'s headline was 'A single incident in a brutal war shocks the American conscience'.

Here, then, was the most appalling story of misconduct by American troops, revealed by the print media (albeit slowly). Nightly television news had to make do with reporting details of the massacre as they emerged.

What happened next showed that America was a deeply divided nation on the rights and wrongs of the Vietnam War.

Some GIs returning home faced hostility. Some were called 'baby killer', and others were spat on. However, not all Americans felt that way. When Calley and some of his men were brought to trial for murder, there was anger at the prosecution of ordinary American soldiers, who many saw as just doing what a GI should do and obeying orders. In the end, only Calley himself was convicted. He was sentenced to life in prison with hard labour. He served three years before he was released.

Of course, support for 'our boys' in the front line didn't necessarily mean people backed the war itself. In fact, it could mean sympathy for young men caught up in a fight which should never have been America's business. The true picture of American attitudes to the war is complex. There are no generalisations which are accurate. Opinion polls at the height of the conflict immediately before the Tet Offensive and the revelations about the My Lai Massacre were confusing. One Gallup survey in 1967 showed half of all Americans had no idea what the war in Vietnam was all about. Another poll commissioned by *Newsweek* magazine in the same year suggested that nightly TV reports from Vietnam had actually encouraged a majority of viewers to support the war.

At one extreme, there were the Hawks who backed the policy of stopping the spread of communism in South East Asia by blocking it in Vietnam. At the other extreme were the Doves, who thought the United States had no right – legally or morally – to be in the conflict. And there was a range of opinions in between.

The anti-war movement itself was vocal, and it got plenty of TV coverage. That was in part because protest rallies were often addressed by liberal-minded entertainment celebrities – Jane Fonda, Joni Mitchel, Jimi Hendrix and others. These were usually peaceful events. In the spirit of the sixties' hippy culture, protesters would place flowers in the gun muzzles of the National Guardsman brought out in case of any violence.

Then came the shocking events on 4 May 1970. At Kent State University in Ohio, during a demonstration against President Nixon's announcement that the war would now be expanded from Vietnam into neighbouring Cambodia, National Guardsmen fired more than sixty rounds into a crowd of students over a period of thirteen seconds. Four students were killed and nine others wounded. No TV cameras witnessed the worst of the violence. There was a limited amount of movie footage of the periphery of the action. It was left to a student stills photographer to capture images of his contemporaries at the moment of their deaths, and he won a Pulitzer Prize for his work that day.

Three days before the Kent State shootings, Nixon had described anti-war protesters as 'bums'. Now, the mother of Allison Krause, one of the students shot dead, went on national television and said, with tears in her eyes, 'My child was not a bum'.

So, on two of the news stories during the Vietnam War that were most likely to influence public opinion against the government – My Lai and Kent State – national television had no pictures of the events themselves. True, most Americans were likely to have learned the details of what happened in both incidents from reporters on their TV screens, and when, three days after Kent State, 75,000 peace protesters came to Washington to hear speeches calling for an end to the war before marching on the White House, it was the lead story on all the national television news shows.

However, the third news story that fed the anti-war movement was entirely down to a newspaper scoop. TV played no part in revealing the details of what became known as the Pentagon Papers. On 13 June 1971, the *New York Times* began publishing a series of articles based on a 7,000-page, official, top-secret study of American covert involvement in Vietnam decades before the public knew about it. The study was leaked by one of its authors, Daniel Ellsberg. President Nixon's administration wanted further publication of the papers stopped – they seemed to show the Vietnam War was unwinnable.

When a lower court banned the *New York Times* from publishing more, the *Washington Post*, led by its publisher Kay Graham and editor Ben Bradlee, took on the campaign. The *Post* fought the legal ban and won what's regarded as a landmark press freedom decision, with the US Supreme Court ruling against the government. Justice Hugo Black declared:

> Only a free and unrestrained press can effectively expose deception in government. And paramount among the responsibilities of a free press is the duty to prevent any part of the government from deceiving the people and sending them off to distant lands to die of foreign fevers and foreign shot and shell.

Among the many damning revelations that now emerged was that the US had secretly bombed Vietnam's neighbours, Cambodia and Laos, and that President Johnson's administration had 'systematically lied, not only to the public but also to Congress'.

* * *

By the early 1970s, a growing number of Americans were starting to believe that the US should get out of Vietnam. The historian Michael Mandelbaum believes that was because they felt that too many lives were being lost and too many taxpayers' dollars being spent:

> The United States lost the war in Vietnam because the American public was not willing to pay the cost of winning, or avoiding losing. The people's decision that the war was not worth these costs had nothing to do with the fact that they learned about it from television.

It's difficult, though, to believe that TV coverage played no part in moulding opinion in the US. There were the nightly images of body bags, each one somebody's son, brother or husband killed in a distant war. And there were those TV pictures of Vietcong guerrillas on American soil at the Saigon Embassy, and the words afterwards of the much-loved TV commentator Walter Cronkite that the world was 'closer to the brink of cosmic disaster'.

The television news that day almost certainly helped turn people against the war. President Johnson believed it did. He recognised that public support was vital if the war was to be won, and so he went on national television to announce that he wouldn't seek another term as president. He was quitting office. The next day, he told a meeting of the National Association of Broadcasters:

> As I sat in my office last evening, waiting to speak, I thought of the many times each week when television brings the war into the American home. No one can say exactly what effect those vivid scenes have on American opinion. Historians must only guess at the effect that television would have had during earlier conflicts on the future of this Nation ... the Korean War, for example ... or World War II.

But it almost doesn't matter whether in the end it was TV news coverage that played a major role in defeating the government and losing the war for America. What matters is that the mighty – in the world's mightiest nation – *thought* they'd been beaten by the media. And this victory, empty as it may have been, would influence the future behaviour of the mighty in other conflicts.

On 21 October 2003, at the start of the Iraq War – twenty-eight years after the end of the Vietnam conflict – the *Washington Post* correspondent, Dana Milbank wrote:

Since the end of the Vietnam War, presidents have worried that their military actions would lose support once the public glimpsed the remains of U.S. soldiers arriving at air bases in flag-draped caskets.

To this problem, the Bush administration has found a simple solution: It has ended the public dissemination of such images by banning news coverage and photography of dead soldiers' homecomings on all military bases.

***

For President Nixon, however, it wasn't the Vietnam War and the country's hostility to it that forced him from office, and it wasn't television news either. It was old-fashioned newspaper journalism, carried out with care, determination and a refusal to back down, that defeated the mighty in the media's most celebrated of all victories – Watergate.

16

WATERGATE

Deep Throat and Dirty Tricks

A cantankerous press, an obstinate press, a ubiquitous press must
be suffered by those in authority in order to preserve the even
greater values of freedom of expression and the right of the
people to know.

US Judge Murray Gurfein (1907–79)

Frank Wills didn't think it was much of a job, on the nightshift
in a place where nothing ever happened. As a black kid born in
Savannah, Georgia, he'd had a difficult start in life. He'd dropped out
of high school, then moved to Michigan where he studied heavy
machinery operation but couldn't find work after he was barred
from union membership. Then, on to Washington DC where, now
aged 24, he got a position as security guard at the Watergate complex, the vast, curving, modernistic set of buildings that houses one
of the US capital's plushest hotels, several hundred balconied apart-
ments overlooking the Potomac River, as well as various offices.

The management issued Wills with just a mace spray and no
other weapon. The role of security guard in the garage there
wasn't considered high risk. Wills felt his career was going
nowhere, and he confessed later that his only thought was
'getting a better job and making some money'.

But on the night of 17 July 1972, Frank Wills was to become the unlikely hero in a drama that would rock the world. A real-life drama that would begin with a no-holds-barred battle between the media and the mighty, and climax with the downfall of the US President. Wills was working the midnight to 7 a.m. slot. He set off on his rounds as usual – all quiet, but he did notice some paper had been taped to two doorframes so the doors from the hotel garage into the stairwell would close but not lock. 'I figured someone had been moving during the day,' he explained later, 'and put the tape on so they could get back in.'

He removed the obstructions, then went to get himself a snack from a restaurant across the street. When he returned, ten minutes later, he passed the doors again and saw that the tape had been stuck back on. Now he became suspicious. 'I got to thinking,' he said, 'there's somebody here beside me.' He remembered what he'd been told: Don't be a hero in case of trouble. 'That's the instructions,' he said, 'With just a can of mace, I couldn't confront a burglar who might have a gun.' So, he rushed up to the lobby and phoned Washington's Second Precinct Police Department. It was now 1.55 a.m.

Three plainclothes officers from the tactical force team arrived in minutes. Wills showed them the door from the garage, still taped open. Inside, the policemen began a search, and as they climbed the stairs, they found the door leading to the hallway on each level taped in the same way. The sixth floor housed the offices of the Democratic National Committee, and there they discovered that the main door had been forced. They drew their weapons and, wary of what they might find, went in. Suddenly, from under one of the desks, a man jumped up with his hands in the air, and shouted, 'Don't shoot!' And within seconds, four other men came out of hiding too, and gave themselves up.

The suspects were all wearing rubber surgical gloves. The officers searched them and found two bugging devices capable of picking up and transmitting any nearby conversations, including those by phone. The men also had with them almost $2,300 in cash – most of it in $100 bills with sequential serial numbers – a walkie-talkie, a shortwave radio for monitoring police calls, forty rolls of unexposed film and two 35mm cameras.

Wills, who was waiting in the main lobby, watched as the suspects were brought out in handcuffs. He'd expected to see a bunch of scruffily dressed thugs, but he got a surprise. The men were in business suits and ties. 'All were well dressed,' he said. 'I couldn't make heads or tails out of the arrests.'

* * *

At 9 a.m. the following morning – it was a Saturday – the phone rang in the one-room apartment of *Washington Post* reporter, Bob Woodward. It was the city editor. There'd been a break-in at the Democratic Party headquarters. Could Woodward come in and cover it? The young reporter – he'd been with the *Post* only nine months – agreed, though with some reluctance. It sounded much like many of the other insignificant, down-page stories he'd been given so far, and he was always hoping to be assigned something that would move his career forward.

When he arrived in the newsroom an hour or so later, he discovered his mistake. He'd wrongly assumed that it was some small local Democratic office that had been burgled. Instead – as he was now told – it was the headquarters of the party's National Committee. After making several phone calls, Woodward discovered the five arrested men would appear later at the Fifth Street Courthouse, and that was where he headed off in the early afternoon.

At 3.30, the five accused were led in, still in business suits although stripped now of their ties. The judge asked them their professions. One of them spoke up and answered that they were 'anti-communists'. The others nodded their agreement. The judge – clearly puzzled by this response – repeated his question, this time addressing the tallest of the five men, who'd given his name as James W. McCord Jr.

'Security consultant,' replied McCord, adding that he'd recently retired from government service.

'Where in government?' asked the judge.

'CIA,' came the almost whispered answer.

Woodward gave a jolt, muttering, 'Holy Shit!' under his breath. And once the short hearing was over, he scrambled back to the office and reported McCord's statement. 'That's a hell of a story,' exclaimed the managing editor, and it was moved to the front page. Woodward was now one of eight *Post* reporters working on it. They included the man whose name would be linked forever with that of Woodward over the coming months and years, Carl Bernstein.

The next morning, the *Post* told its readers:

> Five men, one of whom said he is a former employee of the Central Intelligence Agency, were arrested at 2:30 a.m. yesterday in what authorities described as an elaborate plot to bug the offices of the Democratic National Committee here.

The story went on to report the hearing, then added details that the reporting team had gleaned from their contacts:

> According to police and a desk clerk at the Watergate, four of the suspects – all using fictitious names – rented two rooms, Nos 214 and 314, at the Watergate Hotel around noon on Friday. They were said to have dined together on lobster at the Watergate Restaurant on Friday night. Yesterday afternoon, the U.S. Attorney's office obtained warrants to search the hotel rooms rented by the suspects. They found another $4,200 in $100 bills of the same serial number sequence as the money taken from the suspects.

Carl Bernstein, left, and Bob Woodward, May 1973. (© Associated Press)

It was now clear. These were no run-of-the-mill burglars. This was no ordinary break-in by thieves. And then there was McCord's link to the CIA. It was a mystery. All the *Post* story could do was to note, 'There was no immediate explanation as to why the five suspects would want to bug the Democratic National Committee offices or whether or not they were working for any other individuals or organisations.'

It was at this point that the *Post*'s staff missed a trick. Any first-year student journalist would realise that it was urgent now to track down anything about this McCord and find out who he was working for. But Woodward and the rest of the team didn't – they congratulated themselves on a job well done and at 8 p.m. left the office.

The next morning, an Associated Press report dropped on the city editor's desk. It made it embarrassingly clear why the *Post* should have been on the case the night before. The AP story showed that McCord wasn't just an ex-CIA man. He was also – currently – the security co-ordinator for a key Republican Party organisation popularly known as CREEP, the Committee for the Re-Election of the President, Richard M. Nixon. It was election year and the country would be going to the polls in just five months' time. The obvious theory – shocking, if it were found to be true – was that the burglary was a criminal attempt by Republican Party members to find out what their Democratic rivals were up to. The city editor was on the phone again, and Woodward and Bernstein were summoned back to the office.

To link the burglary of the Democratic Party HQ to a Republican organisation working for the president was a very serious allegation, and the president's election campaign manager, John Mitchell – a former US Attorney General – felt the need to hit straight back. Within hours he issued a statement:

> We want to emphasize that this man [McCord] and the other people involved were not operating on either our behalf or with our consent. There is no place in our campaign or in the electoral process for this type of activity, and we will not permit or condone it.

✳ ✳ ✳

The fact that McCord worked for CREEP didn't of itself prove the president's re-election campaign was behind the attempt to bug the Democratic Party HQ – McCord worked for several organisations. Nevertheless, over the coming days, the FBI were called in to investigate further. They looked to the old rule – follow the money – and the trail led them right back to CREEP. The federal agents turned up clear evidence that another of the Watergate burglars was being paid from a fund controlled by the Nixon campaign's finance committee.

This information was not immediately disclosed by the FBI, but Woodward and Bernstein got to hear of it through their contacts and, on 1 August, the following story appeared in the *Post*:

Bug Suspect Got Campaign Funds

A $25,000 cashier's check, apparently earmarked for President Nixon's re-election campaign, was deposited in April in a bank account of one of the five men arrested in the break-in at Democratic National Headquarters here June l7.

And the two *Post* correspondents also had information that seemed to connect the burglary to the heart of government itself. They reported that a notebook seized from one of the suspects contained the telephone number of an E. Howard Hunt Jr, who turned out to be working as a consultant at the White House. This was so serious that the president himself could no longer ignore it, and he now gave a speech in which he swore that his staff had not been involved in the break-in.

Woodward and Bernstein's information to the contrary, as well as many other revelations over the next seven months, came from a highly placed anonymous source. In their jointly authored book, *All the President's Men*, Woodward mentions contacting 'an old friend and sometimes source who worked for the federal government and did not like to be called at his office'. His meetings with the man were the stuff of cloak-and-dagger spy novels.

Former Attorney General, John N. Mitchell, who made crude threats against the *Washington Post*.

Woodward says he'd signal he wanted a face-to-face with his source by moving a flowerpot topped with a red flag to a different position on the balcony of his apartment. And when the man himself had something to relay to the *Post* reporter, he'd go in the early morning to Woodward's apartment block, find his copy of the *New York Times*, then go to page 20 and draw clock hands to indicate the hour of the get-together. The usual time was 2 a.m., and the meeting place was often the bottom level of an underground car park across the Potomac River in Arlington.

In the *Post's* newsroom, the anonymous source was given the nickname 'Deep Throat', the title of a popular porn movie of the time, though also implying a deep insider knowledge. Woodward wrote later about Deep Throat, 'His one consistent message was that the Watergate burglary was just the tip of the iceberg'.

Deep Throat's identity remained a secret for thirty-three years and was the subject of much speculation during that time, but in 2005, William Mark Felt Sr, Deputy Director of the FBI in 1972 and the second highest official in the FBI during the Watergate investigation, came out as the *Post's* anonymous source, and Woodward and Bernstein then confirmed that he was the one who'd leaked all the information to them.

The revelations kept coming. On 29 September, the *Post* ran a story that pointed an accusing finger at a very senior named individual:

John N. Mitchell, while serving as U.S. Attorney General, personally controlled a secret Republican fund that was used to gather information about the Democrats, according to sources involved in the Watergate investigation.

Beginning in the spring of 1971, almost a year before he left the Justice Department to become President Nixon's campaign manager on March 1, Mitchell personally approved withdrawals from the fund, several reliable sources have told *The Washington Post* …

> Last night, Mitchell was reached by telephone in New York and read the beginning of *The Post*'s story. He said: 'All that crap, you're putting it in the paper? It's all been denied. Jesus.'

The *Post* then reported what amounted to a threat from Mitchell: 'Katie Graham [Katharine Graham, publisher of the *Washington Post*] is gonna get caught in a big fat wringer if that's published'. Mitchell's actual words had been rather more crude, indicating that a certain delicate part of Ms Graham's upper anatomy would 'get caught in a big fat wringer' if the story were published, but the quote had been toned down by the *Post*'s editors.

On 10 October, Deep Throat gave Woodward and Bernstein access to FBI files which not only linked the break-in to CREEP, but showed it was only a small cog in a much bigger ruthless machine:

FBI Finds Nixon Aides Sabotaged Democrats

FBI agents have established that the Watergate bugging incident stemmed from a massive campaign of political spying and sabotage conducted on behalf of President Nixon's re-election and directed by officials of the White House and the Committee for the Re-Election of the President.

The activities, according to information in FBI and Department of Justice files, were aimed at all the major Democratic presidential contenders and had been a basic strategy of the Nixon re-election effort since 1971.

During their Watergate investigation, federal agents established that hundreds of thousands of dollars in Nixon campaign contributions had been set aside to pay for an extensive undercover campaign aimed at discrediting individual Democratic presidential candidates and disrupting their campaigns. When the *Post* put these accusations to officials at CREEP, a spokesman there said, 'The *Post* story is not only fiction but a collection of absurdities'.

Meanwhile, Deep Throat warned Woodward that the FBI were getting concerned that so much of their investigations which they didn't want disclosed at this stage were being leaked, and they were trying to find out who was responsible.

During the first months after the Watergate break-in, the *Washington Post* was almost alone in pursuing the scandal. Most papers and TV news channels either ignored or downplayed the revelations. The *Los Angeles Times* even ran stories discrediting the *Post*'s articles. The *Chicago Tribune* and the *Philadelphia Inquirer* both, on occasions, published White House statements denying the *Post*'s stories but without repeating the original allegations.

White House officials, meanwhile, took every opportunity they could to attack the *Post*. They accused it of having a liberal bias against the administration, and claimed it was conducting a lone vendetta, calling it 'outrageous, vicious, distorted reporting'. On 16 October, the chairman of Nixon's re-election committee told reporters, 'The *Post* has maliciously sought to give the appearance of a direct connection between the White House and the Watergate – a charge the *Post* knows – and a half dozen investigations have found – to be false'.

The government was winning the first round of the battle. An opinion poll at this time showed that public distrust of the media topped 40 per cent. On 7 November, four and a half months after the Watergate break-in, President Richard Nixon was re-elected in one of the biggest landslides in American history.

***

On 30 January 1973, ten days after Nixon's presidential inauguration ceremony, the five Watergate burglars were convicted and sent to prison, and for the next couple of months the scandal quietened down. By April, however, it burst back into the news, and was screaming from the headlines when one of the convicted burglars opened up a gap in the wall of silence that the White House had built around the misdeeds.

James McCord, the man who'd declared himself to be an ex-CIA man at the first hearing, now sent a letter to the trial judge, stating that 'political pressure' had been applied to the Watergate defendants to get them to plead guilty and keep quiet. McCord alleged that government witnesses had committed perjury and that there'd been a widespread conspiracy.

Now the pressure was on, and the first to crack was the deputy director of CREEP, Jeb Magruder. He could see the writing on the wall and in an attempt to do a deal with the prosecutors, Magruder confessed that he'd not told the truth during his testimony at the burglars' trial, and he pointed the finger of blame higher up the ladder to his boss at CREEP, John Mitchell, as well as at White House counsel, John Dean. Dean then, in turn, decided to co-operate with the Department of Justice and tell what he knew.

By 17 April, officers of the US Attorney's Department had enough evidence to be able to advise the president that his chief of staff, H.R. Haldeman, his legal advisor, John Ehrlichman, and several other senior presidential aides were, one way or another, implicated in the break-in or a subsequent cover-up.

Two weeks later, Nixon – in an attempt to fix all the blame on those around him – 'accepted the resignations' of his attorney general, Richard Kleindienst, and Haldeman and Ehrlichman, as well as Dean himself. And in a TV address, the president presented himself as the good guy cleaning out the stables. 'There can be no whitewash at the White House,' he told the nation, and he pledged to take steps to purge the American political system of the kind of abuses that emerged in the Watergate affair.

The *Washington Post*, however, told its readers that the firings still left many questions unanswered:

Ahead are the prospect of indictments, criminal trials, heavily publicized Senate hearings and the ever-haunting question of presidential involvement.

And the *Post* pointed out that the president's popularity ratings were now dropping. It ended the report by patting itself on the back:

It is a matter of history that the *Washington Post*, and particularly two young reporters on its metropolitan staff, Carl Bernstein and Bob Woodward, provided much of the material that made Watergate a name known around the world.

A month later, in May 1973, enough members of Congress started to believe the full truth had yet to emerge that it was agreed to set up a special Senate Committee to investigate further. That committee, in turn, insisted on the appointment of Archibald Cox, a former solicitor general, as special prosecutor, with the widest possible brief to examine 'all offenses arising out of the 1972 election … involving the president, the White House staff or presidential appointments'.

Within days, Woodward and Bernstein got an insight into just how high up the investigations were heading, and told *Post* readers:

Former presidential counsel John W. Dean III has told Senate investigators and federal prosecutors that he discussed aspects of the Watergate cover-up with President Nixon or in Mr. Nixon's presence on at least 35 occasions between January and April of this year, according to reliable sources.

… Dean has told investigators that Mr. Nixon had prior knowledge of payments used to buy the silence of the Watergate conspirators and of offers of executive clemency extended in his name, the sources said.

This was explosive. However, the fact that Dean had made these claims wasn't proof they were true. So, where would that proof come from? The answer was to be one of the biggest surprises of the whole Watergate saga. Every minute of the Senate Watergate hearings was being shown live on public broadcasting TV, and when viewers saw Dean take the stand, they heard him reveal that Nixon had secretly tape recorded every conversation that took place in the Oval Office over a number of years. Other White House aides confirmed it. The recordings would show who was telling the truth.

Now came a bitter fight, with Special Prosecutor Cox demanding that the president hand over the tapes. In October, Nixon used his executive power to fire Cox, then declared in a televised interview, 'I am not a crook'.

The US Supreme Court, however, unanimously ruled that the president was obliged to release the tapes. Nixon still dragged his feet. At first, he made available written versions with gaps where, it was claimed, expletives were deleted. As Members of Congress and the American people read the transcripts, his support waned. Even the vice president, Gerald Ford, was starting to distance himself from his boss, 'While it may be easy to delete characterization from the printed page, we cannot delete characterization from people's minds with a wave of the hand'.

And newspapers which had previously supported Nixon, now turned against him. One such was the *Chicago Tribune,* which wrote:

> He is humorless to the point of being inhumane. He is devious. He is vacillating. He is profane. He is willing to be led. He displays dismaying gaps in knowledge. He is suspicious of his staff. His loyalty is minimal.

The *Providence Journal* declared:

Reading the transcripts is an emetic experience; one comes away feeling unclean ... While the transcripts may not have revealed an indictable offense, they show Nixon contemptuous of the United States, its institutions, and its people.

On 30 July 1974, the Supreme Court ruled that the tapes themselves must be released. Now Nixon had no option and he complied. What the recordings – now broadcast on national TV and radio – did seem to show was that Nixon himself had no prior knowledge of the break-in. At a point, five days after the burglary, he could be heard asking his chief of staff, H.R. Haldeman, 'Who was the asshole who ordered it?' However, other recordings left no doubt that he was involved in the cover-up.

The nation now heard the unmistakable tones of the president – six weeks after the break-in – agreeing with his chief of staff that the burglars' silence had to be bought, 'Well, they have to be paid. That's all there is to that. They have to be paid.' In another conversation, Dean tells Nixon that Howard Hunt – the White House consultant who'd organised the burglary – was now demanding large sums in return for his silence. Nixon replies, 'Just looking at the immediate problem, don't you have to handle Hunt's financial situation damn soon? You've got to keep the cap on the bottle that much, in order to have any options.'

***

The net was closing in and, in July, the House Judiciary Committee recommended the president be impeached for obstruction of justice, abuse of power and contempt of Congress. Then, on 5 August, a previously unheard section of the tape was discovered. It became known as the 'smoking gun'. It had been recorded only six days after the break-in. Haldeman can be heard discussing with the president how to put a stop to the FBI investigation. He suggests getting the CIA to intervene and tell the FBI to drop it. Nixon approves the plan, telling Haldeman, 'You call them in. Good. Good deal. Play it tough. That's the way they play it and that's the way we are going to play it.'

Nixon later denied this was an obstruction of justice, but he couldn't get around the fact that he'd been involved in the cover-up almost from day one. His own lawyers now said, 'The President lied to the nation, to his closest aides, and to his own lawyers – for more than two years.'

Four days later, on 9 August 1974, the *Washington Post* reported that at 2:20 p.m. on the day before, Nixon's press secretary, Ron Ziegler, walked into the press room and, struggling to control his emotions, read a statement which ended, 'Tonight, at 9 o'clock, Eastern Daylight Time, the President of the United States will address the nation on radio and television from his Oval Office'.

The *Post* added that, although Ziegler's voice shook, it did not break.

> As soon as he had finished, he turned on his heel and left the room, without so much as a glance at the men and women in the room who wanted to question him …
>
> Thursday was a wet, humid August day but, despite intermittent rain, the crowds packed the sidewalks in front of the White House. It was an orderly crowd, resigned and curious, watching newsmen come and go and being a part of a dramatic moment in the life of the nation.

The headline over the story read simply:

NIXON RESIGNS

* * *

Nixon never admitted any criminal wrongdoing, though he did acknowledge using poor judgement. Six weeks after his resignation, the new president, former Vice President Gerald Ford, pardoned him for any crimes he had committed while in office. Other lesser mortals were not so lucky. In total, sixty-nine government officials were charged in the wake of Watergate, forty-eight were found guilty. They included:

- John Mitchell, the director of CREEP, who spent nineteen months in jail for perjury.
- H.R. Haldeman, Nixon's chief of staff, convicted of being a conspirator to the break-in, obstruction of justice and perjury. Served eighteen months in prison.
- John Ehrlichman, counsel to Nixon, guilty of the same charges as Haldeman. Eighteen months in prison.
- John Dean, counsel to the president, convicted of obstruction of justice, later reduced to lesser offences. Four months in prison.

The five burglars themselves spent between two and eighteen months in jail.

And what happened to Frank Wills, the young black security guard, without whose alert action the biggest scandal in American political history might never have come to light? His employers promoted him and gave him a 3 per cent pay rise. A few minutes of fame came when he played himself in the film version of the Watergate story, *All the President's Men*, but he then fell on hard times. In 1993, when his mother died, he had to donate her body to medical research because he couldn't afford to bury her. In 2000, at the age of 52, he died of a brain tumour.

Bob Woodward and Carl Bernstein were awarded the Pulitzer Prize for excellence in journalism, and they shot to international fame, in part through the film, where they were played by Robert Redford and Dustin Hoffman. The two *Post* reporters are seen as being among the greatest heroes in the media's long war with the mighty, fearlessly seeking out the truths that the most powerful man in the world found so uncomfortable.

So, is their reputation wholly deserved?

The Harvard University political science professor, Edward Jay Epstein, argues that the Watergate Scandal was, in fact, 'uncovered by government institutions' and, anyway, 'would have come to the public's attention when the cases came to trial'. Epstein says the Watergate conspiracy was actually smashed by:

> ...the investigations conducted by the FBI, the federal prosecutors, the grand jury, and the Congressional committees. The work of almost all those institutions, which unearthed and developed all the actual evidence and disclosures of Watergate, is systematically ignored or minimized by Bernstein and Woodward.

Another argument put forward to undermine the role of the two *Post* journalists is that their attacks on the government were simply part of a long-running witch-hunt by the liberal press. Paul Johnson, in his *History of the American People*, claims that the US East Coast daily newspapers had for the past decade or more had it in for Nixon, and that they'd colluded with the Kennedy administration and later with high-placed opponents of Nixon to undermine him. When it came to Watergate, Johnson says, the Congressional Committee and the Special Prosecutor '... had between them over 200 lawyers and special assistants working for Nixon's downfall, and feeding all the damaging material they could muster to an eager anti-Nixon media'.

There's a grain of truth in both these arguments. Much, though not all, of the real legwork in unearthing the conspiracy, was – it's true – carried out by government investigators, especially the FBI in the early stages. And it's also true that if Woodward and Bernstein had not been working for a liberal-leaning paper, they wouldn't have been allowed to keep up their relentless pursuit of the truth. If they'd been at a paper that favoured the Republican Party, the editor and publisher would undoubtedly have told them to drop it and move on to other stories.

However, neither of the arguments put forward by Epstein and Johnson stands up to detailed scrutiny. Epstein's theory that the investigations carried out by government agencies would have emerged anyway without being published in the *Washington Post*, has a fundamental flaw. It assumes the FBI, for instance, would automatically make all their findings public, and that all would be revealed when the burglars and conspirators came to trial. Epstein ignores the fact that Nixon and his aides were trying to get the CIA to lean on the FBI to hold off in their investigations. And he ignores the fact that the government was bribing the miscreants to keep their mouths shut.

It was these very real threats that persuaded the second most powerful man at the FBI, William Mark Felt, alias Deep Throat, to leak the bureau's findings to Woodward. He wanted to make sure that no White House dirty tricks would stop the truth about the conspiracy from emerging. In a country without assiduous journalists like Woodward and Bernstein, the government cover-up might have stayed covered up from public view.

And what about Johnson's claim that the *Post*'s investigation was simply a witch-hunt? America has known many witch-hunts in its history. Most recently, there'd been Senator Joseph McCarthy's ruthless pursuit of anyone in public office who might ever have said anything which could imply they had communist sympathies or anything that could be interpreted as anti-American. In order to put the Watergate investigation in the same box as McCarthyism, Johnson would need to show that Nixon and his aides were the innocent – or near innocent – victims of an inquisition.

That, of course, was far from the case. Serious crimes were committed. So, the fact that it took a liberal-leaning newspaper to help reveal those crimes to the people is hardly relevant.

In fact, it tells us more about the tendency of the more right-wing press – in the early stages of the scandal – to allow themselves to be taken in and hoodwinked by the White House.

Almost all the revelations in stories written by Woodward and Bernstein turned out in the end to be true, and that was a tribute to their professionalism. They adopted a rule: any allegation that could be considered criminal would be printed only if it could be corroborated by two sources. And that applied to information provided by Felt as much as that from any other of their contacts in CREEP, the investigating agencies or the White House. It was only in that way that the two correspondents could be confident that their published reports were as accurate as possible.

***

We've seen few periods during the 500-year history of the war between the media and the mighty when the media won an out-and-out victory. In fact, as we've seen, there've been many times when reporters and editors have ducked the truth and backed a deceitful government. Watergate showed that when reporters and editors are fearless and determined in their search for the truth, journalism can be a force for democracy. By 1974, many Americans had a renewed trust in the news media, and applications to journalism schools suddenly spiked to an all-time high.

So, did Watergate now set a pattern in the Western world, of responsible journalists holding the mighty to account? To find out, we're going to cross the Atlantic again. Not just to Europe this time, but 8,000 miles away, to the south of that ocean, where a war was about to be fought.

The Falklands War would be the reporters' ultimate test – a conflict on a remote set of islands far from any supporting newsroom, and a place which only a few correspondents could reach, and then would be dependent for almost every element of their professional lives on the very military and political leaders whose actions it was their job to report.

But first, to start the next stage of our journey, we're going to a quiet spot in the English countryside where the only challenge was a cantankerous cow.

17

THE FALKLANDS WAR

A Quick Win (for the Mighty)

> I will never forget it. How could the bloody BBC question
> the integrity of the military?
>
> *Sir Denis Thatcher (1915–2003)*

Michael Nicholson confessed in his memoirs that if it hadn't
been for one pregnant cow he'd never have gone to the Falkland
Islands. During the first week of April 1982, Nicholson, a senior
ITN reporter, was on holiday with his wife Diana and their two
sons in the Lake District. They were out walking for the day
near Ullswater when they came face to face with a very pregnant and very bad-tempered cow. They decided not to risk it,
and turned back. Their new route took them close to where
they were staying, and as they got near, they suddenly saw one
of the hotel staff running up the path towards them. He panted
that a phone call had just come through from ITN in London,
and could Mr Nicholson please call them straight back.

Nicholson – like the rest of the nation – knew that Argentine
troops had just invaded the British Falkland Islands in the South
Atlantic, forced the governor to surrender and hoisted the Argentine
flag over the capital, Port Stanley. So, he could guess what the call
was about. And when he spoke to the foreign editor, he was told

ITN foreign correspondent Michael
Nicholson. (© Press Association)

that the House of Commons had, minutes earlier, ended an emergency debate. Tory back-benchers had demanded that gunships be sent, and the prime minister, Margaret Thatcher, had ordered that a naval task force set sail as soon as possible.

Within half an hour, Nicholson was on his way by car to a small airfield near Carlisle where ITN had a light plane waiting to take him to Southampton. The next morning, he was onboard the aircraft carrier HMS *Hermes* in Portsmouth Docks. Such was the haste, that if Nicholson hadn't got straight back to the ITN foreign desk that day in the Lake District, he would have missed his chance, and the foreign editor would have called the next reporter on the list.

On the following day, 5 April, ITN carried live pictures of tens of thousands of people lining the Portsmouth quayside and cheering as more than 100 naval vessels and civilian supply ships set sail. TV pictures showed tugs chivvying the two aircraft carriers into the sea lane, as sailors lined the edge of the decks, all with Royal Tournament precision.

* * *

On the face of it, the Falklands looked like it could be Britain's Vietnam. It had many of the makings of a similar defeat. Both wars were conducted far from home shores – with an 8,000 mile or more supply line – and both were fought for a cause that had no direct bearing on the safety, wealth or future of the nation back home. In Vietnam, the objective had been to stop the spread of communism in South East Asia, while in the Falklands the aim was to prevent 1,800 English-speaking islanders from being absorbed into Argentina. In Vietnam, the loss of many American lives couldn't, in the end, be justified. US opinion about the rightness of the fight became split, and defeat followed. Now, seven years later, would the same happen to Britain in the South Atlantic?

As it would turn out, however, there were crucial differences between the two conflicts. In Vietnam, American troops were worn down by the constant hit-and-run tactics of guerrilla fighters. The Falklands was a more conventional battle between two armed forces. But what also set the Falklands apart was the way the media covered it – or were prevented from covering it. As we've seen, in Vietnam, reporters and TV news crews had more or less complete freedom to roam the warzone looking for stories, and censorship was rarely imposed on what journalists wrote or filmed. By stark contrast, in the Falklands it was easy for the government to manage the news. The very remoteness of the theatre of war – on and around tiny islands hundreds of miles from any mainland – meant that the only way that the news media could get anywhere near the action was on board one of the task-force ships at the invitation of the Royal Navy.

And that was only the half of it. TV crews, stills photographers and press reporters would then be entirely dependent on the military to get their pictures and reports back to the UK. The whole set-up was one where the military were in control. The ability to censor and manage the news fell into their laps. It was a gift they grabbed without much hesitation.

The first thing Nicholson, as well as the BBC's man, Brian Hanrahan, and a handful of other reporters, found on board HMS *Hermes*, was a piece of paper they had to sign. It was the Official Secrets Act, which reminded them that it would be a criminal offence to disclose information, documents or other articles relating to security or intelligence. Then they were handed a tiny green booklet entitled *Regulations for Correspondents*, which had been printed in 1956 for the Suez invasion. It read, 'The essence of successful warfare is secrecy. The essence of successful journalism is publicity' and it called for 'mutual co-operation in the task of leading and steadying public opinion in times of national stress or crisis'.

The Royal Navy, according to Nicholson, would have far preferred not to have any journalists with them. Its commander-in-chief, Admiral Sir John Fieldhouse, had gone on record that journalists were 'the newly invented curse to armies'. To their credit, it was Prime Minister Margaret Thatcher and her press secretary, Bernard Ingham, who had overruled the naval hierarchy and insisted the news media should accompany the task force – though with suitable constraints on what they could report. Only thirty journalists – including TV cameramen from ITN and the BBC – were allowed on the ships. All British. No foreigners, who might want to be more critical of what they saw.

Over the next few weeks, Nicholson and Hanrahan faced a series of obstacles, delays and bullying. Their reports were censored, held back, occasionally lost, and at best sent slowly. First announcements of developments in the fighting often came not from these correspondents in the South Atlantic, but from the lugubrious mouth of the Ministry of Defence spokesman in London, Ian McDonald, who was described as having 'all the charisma of a speak-your-weight-machine'.

The job of the correspondents with the task force was often reduced to confirming later what the public had already been told. They had to submit what they wrote to one of the officers on *Hermes*, who had the job of censoring – or sometimes blocking their reports altogether. On 6 May, for instance, two Harrier jump jets collided in fog, and both pilots were killed.

Nicholson and Hanrahan were forbidden to report it. Then, that night when they sat around listening to a BBC World Service Radio broadcast – there it was, being officially announced in London.

Nicholson wrote later how the two TV correspondents and their cameraman on *Hermes* were loathed by the ship's officers, who accused them of 'giving too much away' and even of acting like Argentine spies. He added, 'They suffered from the Vietnam syndrome. The analogy was made frequently, and the spectre haunted those in charge of us: the Vietnam War was a television war and it was lost; ergo all television wars are lost.'

He had himself covered Vietnam and taken advantage of the freedom there to do his job with little hindrance. Now, he was climbing the bulkheads in frustration. After weeks of official interference, he sent a radio message to ITN in London telling them that all his reports were being censored and he urged them to make that clear to viewers. But the message never got through: the censor on board censored the word 'censored'.

The restrictions became ever tighter and spread beyond deleting information that might have helped the enemy. When one of the dead from HMS *Sheffield* was buried at sea, the cameraman, who was working jointly for both ITN and the BBC, was not allowed to film the ceremony. The padre said it wouldn't be decent. Nicholson and Hanrahan found it more and more difficult to get a helicopter ride to the radio transmission station. The officer in charge of flight schedules told the TV men, 'You bastards are the lowest priority rating – at the bottom of the list, and as long as I'm here, that's where you'll remain!'

Journalists faced threats and intimidation. One of Nicholson's reports – which had been passed by the censor – mentioned that Royal Navy frigates had crept to within a mile of the Falklands and bombarded Argentine positions. He ended it, 'With that kind of cheek, they may well be encouraged to have another go sometime soon.'

Admiral Fieldhouse, the commander-in-chief in London considered this a breach of the rule against revealing secret information and, on board *Hermes*, Nicholson was summoned to Admiral Sir John Woodward's day cabin. There, he was told to prepare to be helicoptered off to a ship bound for home. 'I'm going to sack you', were the admiral's words, and the message was then broadcast by loudspeaker across the entire ship. Nicholson, battle-hardened as he was, was shocked, and he found himself being physically threatened by both officers and junior ratings for 'endangering lives'. In the end, for whatever reason, no official action was taken, and Nicholson stayed on.

For the first fifty-four days of the conflict, no pictures reached the British viewing public. There were two TV cameras with the task force, one ITN and one BBC, on different ships – with the agreement between the two organisations that their pictures would be shared. Both started out using the latest video technology, but when ITN's equipment broke down, its cameraman had to switch to old-fashioned 16mm film. Stewart Purvis, editor of ITN's *News at Ten* at the time and later the company's editor-in-chief, recalls what a lengthy and cumbersome process it was to get the pictures back to London:

> Each piece of video or film was helicoptered between ships until it reached one going to Ascension Island. There, the video was satellited back. But because there was no film processing on the island, the film had to be shipped on to London either by sea or air. So it was literally sometimes weeks between shooting the story and transmission on the news.

ITN had sent out its most talented field engineer, Peter Heaps, to try to install a satellite up-link from one of the support vessels, so that video could be more directly transmitted to London. Heaps got it to work, but was prevented from using it to send video reports to London because the navy said they'd have to turn off some of their own equipment at the same time, and they refused to do that. Whether this was a genuine technical problem or whether it was the navy being obstructive, isn't clear.

So, Nicholson and Hanrahan of the BBC relied more and more on imageless voice reports. 'I decided this was going to be a radio war,' said Nicholson. Once on the Falklands themselves, the two TV correspondents were allowed to report what they saw so long as they didn't give any specific locations or any details of the strength of British forces or their tactics. On 21 May, Nicholson radioed:

> At one of the unopposed landings near a small village, a cluster of white stone buildings, troops found thirty-one Falklanders in their own makeshift shelter, among them fourteen children. All safe ... Just after ten o'clock here – that's one o'clock British time – with the winter sun low and dazzling, the Argentines began their air attacks, the first in a long, long day of them.

By the end of that day, all correspondents with the task force knew how many British lives had been lost. They were not allowed to report it.

TV correspondents in the Falklands – despite what the navy or the MoD claimed – were not, however, anti-war agents. They recognised genuine bravery and heroism when they saw it, and reported it accordingly. When, on 9 June, the British ship *Sir Galahad* was hit in an Argentine air attack and immediately burst into flames, Hanrahan reported for the BBC on the efforts to rescue the wounded:

> Despite the risk, the helicopters disappeared into the black cloud trying to pull men from the waters. Again and again the pilots risked their lives to save others.

Nicholson ended his report of the same action:

It was a day of tragedy, but I vouch it was a day of extraordinary heroism and selflessness by every man who witnessed it.

* * *

The editorial management at both the BBC and ITN believed their job was to report the war as accurately as they could. That was what was required of them by their founding constitutions, the BBC Charter and, for ITN, the Television Act. In order to fulfil that need, both organisations had sent correspondents to Argentina, from where they sent back regular – and, of course, prompt – reports from Buenos Aires. So, viewers got to hear the Argentine version of the latest fighting and the reaction of the government there, alongside the official British account.

At the same time, the editors of both TV news channels did their best to piece together all the information available. David Nicholas, the editor-in-chief of ITN, gave military analysts regular slots on *News at Ten*, to speculate about the significance of the latest raid. They showed viewers maps and models of the positions of the sea and land forces of both sides, and they indicated where and how the latest air attacks had taken place. The BBC did the same. Every night, on the TV screens of the nation – despite the censorship and obstacles in the South Atlantic – both channels tried to paint a graphic overall picture of the progress of the fighting.

Many in Parliament felt this was wrong, and harmful to the war effort. Prime Minister Margaret Thatcher hated the way the two channels spoke of 'British soldiers' or 'British sailors', rather than talking about 'our boys'. And she noted afterwards:

Many of the public (including me) did not like the attitude particularly of the BBC and I was very worried about it. They were sometimes reporting as if they were neutral between Britain and Argentina. At other times we felt strongly that they were assisting

the enemy by open discussions with experts on the next likely
steps in the campaign. My concern was always the safety of our
forces. Theirs was news.

She added that her criticisms also applied to ITN, but only
singled out BBC broadcasts. She was so angry with the BBC
that she put pressure on the Home Secretary, Willie Whitelaw
to take the corporation into the government's direct control for
the duration of the war. The BBC's director general designate,
Alasdair Milne, and its chairman, Lord Howard, appeared
before a session of the Tory MPs' Media Committee in order
to defend their news coverage, and they faced the accusation
that the corporation was 'obsequious' towards Argentina.
Whitelaw himself could see that any attempt to turn the BBC
into a government mouthpiece would be a step too far, and
he managed to head it off. Whether the threat was ever meant
seriously, or whether it was a crude attempt to bully the BBC
management, we don't know.

As the war ended, there was one final snub to the media, and it
was Nicholson on the receiving end. It was nigh on impossible to
get a scoop in the Falklands, with all the journalists packed together
and under the tight control of the authorities. But Nicholson had a
world exclusive – or thought he did. Separated on the island from
his fellow reporters, he came across General Jeremy Moore, who –
he discovered – was on his way to accept the formal surrender of
the Argentine commander, General Menendez.

So, it was all over, and Nicholson had the story to himself.
Now, he needed to get the news back to ITN. He thumbed lifts,
'borrowed' a dinghy, and used every ounce of his ingenuity to
get himself to the radio transmission station on board a British
ship just offshore. He arrived there with only ten minutes to go
before *News at Ten*. He was going to break the story to the world.
Wrong! The Ministry of Defence had imposed a news blackout.
Nicholson's report was blocked. Prime Minister Thatcher had

decided that she alone would announce the good news to the nation. And that's what she did in Parliament the next day.

***

A later parliamentary enquiry into the way the government had handled media relations during the conflict reached a muddled conclusion. It accused the Ministry of Defence of 'inconsistent and unnecessarily strict censorship which caused gratuitous delay in the reporting of events', as well as 'managing the news and disseminating misinformation about operational matters'. At the same time, the enquiry's authors managed the amazing acrobatic feat of riding two horses going in opposite directions at once by claiming that 'in the main ... the credibility of the information issued by the Ministry of Defence was sustained throughout the campaign'.

In Vietnam, as we've seen, the American Government had chosen not to censor or control the media, even though many of those in power, including at least two presidents, believed – over-simplistically – that nightly TV coverage was sapping the American nation's morale and hastening defeat. And many in the British military came to a similar view.

In the immediate aftermath of Vietnam, Brigadier F.G. Caldwell, a senior director at the Ministry of Defence, wrote, 'If Britain were to go to war again, we would have to start saying to ourselves, are we going to let the television cameras loose on the battlefield?' In the Falklands, it was easy to keep TV crews on a tight leash, and it became – in Nicholson's phrase – 'a radio war'.

Did that help in corralling British public opinion firmly behind the war effort? We can't know. Unlike Vietnam, which ground on for sixteen years, the Falklands lasted a mere seventy-four days before the Argentine enemy was defeated. That was not long enough for public support to wane, especially given the enthusiasm for the fight in the populist press. With the exception of the *Financial Times*, the *Guardian* and the *Daily Mirror*, the national newspapers were flag-toting, patriotic cheerleaders for Britain's soldiers, sailors and airmen.

The height of this euphoria came on 4 May, with the *Sun's* front-page report on the sinking of the Argentine cruiser, General Belgrano:

GOTCHA
Our lads sink gunboat and hole cruiser

And before any idea could start to dawn on people back home that 260 British service personnel had been killed and 777 wounded, solely to preserve the way of life of just 1,800 islanders, the Argentines had raised a white flag over Port Stanley and the glory of victory was the story of the day.

Who knows what might have happened if the Falklands War hadn't been a quick win – if it had dragged on for years into a costly stalemate. Would then there have been a public demand to be told the truth, rising to a clamour that couldn't be ignored? The suppression of TV news coverage might have become an issue in itself, and there might have been demands for free reporting of the war on TV and in the press so that the people could exercise their democratic right to make up their own minds. But this is conjecture. The war lasted just ten weeks and four days. And the mighty got away with it.

***

Twenty-one years later, the UK went to war again, and once more the fight was far from home. This time, however, it was a land war, and provided there were news crews around prepared to risk their lives – which there were – there wasn't much the government or the military could do to rein them in or control what they reported. But the real problem, this time, for the mighty wasn't out there on the front line, it was back home in Britain. There wasn't any obvious reason why British troops should be sent to fight and some, as ever, to die. That was the tricky question facing the prime minister, Tony Blair, in the run-up to the invasion of Iraq in 2003. His solution would be catastrophic in its consequences – for Blair himself, for parts of the media, and for many ordinary citizens who lost trust in them both.

So, what happened, and who was to blame? That's what we're going find out next.

18

BLAIR AND IRAQ

The Dodgy Spinners

Today's media … is like a feral beast just tearing people
and reputations to bits.

Tony Blair (1953–)

On 22 May 2003, two men arrived, one after the other, at that
grand survival of the Victorian railway age, London's 150-year-
old Charing Cross Hotel, now glitzed up and modernised to
become a favourite with overseas tourists who want to be handy
for Trafalgar Square, a few steps away. The men met in the first-
floor bar and sat down to talk.

Anyone who'd walked in and glanced at the two of them that
morning would have noticed nothing exceptional. Just a couple
of old friends, or colleagues, maybe – one in his thirties, round-
faced, balding and in frameless spectacles, the other much older, in
his late fifties, a greying trimmed beard below owl glasses. In fact,
anyone who'd wandered over and eavesdropped on the first few
minutes of their conversation would have just caught snatches of
them having a moan about the poor state of Britain's railways.

No one in the bar that day could have guessed they were witnessing something that would trigger an explosive battle which
would hit the nation's headlines, and pit the government, the

BBC and Britain's intelligence services at each other's throats. The bitter three-way fight would leave them all with their reputations badly wounded, and one man, caught in the crossfire, would be dead. That man was here now in the hotel bar – he was the older of the two, the one with the greying beard. He was Dr David Kelly, a leading expert on biological warfare. The man sitting opposite him was a BBC Radio reporter named Andrew Gilligan.

Two months before this meeting, UK forces alongside American troops had invaded Iraq and rapidly toppled the government of Saddam Hussein. In the previous September, an intelligence report, endorsed by Prime Minister Tony Blair, had been made public. It stated that Iraq had weapons of mass destruction which threatened the safety of the West and, in addition, Saddam could deploy and activate chemical weapons within forty-five minutes of an order being given. The report was presented by the Blair government as a justification for the war.

The Sun newspaper – owned by Rupert Murdoch, who Blair had persuaded to support him – put a photo on its front page of people sunning themselves on a beach. The headline screamed:

Brits 45 Mins from Doom
   BRITISH servicemen and tourists in Cyprus could be annihilated by germ warfare missiles launched by Iraq, it was revealed yesterday.

Other parts of the more Tory-leaning press weren't so convinced. In January 2003, the *Daily Mail* told its 2.5 million readers that Britain was 'stumbling along the road to war':

The closer the military action looms, the less convincingly warranted it seems. And the more ethically dubious the case that Mr Blair puts for it seems.

The invasion had lasted just six weeks, until 1 May. Unfortunately for Tony Blair and the government, once Western troops had overrun the country and searched for evidence of the weapons of mass destruction – WMD, as everyone had got used to calling them – none was found. The suspicion was mounting that the nation had been hoodwinked by a prime minister too eager to go to war alongside his friend President George W. Bush, and the media christened the report that had been used to justify Britain's involvement as the 'dodgy dossier'.

Andrew Gilligan, the BBC man at the Charing Cross Hotel, was trying to get to the bottom of it, to discover exactly how the government had been involved in producing the dossier, and whether the forty-five-minute threat was real. That's why he'd called Kelly to arrange the meeting. He'd consulted the scientist before to get background information for his radio reports.

Kelly's knowledge of biological weaponry was unmatched. In his earlier career, he'd helped investigate Soviet violations of the Biological Weapons Convention. Then, following the Gulf War in the early 1990s, he'd worked as a UN weapons inspector, and his success in uncovering Iraq's biological weapons programme had even led to a nomination for the Nobel Peace Prize. Saddam's germ warfare capability was supposed to have been destroyed after that.

In the lead up to the Iraq invasion of 2003, Kelly was working for the Defence Intelligence Service, a section of the Ministry of Defence, though he was also called in at times to assist MI6. He'd proofread parts of the so-called 'dodgy dossier', but had had nothing to do with writing it. It had been produced by the Joint Intelligence Committee, which was the Cabinet's own body responsible for analysing intelligence information. But Gilligan thought that Kelly, as an insider in the intelligence community, might be aware of who knew what about the dossier's claims, and when.

Their meeting at the Charing Cross Hotel was described as 'longish'. Gilligan didn't make a voice recording of what Kelly told him, but he tapped out some notes on a small electronic personal organiser. He'd made it clear to Kelly that anything he said would be 'non-attributable', in other words, Gilligan could report Kelly's comments but not reveal who'd made them. When the two men parted, the BBC correspondent didn't go on air immediately to tell listeners what he'd discovered from Kelly. He sat on it for the moment, waiting for a suitable news peg – in other words, for a news story to break that would make it more relevant.

***

Seven days later, Prime Minister Blair accompanied by his director of communications, Alastair Campbell, stepped out of an RAF plane into the desert heat of Basra in southern Iraq. Blair was there to congratulate the troops on their rapid victory and, of course, to get some favourable publicity by being associated with their success.

Alastair Campbell and Tony Blair in the prime ministerial car. (© Press Association)

Campbell was a long-time ally of Blair's. He'd come from the world of journalism himself, and in his early adult life had had to overcome severe personal difficulties. He'd struggled with a mental breakdown and alcoholism but, after a lengthy recovery, he'd rebuilt his career to become political editor of the *Daily Mirror*. When Tony Blair became Labour leader in 1994, Campbell joined him as his press secretary. It was he who coined the phrase 'New Labour' to denote the modernised party that Blair was creating.

Along with Peter Mandelson, he'd co-ordinated Labour's 1997 general election campaign that put Tony Blair's government in power. Campbell brought the word 'spin' to British politics – meaning to give a positive twist to government announcements without too much regard always for the truth. And he'd put the backs up of journalists right across the media with the relentless and ruthless way he'd spun the ups and downs of the Blair government. Campbell's enemies called him 'the real deputy prime minister'. The 'dodgy dossier' and all the allegations of deceit and lies that surrounded it, were to be by far the biggest challenge of his career.

Blair, advised by Campbell, had maintained a consistent position whenever reporters asked him about the absence of WMD, and he'd reply, 'I'm absolutely confident that the weapons will be found'. However, that morning as Blair and Campbell celebrated victory in southern Iraq, it was all suddenly about to get a whole lot harder to trot out that line. One of the prime ministerial aides came up to Blair and told him of news just in from the US. The American Secretary of Defense, Donald Rumsfeld had stated in public that Saddam's WMD would probably never be found, because he possibly had never possessed any.

That was bad enough (Campbell muttered, 'What a clot ... really irritating'), but there was worse to come. An hour or so later, there was a second bit of breaking news, and this time it pointed an accusing finger at Blair and Campbell for having deliberately deceived the British people. At 6.07 that morning, Gilligan had spoken on the BBC Radio *Today* programme, and in a question-and-answer session he'd revealed – without naming his source – what Kelly had told him in that conversation at the Charing Cross Hotel. First, he'd reminded listeners that a central claim of the dossier had been that weapons of mass destruction would be ready to fire in forty-five minutes, then he continued:

> ... what we've been told by one of the senior officials in charge of drawing up that dossier was that actually **the government probably knew that the 45-minute figure was wrong even before it decided to put it in** [my emphasis] ... Downing Street, our source says ... ordered it to be sexed up, to be made more exciting and ordered more facts to be discovered. Our source says that the dossier as it was finally published made the intelligence services unhappy ... the 45-minute point was probably the most important thing that was added ... and the intelligence agencies don't really believe it was necessarily true ... The 45 minutes isn't just a detail, it did go to the heart of the government's case that Saddam was an imminent threat.

And Gilligan's conclusion would be the understatement of the war:

> But if they knew it was wrong before they actually made the claim, that's perhaps a bit more serious.

Gilligan was claiming that he had inside knowledge that showed Tony Blair's government had probably lied and distorted the truth to justify the invasion. Campbell was incandescent with rage, and he had a quick phone conference with the Downing Street early-shift press officers, ordering them to put out an immediate denial. The result was a garbled official statement that read, 'Not one word of the dossier was not entirely the work of the intelligence agencies' – which was trying to say that it had all been written by the intelligence services, and was nothing to do with the government.

At 7.32 in London, Gilligan was back in front of the microphones in the *Today* studio. John Humphrys, the presenter, introduced him with a fresh allegation:

Our defence correspondent Andrew Gilligan has found evidence that **the government's dossier** on Iraq that was produced last September **was cobbled together at the last minute** with some unconfirmed material that had not been approved by the security services [my emphasis].

Humphrys then asked Gilligan:

Are you suggesting, let's be very clear about this, that it was not the work of the intelligence agencies?

Gilligan replied:

No, the information which I'm told was dubious did come from the agencies, but they were unhappy about it, because they didn't think it should have been in there.

But he went on to point out that the dossier's contents were fully endorsed by the government:

And you open up the dossier and the first thing you see is a preface written by Tony Blair that includes the following words 'Saddam's military planning allows for some weapons of mass destruction to be ready within 45 minutes of an order to deploy them' ... But you know, it could have been an honest mistake. But what I have been told is that **the government knew that claim was questionable**, even before the war, even before they wrote it in their dossier [my emphasis].

With that word 'questionable', Gilligan slightly toned down his accusation against the government. He was no longer saying – as he had an hour and a half earlier – that the government 'probably knew' it was wrong. He was now saying they'd had doubts, but had still gone ahead with publishing the dossier anyway.

All BBC bulletins for the rest of the day led with the news that – according to BBC sources – Tony Blair's government had gone against the advice of the country's spy chiefs and authorised a report with dubious evidence in order to fool the public into thinking the war was necessary. The repercussions of the story were rarely out of the headlines for weeks, and months, to come.

Blair himself immediately tried to stamp out the allegations. He told journalists accompanying him on his Iraq tour, 'The idea that we authorised or made our intelligence agencies invent some piece of evidence is completely absurd'.

But Gilligan had more shocks to deliver. He followed up his *Today* programme revelations with an article in the *Mail on Sunday* based on his conversation with Kelly. First, he quoted his anonymous source as saying that, although conventional missiles could be launched in forty-five minutes, there was no evidence for the claim that this applied to weapons of mass destruction. Then he exploded another bombshell. He described how his source had talked about the way Downing Street had exaggerated the case for war. Gilligan told *Mail on Sunday* readers:

> I asked him how this transformation happened. The answer was a single word. 'Campbell'.
> What? Campbell made it up?
> 'No, it was real information. But it was included against our wishes because it wasn't reliable.'

Gilligan was saying that the prime minister's close associate, his director of communications, his 'real deputy prime minister',

Alastair Campbell, had bent the truth in order to persuade the country to back the invasion.

Blair felt this was a dangerous assault on himself, and the assailant was the BBC, seen as the most reliable organisation in the British media. He told Campbell, 'It's another attack to go to the heart of my integrity ... It's grotesque. There's no story here at all, but it's being driven by the BBC as a huge crisis for us.'

A week later, Gilligan returned to the *Mail on Sunday*, this time to present himself as a victim of government harassment, describing the day that 'hurricane Alastair and tropical storm Tony blew into my life' – reference to Campbell's briefing of other journalists about what he claimed were a series of inaccuracies in Gilligan's original report.

Over the following month, the prime minister's director of communications became more and more desperate in his attempts to refute the BBC reports and establish his innocence. On 25 June, he appeared before the Parliamentary Foreign Affairs Committee. He told MPs:

I simply say in relation to the BBC story, it is a lie, it was a lie. It is a lie that is continually repeated, and until we get a public apology for it, I will keep making sure that parliament, people like yourselves and the public know that it was a lie.

Two days later, he turned up, unexpected, at the *Channel Four News* studio just as their nightly programme was going out. He was ushered in front of the cameras, and over the next ten minutes in an angry exchange with the presenter, Jon Snow, Campbell attacked not only the BBC, but much of the rest of the media too:

You can say whatever you want on the television because somebody said it to you. [He was forgetting that Gilligan's claims had been made on radio and in the press] It doesn't matter if it's true ... A lot of journalists see their mission as to discredit

politicians and the political process ... People who have been
opposed to this conflict from the word go are now seeking
to change the ground and to say the Prime Minister led the
country into conflict on a false basis, and you're deliberately
conflating two issues ... Get your facts right before you make
serious allegations.

***

In the storm of accusations and counter-accusations of lying
that blew up immediately after the Gilligan radio and press
reports, both sides started to agree on one thing. They both
– for their own very different reasons – wanted Gilligan's
secret source unmasked. It would suit the BBC's radio reporter
because he wanted to prove he hadn't been making it all up,
and Blair and Campbell wanted to challenge the informant
in public so they could – they hoped – prove the opposite,
that the source was unreliable, so demonstrating that they
hadn't had any hand in writing the dossier. 'The biggest thing
needed,' wrote Campbell later, 'was the source out', that would
'open a flank on the BBC'.

In fact, it was Kelly himself who came forward, in order to
clear his name. He went to his line manager at the Ministry
of Defence. Yes, he confessed, he had briefed Gilligan – it was
part of his job description to talk to journalists on areas of his
expertise. But, no, he told his employer, he most certainly had
not alleged that Alastair Campbell had insisted on the forty-
five-minute claim being inserted in the dossier. But the MoD's
personnel director accused Kelly of not getting higher-up clear-
ance before meeting the BBC man, and he threated the highly
respected scientist with the sack and even losing his pension if
any further misconduct came to light, in this or any other case.

Kelly's passion was his work. A friend described him as a
'quiet, self-effacing and serious man'. The manoeuvrings of

politicians were foreign to his nature, but he now found himself in the middle of a vicious political scrap.

And it's at this point that we must introduce a new character into the drama, the man who had produced the dossier, the Chairman of the Joint Intelligence Committee (JIC), John Scarlett. Before his move to the JIC, Scarlett had had an outstanding career in Britain's overseas spying organisation, MI6. His ambition was to become its chief. There's no evidence that this influenced any of his decisions over what went into the dossier. However, it's certain that Scarlett had a warm relationship with Downing Street. He got on well with Campbell, who referred to him as 'a mate'.

Now Scarlett, like Blair and Campbell, was under direct fire from the Gilligan revelations. His intelligence in the 'dodgy dossier' had been wrong, there was no WMD and the forty-five-minutes claim was fantasy. So, he too had everything to gain by discrediting Gilligan's source. Hence, Scarlett now heaped his weight onto the

Dr David Kelly appearing before the House of Commons Foreign Affairs Select Committee. (© Press Association)

unfortunate Kelly. He wrote to the Cabinet Office's co-ordinator
of security and intelligence, saying, 'Kelly needs a proper security
style interview in which … inconsistencies are thrashed out …
I think this is rather urgent. Happy to discuss.'

According to Tony Blair's biographer, Tom Bower, the prime
minster himself then agreed that the MoD should release the
name of Gilligan's informant – Blair himself always denied that.
Nevertheless, it did happen, and it was done in a roundabout way.
Kelly's name started to leak out, and whenever journalists asked
if he was the BBC's source for the accusations about WMD and
the forty-five minutes, the MoD Press Office confirmed it.

Kelly himself was mortified and, in an agitated state, on
15 July he was summoned before Parliament's Foreign Affairs
Committee. He was interrogated on every detail of what
Gilligan had claimed he'd said. And he was also questioned
about another report by an entirely different BBC correspondent, and was asked if he had been the source for that too. He
gave a vague answer. That was a mistake. It soon became clear
that he had, in fact, been that reporter's source as well. It looked
like he'd lied to the MPs.

Two days later, Tony Blair and his wife Cherie were in
Washington boarding a plane for Tokyo after a celebratory
dinner with the Bushes at the White House. The prime minister
slept on the flight, until he was woken by an aide. 'Very bad
news,' he was told, 'David Kelly has been found dead in woods
near his home. Suicide is suspected.' Blair immediately spoke by
phone with the Lord Chancellor, Charlie Falconer. They agreed
that the inquest into Kelly's death should be chaired by a leading
judge, Brian Hutton – it was the birth of the first of the three
official enquiries into various aspects of the Iraq invasion and its
aftermath. With that, the prime minister walked to the back of
the plane to announce the news to the correspondents accompanying him on his overseas tour. One of them, Paul Eastham of
the *Daily Mail*, tackled him straightaway.

'Why did you authorise the leaking of the name?' he asked.

'That's completely untrue,' replied Blair.

'Have you got blood on your hands?' asked Eastham. Blair turned and left without answering.

The *Daily Mail* had never concealed its hostility to the New Labour leader, and the next day, it went for the jugular:

> There have been calls for Mr Campbell's resignation for weeks, partly because of his casual relationship with the truth, partly because of his lack of accountability. If he didn't feel compelled to resign for lying, surely Dr Kelly's death is reason enough for him to leave public life.

The *Mail* even made comparisons with the darkest days of Soviet oppression:

> There is a horrible echo in all of this of the methods of Beria, Stalin's secret police chief, who, as well as simply ordering executions of those who upset the regime, would blacken, smear, threaten and humiliate individuals until they chose to kill themselves.

But the article saved its most poisonous barbs for the highest target:

> There is, however, a more important figure in this tragedy, and that is the prime minister ... ultimately responsible for the death of Dr Kelly. As one lie after another has been exposed, Mr Blair's silken pose as a decent Christian gentleman has looked increasingly threadbare. His personal probity and the integrity of his administration are in shreds. He does not deserve to survive this shocking incident, and if his party lets him, it does not deserve to survive in government either.

Once back home from the overseas tour, Campbell set his staff to putting out the word: it was the BBC, the *Daily Mail* and the rest of the media that had driven Dr Kelly to kill himself. But it was Campbell himself who was to be the first casualty of this battle. A month later, he resigned. The *Guardian* believed the reason was long-term, widespread discontent with the director of communications, who 'has become the centre of criticism about the government's preoccupation with spin and media presentation for at least the past three years'.

The *Daily Telegraph* later gave a very different explanation:

> Tony Blair was forced to sack Alastair Campbell as his director of communications because he was 'deranged, vindictive, and out of control', the former director-general of the BBC claimed yesterday.

'Former' director general because the man who'd held that post, Greg Dyke, had himself followed Campbell out of the door. The Hutton Report had slated him for his 'defective' approach to checking news stories. The chairman of the BBC's Board of Governors and Gilligan himself resigned at the same time. The BBC – supposedly the part of the media that people could trust to tell the truth – had got it wrong. It had failed its audience.

* * *

So, who was most to blame in all this? The media? Or the mighty?

The answer isn't simple. Both sides made bad mistakes – lied maybe – at least some of the time. Let's take the BBC Radio reporter, Andrew Gilligan. He made two mistakes.

One – he was just plain wrong about Kelly's role in producing the dossier. Kelly had not – as Gilligan inaccurately told BBC Radio listeners – written *any* of the 'dodgy dossier', and he was not part of the Cabinet's Joint Intelligence Committee which had produced it. Yes, he'd been asked to read part of it in advance, and as an insider, he was familiar with the intelligence community, but he had no direct knowledge of who wanted what included in the dossier.

Two – Gilligan had no proof that Campbell had meddled with the dossier. This was the most damning element of his allegations. All he had was what he claimed Kelly had told him, and Kelly, of course, later denied he'd ever pointed the finger at the prime minister's director of communications. Gilligan had no other evidence for this accusation.

So, what about the government and the intelligence services? Had they lied? Had they bent the truth? Or had they made honest mistakes?

In the months following the end of the invasion, it was proved beyond doubt that the central claims of the 'dodgy dossier' were worse than dodgy. The UN had dispatched 1,400 weapons experts – the Iraq Survey Group – to scour Saddam's conquered land for any evidence of WMD. In January 2004, its director told the US Congress that, despite all the pre-invasion intelligence, there were no weapons of mass destruction in Iraq.

In the wake of the Iraq invasion, the three official enquiries – the first, already mentioned, chaired by Sir Brian Hutton, former lord chief justice of Northern Ireland, and the other later two by high-ranking civil servants, Baron Butler of Brockwell and Sir John Chilcot – published their conclusions over a period of many years. Some in the media, and in the country at large, sometimes wondered whether these three report chairmen saw themselves in the ranks of the mighty and had pulled their punches.

Hutton ducked any criticism of the government, and concluded that John Scarlett – the author of the dodgy dossier – had only been 'subconsciously influenced' by Campbell, while reserving condemnation for Gilligan and the BBC. Much of the press slated Hutton's conclusions as an 'Establishment whitewash'. That was perhaps to be expected of the populist Tory *Daily Mail*, which declared:

We're faced with the wretched spectacle of the BBC chairman resigning while Alastair Campbell crows from the summit of his dunghill. Does this verdict, my lord, serve the real interest of truth?

But even the more moderate, unaligned *Independent* newspaper said much the same in its own dramatic fashion. It left half of its front page a white blank, just with the words 'WHITEWASH?' in red, and 'THE HUTTON REPORT', in tiny letters in the middle.

The second enquiry, the Butler Report in July 2004, was also seen by many as a fudge. The *Guardian*'s Jonathan Freedland pointed out the contrast with the robust way that a similar enquiry by the US Congress had dealt with the same dodgy intelligence in the United States. That report had condemned the CIA for 'the biggest intelligence failure in our nation's history'. Freedland said it was as though Lord Butler had laid out a boxful of knives which he daren't use himself, but left them kicking around buried in the detail for others to pick up and do the stabbing. Freedland wrote:

> The report includes a handy appendix laying out the raw intelligence material alongside the finished, political product. It makes clear how almost all the qualifiers – the maybes and possiblys – were removed, giving the impression the government had a much firmer fix on Saddam's arsenal than it ever did … Many people will regard the removal of these qualifiers, turning possibilities into certainties, as a material change to the document, hardening it up, firming it up – even sexing it up.

But instead of coming out and saying as such, Lord Butler had concluded, 'We have found no evidence of deliberate distortion'.

The *Daily Mail*, like the *Guardian*, trawled through the report's hundreds of paragraphs and found, hidden away, some of those sharp knives that Butler had left ready. The *Mail* didn't hesitate to use them:

> Lord Butler's case against Mr Blair is explosive. He quotes what the JIC actually told No. 10 about Iraq, which was full of caveats about 'sporadic, patchy and limited intelligence'. But no hint of such doubts appeared in Mr Blair's arguments for war. He told

MPs the intelligence was 'extensive, detailed and authoritative'.
At the very least, those statements were damningly misleading ...

Will anyone now believe Mr Blair if he warns of a genuine
threat to national security? Will anyone trust him if he says the
intelligence was compelling, as next time it might be?

***

So, who were the real casualties of this war between the media
and the mighty?

The most tragic was Dr David Kelly. On the verge of retirement after an outstanding career as a scientist and international
peacemaker, now threatened with disgrace and the loss of his
pension, this self-effacing man had been found dead in the
woods near his home with his wrists cut. Later, various conspiracy theories were put forward to explain his death. His family
were certain it was suicide.

Others of those in the front line of the fight were more for-
tunate. Andrew Gilligan was recruited by the then editor of *The
Spectator*, Boris Johnson. From there he moved to the London
Evening Standard, and in 2008 was nominated Journalist of the
Year at the British Press Awards for his investigations into the
London mayoral elections.

Greg Dyke, the BBC director general, became chancellor
of York University and chairman of the Football Association.

John Scarlett fulfilled his dream of becoming chief of MI6,
and was knighted for his services.

And the government double act, Campbell and Blair? After
he resigned, Alastair Campbell went back to journalism, writing
mainly on sport and politics. He advised subsequent Labour leaders on strategy, appeared on many TV programmes – including
one called *Cracking Up*, about his own early years struggle with a
breakdown and alcoholism – and he's worked as an ambassador
for mental health charities such as Alcohol Concern.

Tony Blair survived in government for four years after Dr Kelly's death. A decade later, the Chilcot Inquiry found the former prime minister had deliberately exaggerated the threat posed by the Iraqi regime in order to get MPs and the public to back the invasion. Blair then expressed 'sorrow, regret and apology', but added, 'I did not mislead this country … the intelligence was not falsified and the decision was made in good faith'.

But Blair's reputation was incurably maimed way before then. It didn't matter that he could trumpet many worthwhile achievements during his time in power, what many British people remembered ever after was the image of a man who you couldn't believe. Much of the reason for that was Blair's own fault. He chose Alastair Campbell as his general in the war with the media. There was little finesse about Campbell, and his relentless bending of the facts, in the end, fooled no one. At the turn of the twenty-first century, the mighty needed to employ a degree of subtlety to win over the media. Campbell never recognised that. Even when he was telling the truth, journalists tended not to believe him, and they passed their doubts on to their readers, viewers and listeners.

What will forever be known as the 'dodgy dossier', we have to remember, was not some academic report for the eyes of the government ministers only. It was a public document. It was a press release under a different name. ITN's former editor, Nigel Ryan, pointed out that the profound damage that had been done went far beyond the reputation of one prime minister. 'Downing Street,' said Ryan, 'is renowned for sometimes being economical with the truth – but not on the whole for crossing the line into overt lying.' Then, noted Ryan, 'the first casualty of the public lie is the public trust'.

Ryan's remark could apply just as well to the other side in the media–mighty conflict. The journalist at the heart of the dodgy dossier story, Andrew Gilligan, had failed to live up to the principles of his trade. He'd failed to report accurately what his source told him, and he'd failed to find any other evidence to support the main allegations he claimed Kelly made. The BBC management, in turn, failed to challenge their reporter on a story which would clearly send shockwaves through the country. And so again, the casualty was 'public trust' – in what had become the most respected arm of the media, the BBC, as well as in the mighty.

It's the same in all wars, it's always the civilians who suffer most. During the whole sorry scrap over the dodgy dossier, the real losers were ordinary people who wanted to know what was going on. They, more and more, felt they couldn't rely on either the media or the mighty to tell them the truth. And so they were led blindfold into a war they had little chance of understanding.

* * *

During the fifteen years that followed the dodgy dossier, the big question many are asking is – has public trust in governments and the media been re-established? The answer has got a lot more complicated since the 2003 Iraq invasion. The reason is an age-old one – new technology. Social media – *Twitter, Facebook, YouTube* and others – has brought an information revolution to our planet unmatched since the invention of the printing press in the fifteenth century. And all the talk now is of 'fake news' in a 'post-truth' world. So, are we civilians who, as ever, are caught in the crossfire of the media–mighty war, now doomed? Or is there some hope for us? That's what we're going to investigate next.

19

THE SOCIAL MEDIA REVOLUTION

Trump, Tweets and Fake News

> One of the dangers of the internet is that people can
> have entirely different realities. They can be cocooned in
> information that reinforces their current biases.
>
> *Barack Obama (1961–)*

Edgar Maddison Welch woke up on Sunday and told his girlfriend and their two young daughters that he'd be away for the day – he had 'some things to do'. With that, he collected his 9mm semi-automatic rifle, his Colt .38 handgun, and his 12-gauge shotgun, along with a loaded ammunition belt and a box of bullets, then he got in his Toyota Prius and began the 350-mile drive to Washington DC. It was 4 December 2016, one month after Donald Trump had beaten Hillary Clinton in the race to become US President.

At the age of 28, Welch had a reputation as a soft-spoken, polite, churchgoing man in the quiet little town of Salisbury, North Carolina – locals called it 'Smallsbury'. He wasn't much interested in politics. He hadn't voted for Trump, he hadn't voted for Clinton either, though, as he said later, he was just praying that Mr Trump would take the country in the 'right direction'.

Earlier in his life, he'd been arrested and convicted of marijuana possession and public drinking, and had undergone a substance abuse programme. Now though, those troubles seemed to be behind him, and in recent years religion had become more and more important to him. He'd taken to preaching at friends who did drugs, and he'd had some Bible verses tattooed on his back, including the lines, 'Those who hope in the Lord will renew their strength. They will soar on wings like eagles; they will run and not grow weary, they will walk and not be faint.'

Welch had recently had the Internet installed at home, and when someone told him there was a child sex-slave ring operating in Washington with connections to the Clinton campaign, he'd decided to start googling. This, he said, meant he was 'really able to look into it'. He also liked to listen to Alex Jones' radio show. Jones was described by *New York* magazine as 'America's leading conspiracy theorist'. Welch said of him, 'He touches on some issues that are viable, but goes off the deep end on some things.' Jones had posted a *YouTube* video of himself saying:

When I think about all the children Hillary Clinton has **personally** [my emphasis] murdered and chopped up and raped, I have zero fear standing up against her. Yeah, you heard me right. Hillary Clinton has **personally** murdered children. I just can't hold back the truth anymore.

Jones later said he'd been talking about US policy in Syria, but most who saw it heard that word 'personally' repeated, and didn't take it that way. Welch, like many others, found supporting 'evidence' on his computer screen. A white supremacist *Twitter* account claimed the New York City Police Department had discovered the existence of a paedophile ring linked to members of the Democratic Party. He read how the email account of John Podesta, Hillary Clinton's campaign manager, had been hacked, and how Podesta's emails had been found to contain coded messages referring to human trafficking – for instance, that the phrase 'cheese pizza' referred to child pornography because it had the same initial letters. The hacked emails showed that Podesta occasionally dined at a popular pizza restaurant called Comet Ping Pong, in Washington's Chevy Chase District, and the online conspiracy theorists – who were growing in number – pointed out similarities between the restaurant's logo and symbols associated with Satanism and paedophilia.

Welch decided he wanted to 'self-investigate' the paedophile ring, and he began approaching others to see if they'd join him in a 'violent confrontation' at the pizzeria. He texted a friend saying, 'Raiding a pedo ring, possible [*sic*] sacrificing the lives of a few for the lives of many'. Another of his texts spoke of 'standing up against a corrupt system that kidnaps, tortures and rapes babies and children in our own back yard'. But no one wanted to help him. One friend suggested instead that Welch visit the restaurant with a camera to find out what was happening rather than going in with 'guns blazing'. His girlfriend warned him against doing 'something stupid'.

Three days before he drove off fully armed to Washington, Welch had binge-watched *YouTube* videos about the alleged child-trafficking ring. It was now being referred to as 'Pizzagate', according to the over-used fashion to try and put any scandal – or alleged scandal – on a par with Watergate.

Now, on that December Sunday morning, as Welch drove along Highway 95 towards the nation's capital, he felt – as he later told a reporter from the *New York Times* – his 'heart breaking over the thought of innocent people suffering'. He stopped briefly to text his girlfriend with a Bible verse about being anointed by God, and he recorded a message on his phone to his family, saying he loved them and hoped his daughters would understand someday that he was trying to protect the defenceless.

Shortly before 3 p.m., Welch parked his Toyota close to the Comet Ping Pong pizzeria. He left the loaded shotgun and box of shells in the car, and chose instead to strap the holster with the loaded revolver to his hip, draped the ammunition belt across his chest, and picked up the semi-automatic rifle. Thus armed, he marched inside the restaurant, and headed straight towards the rear of the building.

Most of the customers didn't see him, but when one of the waiters told people an armed man had just walked in, there was panic. Parents grabbed their children, and everyone rushed for the door. Welch let them go. They weren't the reason he'd come here. He found a locked door and when he couldn't open it, he raised his rifle and fired several shots at it. At that moment, one of the chefs, who'd been in a back room fetching pizza dough, came in, and as Welch aimed his rifle at him, the man turned and ran for his life.

Welch then started searching for the tunnels where, he'd read on the Internet, children were hidden and tortured. As the minutes passed, it became clear to him that there was nothing here you wouldn't expect to see in a popular pizzeria. The place didn't even have a basement.

By now, police had swarmed over the neighbourhood, everyone was cleared off the streets, and the area was in lockdown. Forty-five minutes after Welch had arrived at the Comet Ping Pong, he gave himself up. He put his rifle on top of a beer keg and his revolver on a table. He came out with his hands in the air. The police ordered him to walk backwards towards them, then lie face down in the street. They handcuffed him, and he was taken away.

At his trial, Welch pleaded guilty and was sentenced to four and a half years in prison. He told the court, 'I wish there were a way that I could offer something other than an apology ... I realize mere words can't undo what happened ... but I am sorry.' The judge told him, 'You do seem like a nice person who in your own mind was trying to do the right thing. But that does not excuse reckless conduct and the real damage that it caused.'

On the day of the attack, the owner of Comet Ping Pong, Mr James Alefantis, had issued a statement:

> What happened today demonstrates that promoting false and reckless conspiracy theories comes with consequences. I hope that those involved in fanning these flames will take a moment to contemplate what happened here today, and stop promoting these falsehoods right away.

Three days later, a Louisiana man named Yusif Lee Jones, phoned another pizzeria on the same block as Comet Ping Pong. He told the owner he was going to 'save the kids' and 'finish what the other guy didn't' and he threatened to 'shoot everyone in the place'. Police tracked him down and he pleaded guilty in the District Court to a charge of interstate threatening communications.

***

Absolutely no evidence has been found to corroborate any part of the Pizzagate allegations. And that includes an investigation by the NYPD. And yet the rumours had spread as fact. Well before Welch walked into Comet Ping Pong, the restaurant was getting as many as 150 threats a day – by phone and online. One of the *YouTube* videos watched by Welch had been uploaded by an account named 'Evil Hillary' and titled 'Podestas, Pizza and Pedos'. Within two weeks, it had been watched over 340,000 times. The Alex Jones video accusing Hillary Clinton of chopping up babies was viewed more than 427,000 times. And thousands of other tweets, Facebook and website pages on similar themes were seen and liked by hundreds of thousands of people.

Pizzagate is only one of many such pieces of fake news about American politics to flood the Internet around the time of the 2016 election. Another, for instance, claimed that 'Hillary Clinton and her State department were actively arming Islamic

Edgar Maddison Welch ordered to walk backwards towards the police after he'd laid down his weapons inside the Washington pizzeria. (© Associated Press)

jihadists, which includes ISIS', and was viewed 789,000 times. A *Facebook* page which proclaimed, 'FBI agent suspected in Hillary email leaks, found dead in apartment murder-suicide', got 567,000 hits.

The most notorious and one of the most damaging pieces of fake news originated on the website *WTOE 5 News* in July 2016:

> News outlets around the world are reporting on the news that Pope Francis has made the unprecedented decision to endorse a US presidential candidate. His statement in support of Donald Trump was released from the Vatican this evening.

The story then quoted the pope as saying that it was the FBI's failure to prosecute Hillary Clinton over her misuse of her personal email account that had led him to back Trump. When the website *Ending the Fed* then repeated the story on *Facebook* in

late September, it was watched 960,000 times. Online corrections, pointing out that the claim was entirely false, got only a
small fraction of that number of views.

***

So how does fake news spread?

Much of it in the Pizzagate affair, according to an analysis
carried out at Elon University in North Carolina, was driven by
computerised programs. These bots would search the Internet
for messages containing keywords such as 'Pizzagate' and 'paedophilia', and automatically redistribute them to thousands of
other – human – Internet users. Then many of those who saw
that a tweet or a video linking Hillary Clinton to a child sex
ring, which had been viewed and liked – apparently – by hundreds of thousands of people, took that to mean it must be true.
So many people couldn't all be wrong.

But it now seems humans are even more to blame. A 2018
study at Massachusetts Institute of Technology, found that
Twitter-users are 70 per cent more likely to retweet false news
than the truth. Why? No one quite knows yet. The theory is
that false news is more spectacular, and we just love to entertain
our friends with an 'Oh-my-gosh tale,' rather than bore them
with dull old reality. This combination of humans and robots
means lies then infect the internet like a plague. But that doesn't
tell us where the fake news comes from in the first place. Who
starts these rumours that get transformed into 'truth'? And what
human hand sets up these bots to do their diabolical work?

No decisive answer has been given in the case of Pizzagate.
But the scandal that erupted in 2018 around the data company
Cambridge Analytica, and the allegations that it interfered in
the election of Donald Trump, showed that spreading fake news
has become a science. CA claims to have devised the 'Crooked
Hillary' campaign aimed at Trump's opponent. The company's

Managing Director, Mark Turnbull revealed to a *Channel 4 News* undercover reporter how it was done:

> We just put information into the bloodstream of the internet and then watch it grow. Give it a little push every now and then, and watch it take shape. And so this stuff infiltrates the online community and expands, but with no branding, so it's unattributable, untrackable.

It's often impossible to come up with specific answers as to who started which rumour, whether it was just a fluke, a meddlesome troublemaker, or someone with more sinister, malicious political motives. During 2017 and 2018, more and more evidence came to light that America's enemies might have used social media to influence the 2016 presidential race. In April 2017, the *Reuters* news agency cited US officials as saying that the Russian Institute for Strategic Studies had organised an online campaign to sway the US election in Donald Trump's favour. In September 2017, *Facebook* directors told Congressional investigators they had discovered that hundreds of fake accounts linked to Russia had bought $100,000 of advertisements targeting American voters, and that 126 million Americans may have seen posts published by Russia-based operatives.

***

Attempting to describe the permeation of fake news on social media is like trying to count snakes in the jungle at night. The very name 'social media' is misleading. *Facebook*, *Twitter* and the rest may have started out solely as a means of chatting with and sending pictures to friends and family, and of course they still do that, but, whatever else they are, 'social media' are still mass communications systems, and ones like no other the world has ever seen. And what's more, they've become weapons with a force beyond the scariest dreams of any of the mighty we've encountered on our long journey.

Technology has always been key to the power of the media. The invention of the rotary printing press in the nineteenth century – able to turn out millions of copies of a newspaper in a few hours – and radio and TV transmission systems in the twentieth century, added the word 'mass' to 'media'. That was real power. But this technology came at a price. It required huge investments of cash, only available to wealthy individuals or large corporations. There was no way that ordinary citizens could have their own version of mass media.

Until along came the Internet. Within a decade, it had invaded almost every facet of our lives, for sharing gossip and family photos, buying, selling and advertising, controlling industrial conglomerates, playing games with someone on the other side of the planet, and – of course – as a means of spreading news, family news, local news, international news, fake news, any news.

The Internet has turned the ages-long battle between the media and the mighty on its head. Now, if you or I can say something sufficiently shocking or exciting on *Twitter, Facebook, Snapchat, YouTube* etc., etc., the world can know about it in seconds. Of course, it's not quite as simple as that. If no one outside our family, friends and work colleagues has heard of us, then the odds are that the pictures of our cat eating cornflakes won't go far. But it's not out of the question. Sometimes, among the billions of posts on the Internet every day, a claim by some unknown Tami, Dick or Harriet that they've just seen Elvis that morning in the local supermarket, or that Hillary Clinton is linked to a paedophile ring, can get picked up and spread across the globe in a trice. It goes viral.

And there is a way that you can guarantee reaching millions of people on social media. It's simple, though not easy. Be famous – be famous for anything – being a footballer, comedian, singer, film star. Or, of course, a politician …

***

And this is what Donald Trump has recognised. He's arguably the most famous person on the planet, and certainly one of the most influential. Trump has understood the power that the new technology gives him. It's a power which has never been available to any world leader before. The power to address the whole nation without the need to go through journalists, editors, newspapers, TV or radio channels. He simply has to pick up his phone and send off a tweet to his followers.

Take a day at random: 10 January 2018, that's yesterday, as I write these words. Many of the president's tweets are simply telling people what's happened and what he thinks is important. At 4.31 p.m., he tweeted:

Today, it was my great honor to welcome Prime Minister Erna Solberg of Norway to the @WhiteHouse

At 6.07 p.m., he told his followers:

The United States needs the security of the Wall on the Southern Border.

Thirty minutes later, it was:

Cutting taxes and simplifying regulations makes America the place to invest!

He posted six tweets yesterday, which is around the daily average.

By January 2018, President Trump's two *Twitter* accounts reached 68.4 million followers, and his *Facebook* posts went to another 24.3 million. So, he can reach a total of 92.7 million people in seconds, and that doesn't take into account that many millions of those followers then retweet or share his messages with others, who then do the same, and so on, and so on. How Henry VIII, not to mention Oliver Cromwell, Richard Nixon and the rest of the mighty we've met on our journey would have envied Donald Trump.

But President Trump does more than bypassing the traditional media to speak directly to Americans, and to the world. He's in no doubt that there's a war between the media and the mighty, and he's made it a vicious war. He discredits newspapers – either by name or as a collective group – and TV news (with the exception of his favourite *Fox News*) almost every day. On 1 August 2017, he tweeted:

> Only the Fake News Media and Trump enemies want me to stop using Social Media (110 million people). Only way for me to get the truth out!

This tweet neatly summarised his strategy in his war against the traditional media. Keep telling people that what you say is the only reliable truth, and keep saying the traditional media are liars. He's carried out almost daily attacks on newspapers and TV news channels as 'fake news', constantly undermining the journalistic reputation of well-known papers such as the *Washington Post* and the *New York Times*. On 28 January 2017, the newly elected President Trump tweeted:

> The coverage about me in the @nytimes and the @washingtonpost has been so false and angry that The Times actually apologised to its dwindling subscribers and readers.

Then, a week later, the president said on *Twitter*:

> After being forced to apologize for its bad and inaccurate coverage of me after winning the election, the FAKE NEWS @nytimes is still lost!

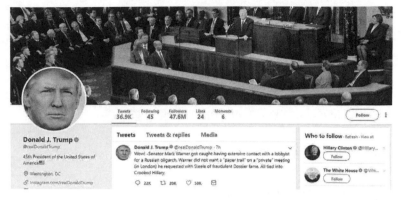

President Trump's personal Twitter account.

Two days later, he went on *Twitter* to accuse the press of failing to cover the threat of terrorism in the USA:

> It's gotten to a point where it is not even being reported. And in many cases, the very, very dishonest press doesn't want to report it.

In response to each of these accusations, the *New York Times* told its readers it had never in fact apologised, as the president suggested, and it gave a list of examples where dozens of terrorist attacks had been reported in the news media.

So, are any of the president's accusations against the mainstream media justified? There's certainly been no believable evidence of fraudulent anti-Trump news being concocted by them, as he constantly alleges. However, what about the tone and virulence of the media attacks on him? Republicans and conservatives have grumbled about unfair coverage from the 'mainstream media' for decades, ever since Watergate, forty years earlier, and before. But when Donald Trump came on the political stage, the pitch of ill-feeling – and hatred – became frenzied. And if the newspapers and broadcast stations can be accused with justice of anything, it is that, on occasions, instead of letting his barbs bounce off them, they've gone over the top in shooting back the insults.

On 25 November 2017, the *Washington Post* called him :

IMPULSIVE, BOMBASTIC and prone to grudges

The *New York Times* on 15 January 2018 wrote:

Trump is a racist. Period.
'Trump is a racist' – we can put that baby to bed. 'Racism' and 'racist' are simply words that have definitions, and Trump comfortably and unambiguously meets those definitions.

While the papers might believe they have evidence to back up such comments, the sort of language they're sometimes choosing helps the president and his supporters to justify their own claims that the mainstream media is biased against him.

***

With both sides in America's media–mighty war each accusing the other of lying, the result has been confusion. A confusion in the minds of many ordinary Americans. People often don't know who to believe, and sometimes it seems the concept of truth itself is a mirage, as though nothing can be proved.

Take, for instance, Donald Trump's remarks in August 2016 during the election campaign. He declared that Barack Obama was 'the founder of ISIS' and its 'most valuable player'. Both were untrue, and this was pointed out by many newspapers. Trump then tweeted:

 THEY DON'T GET SARCASM?

It was an outrageous accusation followed by an ambiguous clarification.

Then there was the row about the crowd size at his inauguration in January 2017. How many people turned out in Washington that day to support the new president? Trump stated:

 Now, the audience was the biggest ever. But this crowd was massive. Look how far back it goes. This crowd was massive.

Aerial photographs produced both by the National Park Service and the Public Broadcasting Service, however, appeared to show crowd numbers to be significantly fewer than had attended Barack Obama's inauguration. Trump's official spokesman, Sean Spicer, nevertheless, in his very first press conference accused journalists of using unrepresentative pictures to 'minimise the enormous support' and added, 'These attempts to lessen the enthusiasm for the inauguration are shameful and wrong'.

One of Trump's top aides, Kellyanne Conway, was then interviewed on NBC's show, *Meet the Press*. The presenter, Chuck Todd, asked her why Spicer had delivered such a 'provable falsehood'. Conway replied, 'You're saying it's a falsehood. And … Sean Spicer, our press secretary gave alternative facts to that.'

Todd snapped back, 'Alternative facts aren't facts, they're falsehoods.'

Was Conway's phrase 'alternative facts' just a sloppy use of language? Or was she deliberately sowing the seeds of chaos in the minds of the public by implying that somehow there could be more than one version of the truth?

In November 2017, Trump retweeted to his tens of millions of followers, messages posted from the UK by the deputy leader of a far-right extremist group called Britain First. One contained a video which the group's deputy leader claimed showed 'Muslim migrants beating up a Dutch boy on crutches'. Dutch police, however, confirmed that the attackers were neither Muslim nor migrants, and the British Prime Minister Theresa May issued a statement saying that Britain First sought to divide communities through its use of 'hateful narratives which peddle lies and stoke tensions', adding, 'It is wrong for the President to have done this'.

Donald Trump then tweeted:

> Theresa, don't focus on me, focus on the destructive Radical Islamic Terrorism that is taking place within the United Kingdom. We are doing just fine!

There was no apology from the president for what appeared to be a clumsy, ill-considered mistake. He simply ignored it. The impression given was that evidence – what convicts people in a court of law – doesn't somehow matter anymore.

So, is this anything new? Or is a disregard for facts simply a more elaborate version of what politicians have always tried to do when they're found out, i.e. deny it and try to change the subject? It could certainly be argued that this is what Tony Blair and Alastair Campbell routinely tried during the various inquiries into the British Government's handling of the Iraq War. The difference is that now instant access to the mass media via *Twitter* has made the technique easier and much more effective. The result is that many ordinary citizens, faced – apparently – with no reliable facts, fall back on their gut instincts. Edgar Welch, for instance, even after his attack on Comet Ping Pong had turned up no evidence of a child sex ring, still refused to dismiss the claims outright. He told a *New York Times* reporter that he'd just not found any facts to support it in that particular building.

And the result is that many now choose to believe the version of events that most closely matches what they'd like to believe is true, regardless of any evidence either way. It's a human failing as old as politics itself. Julius Caesar, more than 2,000 years ago, wrote, 'It's easy for people to believe what they want to believe.' But today, that tendency has been made more common by the sheer profusion of views and opinions on every imaginable subject available on the Internet, and by an atmosphere created by some leading politicians who, in effect, are saying, 'It doesn't matter that I can't prove it. The fact that I – someone important – is saying it, is enough. So believe me.'

In the midst of this confusion about what's true and what isn't, trust in newspapers, as well as in most TV and radio news, has taken a nosedive. In August 2017, the president launched his most damning attack yet on the mainstream media:

 These are really, really dishonest people and they're bad people and I really think they don't like our country.

And it's not just Trump's core base of supporters who've come to believe him. Distrust of the mainstream media has spread to the wider American population. According to Gallup Polls, the president's approval rating during 2017 fell to 32 per cent. During the same period, other polls showed that a larger number – almost half of Americans, 46 per cent – believed that newspapers and broadcasters invented stories which showed President Trump in a bad light. Compare that with mid-1970s after Watergate, when nearly three out of every four people in the US trusted newspapers and broadcast news.

These are not just statistics about what goes on in people's heads. They're reflected in the way they act. Americans in their droves have been abandoning newspapers, and instead turning to social media to find out what's happening in the world. In 2013, just 27 per cent used *Twitter*, *Facebook* and *YouTube* as their sources of news. Four years later, by 2017, that figure had shot up to top just over half the adult population. During the same period, the number of people who rely on traditional newspapers fell from 38 per cent to 22 per cent.

Let's just put this in crude terms. More than half of all Americans now think that anybody – absolutely anybody – out there with a laptop computer or an iPad, including anonymous crooks, liars and their country's enemies, is a better bet to tell them what's going on than professionally trained journalists. It's been called a 'post-truth' world. An ugly phrase – but then it's an ugly place to be.

＊

Is this a purely American phenomenon? No. In fact, in November 2017, the European Union Commission set up a high-level expert group to investigate fake news. The UK's elections regulator is looking at whether Russia tried to use online media to illegally influence the Brexit referendum campaign. And media analysts have found that 20 per cent of news stories circulating in France and Germany during the 2017 leadership elections were classified as 'junk news'. That's not as bad, of course, as the 50 per cent of all news estimated as fake doing the rounds during the US election campaign, but there's a fear that it could get worse in Europe. 'Things are bent here, but in the U.S. they're already broken,' according to the Swedish media analyst, Ehsan Fadakar. The EU Commission President Jean-Claude Juncker said that fake news has become 'almost overwhelming'.

In most European countries, however, reliance on traditional media hasn't tumbled as far as in America. In Scandinavia, France and Germany, a majority of people still trust newspapers, TV and radio to tell them the truth. And it's a similar story in the UK. The annual Edelman survey into which institutions people trust showed in 2018 that fewer than a quarter of Britons have confidence in social media, and that this is, in part, because of their role in spreading fake news. At the same time, trust in newspapers and TV has risen to a six-year high of 61 per cent.

So, does this mean people in the UK can give a big 'Phew!' and say, 'We don't need to worry anymore'? That would be a mistake.

Dig down into these figures for a moment. One in four Britons still putting their faith in social media translates into 13 million people, aged 16 or over, who get their news from *Twitter* and *Facebook* with all the attendant risks about inaccuracy. And then there's that 61 per cent who trust traditional media – papers and broadcasters – in the UK. That, of course, means there are 39 per cent who either don't do so, or who're unsure, and that's more than 20 million people aged over 16 who've lost faith in trained journalists. Add to this that both these sets of statistics have tended to go up and down over the past few years, and we can see it's too soon to conclude there's a favourable trend emerging.

This is serious. We voters need accurate information, if we're to make the right decision at the ballot box. And if many of us don't believe it when newspapers or broadcasters tell us about government corruption or any other misdeeds of those on high, then the mighty will start to feel they can get away with it, and we're on the slippery road to dictatorship.

So, what, if anything, can be done? Is it all gloom ahead? Stick with me now for the final stage of our journey. Don't worry, we'll find there's hope for us yet.

20

THE FUTURE

Wobbling On

Eternal vigilance is the price of liberty.

Wendell Phillips (1811–84), American Abolitionist

In a perfect world – that would be boring, but bear with me – the war between the media and the mighty wouldn't be a war at all. The media would represent the people, giving them the power they need to keep the mighty in their place. The mightiest political leaders would never be corrupt or tell lies or make mistakes (don't scoff, this is a make-believe world, remember) because they would know that the media – reporters and editors – would always get to the truth and find them out.

In the very worst of all worlds, on the other hand, the media are gagged, or tell lies – or at least the people believe they're lying – and that allows the mighty to lie too. The result is that ordinary citizens are either confused, disillusioned or – worst of all – misled. The mighty can then do whatever they like. Democracy crumbles.

It's inevitable that in the real world – at least in Western democracies – we'll usually be wobbling to keep our balance somewhere between the two, and hoping we can stay closer to the perfect end of the tightrope. This has been a conflict like no other. In the century after the birth of the printing press, kings and queens and their advisors started to get nervous. Then they got worried. Then they began to panic, as they realised the potential power of this machine. In the wrong hands ('wrong' in the dictionary of the mighty), it could usurp the government's role in telling the people what to think. As we've seen, the first response of the mighty was to criminalise journalism, except when it spoke in their favour. Then, as societies became more democratic, political leaders were compelled to find more subtle methods of influencing the media.

On the other side, it's been the job of journalists to fight back against any gagging, blindfolding or manipulation by officialdom, at times facing imprisonment, torture or execution for writing what the mighty don't want to read. We've met some heroes along the way. In the eighteenth century, there was John Wilkes in Britain, and Isaiah Thomas during the American Revolution. In the nineteenth century, we've seen John Tyas of the London *Times*, James Wroe of the *Observer* and other journalists fighting the government to reveal the atrocity of the Peterloo Massacre. In the twentieth century, there were the suffragettes battling both the media and the mighty, C.P. Scott defining journalism's high standards, Geoffrey Cox championing television as an instrument of truth, Natalya Gorbanevskaya risking her life to reveal her government's oppression of its citizens, and Bob Woodward and Carl Bernstein helping bring down a crooked president.

At the same time, there have, of course, been plenty of journalists who've not done their job, and we won't name them again. Suffice it to say that it's the rest of us, kept in the dark, who in the end – as always – have been the losers. But it would be misleading to suggest that where we stand on the fake news/accurate reporting tightrope, is just down to a few individual journalists. They're important, but they're not the whole story. And they're especially not the whole story in the complex muddle of social media and traditional media in the early twenty-first century.

There's much that the rest of us can do to move back closer to a world where more of us are able to recognise the truth when we see it, and where fewer of us get sucked in by the lies.

***

But let's start with what we should *not* do.

It's dangerous to think the simple answer is just to make fake news illegal, to slap heavy fines, for instance, on tech companies like *Twitter* or *YouTube* who distribute it. If you do that, you have to recognise that you're on a rocky road. Fake news can be used as an excuse for cracking down on a free press. It's already happening.

In Egypt, for instance, in December 2016, a producer from the Al-Jazeera TV news network was arrested there and imprisoned on charges of 'incitement against state institutions and broadcasting fake news with the aim of spreading chaos'. He'd made a documentary criticising Egyptian military conscription. A former Al-Jazeera editor was also condemned to death in his absence. In the Philippines, the government has proposed a law to impose up to a five-year prison term on anyone who publishes or distributes 'fake news', defined as activities that 'cause panic, division, chaos, violence, and hate, or those which exhibit a propaganda to blacken or discredit a person's reputation'. One Philippines newspaper pointed out that the government could apply the law to suppress the opposition.

It's too easy for those of us who live in Western democracies to forget that, in many countries around the world, journalists are still routinely imprisoned for criticising their governments. According to the Committee to Protect Journalists (CPJ), 262 reporters were behind bars in 2017. Turkey topped the list, with seventy-two journalists imprisoned, followed by China and Egypt. The numbers don't include North Korea either, because its repressive brutality has been entirely effective or because there's no way of knowing the fate of reporters there.

'The political situation in some countries has deteriorated and the tolerance for criticism has decreased,' said the CPJ director, Robert Mahoney. 'Authoritarianism is on the rise and journalists are paying the price.'

We in the West shouldn't feel superior. Can we be sure that in the midst of all our horror at the fake news tsunami, we wouldn't find ourselves sliding down the same slippery slope? Fining or imprisoning those who publish fake news risks throwing out the free press baby with the fake news bath water.

This doesn't mean we have to tolerate fake news. And the glad tidings are that the giant tech companies who control the world's social media – under pressure from their users and democratic governments – are beginning to wake up to their own responsibilities. *Google* has started to kick out publishers who 'misrepresent content'. *Twitter* claims it's suspended

May 5, 2014. Mohammed Fahmy, Canadian-Egyptian acting bureau chief of Al-Jazeera TV News, in a defendant's cage during his trial in Egypt on terror charges. He told the judge, 'I wish there was a single shred of evidence so I could defend myself.' He and three other journalists were sentenced to seven years in prison. (© Associated Press)

hundreds of thousands of accounts. *YouTube* is making changes to its search engine so that unreliable sites are less likely to pop up. *Facebook*'s boss has announced that it plans to return to its roots, cutting the amount of news it feeds, and instead going back to how it started out, as a 'social' media platform. In future, it'll concentrate on being a way for people to stay in touch with family and friends. *Facebook* has come in for special condemnation. First, during the 2016 US elections it was seen to be spreading stories that misled millions of people. Then, in 2018 it was revealed that it had allowed the personal profiles of 87 million of its users to be passed on to election campaigns around the globe. So *Facebook* is now attempting to shine up its reputation. *Facebook*, like most of the tech companies, is also trying to spot fake news by setting up partnerships with fact-checking organisations such as *Snopes*, the *Associated Press*, and *FactCheck.org*, but there are concerns that this doesn't go far enough. One of these fact checkers, working with *Facebook*, told the *Guardian*, 'I don't feel like it's working at all. The fake information is still going viral and spreading rapidly … It's really difficult to hold [*Facebook*] accountable.'

The tech companies need to do more. The pressure on them has to be tightened. But they don't hold the whole answer. It's not enough to try to drain the Internet of the floods of lies. It's good that we're making them less accessible. We have to accept, however, that whatever we do, some fake news will always be out there.

So, we also have to promote the alternative. We have to rebuild the trust in traditional journalism. Governments themselves have to recognise publicly the importance to democratic institutions of a free press. In America, that will have to be left to a post-Trump presidency. In Britain, the government needs to resist all attempts to shackle the news media, and to praise the job done by the BBC, ITN and newspapers when their investigations reveal misdeeds that shame those in power. That may sound strange in a 'war' between the media and the mighty, but in the twenty-first century, we have every right to demand that those who govern us uphold all the principles of democracy, including freedom of expression.

Then there are the news organisations themselves. The highest journalistic standards of accuracy are now needed more than ever. University journalism courses must be encouraged, where students learn about the importance to democracy and to society of the profession they've chosen. Then editors and reporters must do all they can to avoid accusations that they're pursuing witch-hunts, while at the same time always challenging those in positions of power. The media's guiding light through the current murky darkness must be the words of the influential twentieth-century *Guardian* editor, C.P. Scott: 'Comment is free, but facts are sacred'. The two must be kept apart. Support for the Republican Party, the Democrats, the Conservatives or the Labour Party belongs in the editorial and op. ed. columns or broadcast interviews, not in the words of the reporter or presenter. That's a tall order, and if we're realistic, it won't happen, not everywhere, not in that pure form. It's an ideal but it can still be an aspiration.

* * *

However, there's something more that's often been overlooked. That's us, the civilians in this war between the media and the mighty. The Internet has changed the nature of that war, and we – who've always been the ones to suffer when the fighting hots up – now need to learn how to look after ourselves in this new world.

There are techniques that can be learned to help us get suspicious when fake news starts to creep onto our screens. Those techniques need to be made widely known, and especially we must start teaching them to our children in schools. Courses in

'News Reliability' have to be added to the standard curriculum. We need to educate the coming generation about the dangers of fake news, as well as teaching them how to spot the damaging lies online, and how to find trustworthy news sources. A News Reliability course would show students:

1 How widespread and harmful fake news has become.
2 The role of responsible news media in a democracy, to hold governments to account.
3 Which Internet sites or posts – such as those of TV channels with a legal obligation to be impartial, or reputable fact-checker organisations, or leading newspapers or news agencies – have a better reputation for accuracy and fairness.
4 Examples of fake news online, and what to notice about the author's claims and writing style which should make us wary.
5 How to recognise the difference between factual reporting and opinion, and to be suspicious of sites which muddle the two.

The amount of fake news, whether from malicious home-based trolls or organised foreign enemies, is not suddenly going to reduce. In fact, it may even increase as future generations rely more and more on the Internet to find out what's happening around them. So, educating our young people in how to use online media must now be a priority.

And here is a really hopeful chord to end on. On 3 October 2017, the London *Times* reported that more and more young American adults are subscribing to national newspapers and news magazines. They're paying to read the *Wall Street Journal*, the *Washington Post* and the *New York Times*, as well as the *Economist* magazine, usually online rather than buying the old-fashioned printed version. And at the same time in the UK, 40 per cent of all those who read the five national newspapers online are now aged under 35.

Matilda Giglio, one of the founders of *Compass News*, a media digest service aimed at students in the UK, told *The Times* why she thought this is happening. She said the deluge of information and the difficulty of verifying information on the web had persuaded many students to pay for authoritative journalism. *Compass*'s research showed that nearly two-thirds of students at Britain's leading universities would be happy to pay £5–10 a month for 'quality news'. It seems the next generation are more ready than their elders to combat the threat posed to our democracy by the misuse of social media.

What we've seen over the past few years is the media army's supply train being hijacked by a rabble of liars and crooks, sometimes with the aid of the enemy – the mighty. But perhaps, just perhaps, the old-school generals and foot soldiers in the media ranks – the trustworthy editors and reporters – are now poised to regain control. We need them to do that, we civilians. And we need to help them in every way we can.

Reputable journalists are our only hope of knowing what those who govern us are really getting up to because, otherwise, we're lost. And we'll end up back in the ignorant darkness that blanketed the world before a German goldsmith named Johannes Gutenberg in the fifteenth century had an idea one day for a clever machine, a machine that would give its name to journalism. The press.

ACKNOWLEDGEMENTS

My special thanks go to those friends and former journalist colleagues who've kindly pointed me in the right direction and corrected me when I've strayed. They include John Flewin, Ros Gallant, Dina Gould, Pauline Heard, Simon Henderson, Richard Lindley, Mike Morris, Stewart Purvis and Peter Sissons, as well as my son, Dan Cavedon-Taylor.

I've consulted close to a hundred books and academic papers in researching *Fayke Newes*. Many could be singled out, but if I choose one, it's Phillip Knightley's *The First Casualty* for its help on the chapters dealing with conflicts between journalists and governments during wartime.

My agent, Martin Redfern of the Diane Banks Literary Agency, has been encouraging throughout, and Mark Beynon and Jessica Palmer at The History Press are, as always, a delight to work with. Many thanks.

Most of all, I'm grateful to my wife, Maggie, for her patience and determination as my 'first reader'. No jumbled meaning, unsupported conclusion or typo gets past her, and that's invaluable.

INDEX

Note: *italicised* page numbers denote
    illustrations

Adams, John 74–5
Adams, Samuel 65, 74
Al-Jazeera 348, *349*
Albert, Prince *129*, 132
American Civil War 133, 134–49, 169
American Revolution 59, 60–79, 347
Andrews, J. Cutler 146
Antietam, Battle of 134, 135, 138–9, 144
Anzio Campaign 224
Asquith, Herbert 159, 161, 165, 190
Associated Press 142, 212, 257, 258, *258*,
    281–2, 350

Balaclava, Battle of 123–7, 133
Baldwin, Stanley 189, 194–5
Barton, Elizabeth 5–9, *6*, 13–15
Bateman, Viscount 90, 91, 95
BBC 214, 226, 231–3, 237, 238, 239, 242,
    252, 350
    Falklands War 297, 299, 300, 301, 302,
        303, 304–5
    Iraq War 309–10, 311, 314, 315–16, 317,
        318, 320, 321–2, 322, 323, 327
    Second World War 215, 220, 226, 232
Beach Thomas, William 179–80, *180*,
    182, 187
Beaverbrook, Lord 175, 188, 194–5, *203*,
    204, 206–7

Bennett, James Gordon 202, 206
Bennett, Paul 211
Bernstein, Carl 280–95, *281*, 347
Black, Hugo 274
Blackstone, Sir William 53
Blair, Tony 308, 309, 310, 311, 312–14, *312*,
    315, 316, 317, 318, 320–1, 322, 324–5,
    326, 342
Bocking, Edward 5–8, *6*, 14, 15
Boston, America 60–1, 63, 65–72
Boston Massacre 67, *78*
Boston Tea Party 70–1
Bower, Tom 320
Bowles, Samuel 140
Brexit referendum 327
Britain First 341–2
Bush, George W. 276, 311, 320
Butler, Robin (Butler Report) 323, 324–5

Caesar, Julius 342
Caldwell, F.G. 306
Calley, William 271–2
Cambridge Analytica 335
Campbell, Alistair 312–14, *312*, 316–18,
    318, 319, 321–2, 323, 325, 326, 342
Campion, Edmund 21–2
Canning, George 93–5
Cardigan, Earl of 120, 123–4
caricatures 80, 83–95, *91*, *94*
Carlile, Richard 107–8
Carlyle, Thomas 115

CBS 261–2, 265, 266, *266*, 269–70
censorship 22, 170, 255, 276
    American Civil War 142, 144, 145, 148
    in Civil War England 34, 38, 39
    Crimean War 121, 122–3, 131, 133
    Falklands War 299–300, 301, 304, 306, 307
    First World War 173, 176, 177, 178, 179,
        185–6, 187
    Second World War 207, 208, 213, 216,
        221–2, 224, 225
    in Soviet Union 244, 246, 252, 253
    and television 238, 239, 299, 300–1,
        304, 306, 307
    Vietnam War 259, 262, 263–4
Chamberlain, Neville 200–1
Channel 4 317, 335
Charles I, King 27–32, 40
Charles II, King 35, 36, 40, 41
Chenery, Thomas 127–8, 132, 133
Chicago Tribune 286, 289
Chilcot, John (Chilcot Inquiry) 323, 326
China 348
Chronicle (Boston, America) 65, 66, 76
A Chronicle of Current Events 246, 247–8,
    249, 250, 251, 253–4
Churchill, Winston 163, 217–18, 224, 235
Civil War, England 27–41
Clinton, Hillary 328, 329, 332–3, 334–5, 336
Codrington, Sir William 131
Compass News 353
Connor, Bill 230
Conway, Kellyanne 341
Cox, Archibald 288, 289
Cox, Geoffrey 228–9, *232*, 233, 234–6,
    237–8, 239, 240, 241–2, 347
CPJ (Committee to Protect Journalists)
    348, 349
Craig, Edith 158–9
Cranmer, Thomas 13–14, *20*
Crapsey, Edward 143
Crawley, Aidan 233–4, 237
CREEP (Committee for the Re-Election
    of the President) 282, 285, 287, 292, 295
Crimean War 116, 119–33, 147
Cromwell, Oliver 31, 33–4, *33*, 40
Cromwell, Thomas 13–16, 239, 250–1
Cronkite, Walter 266, *266*, 267, 268, 275
Crosby, Brass 57

Daily Chronicle 159, 171–2, 177, 181
Daily Express 158, 161–2, 175, 194, *203*,
    204, 207, 216, 221, 228, 234
Daily Graphic 171
Daily Mail 171, 189, 191, 192, 193, 194,
    197, 198, *199*, 201, 231
    and First World War 175, 176, *180*, 183–4
    and Hitler 196, 198, 200, 201, 202
    and Iraq War 310, 320–3, 324–5
    and Second World War 202, 210
    and the suffragettes 156, 167
Daily Mirror 179–80, 182, 187, 204, 218,
    230, 306–7, 313
The Daily Sketch 162
Daily Telegraph 177, 183, 230, 322
Davison, Emily 161, 163
Day, Robin 227–30, 231, 237, 239–42, 262
Dean, John 287, 288–9, 290, 292
Deep Throat 284, 285, 286, 294
Defoe, Daniel 47
Delane, John 118, 119–21, 122–3, 127,
    128–9, 130, 132, 133, 147
democracy 23, 40–1, 45, 113, 130, 205,
    229–30, 231, 346–7, 352
    and a free press 115, 140, 237, 241–2,
        251, 295, 307, 348, 350–1
    and social media 346, 349, 353
    suffrage 101, 113, 149, 151, 168
    see also suffragettes
Downes, Alan 257–8, 260
Drummond, Flora *160*
Dunkirk 217–19
Dutton, Lida and Lizzie 148
Dyke, Greg 322, 325

Eastham, Paul 320–1
Eden, Anthony 228
Edward VI, King 16, 17
Egypt 348, *349*
Ehrlichman, John 287, 292
Eisenhower, Dwight D. 209, 211–12, 214–15
Elizabeth I, Queen 18–22
Epstein, Edward Jay 292, 293, 294
Evans, Harold 240
Evening Standard 156, 325

Facebook 327, 332, 333–4, 335, 336, 337,
    343, 345, 350

fake news 23, 327, 328–45, 347, 348, 349, 350, 351–2
Falklands War 295–6, 297–308
Fawcett, Millicent 151, 153–4, 156
Felt, William Mark 284, 294, 295
Fieldhouse, Sir John 300, 302
First Amendment 77, 140, 141, 221–2, 262
First World War 151, 166–7, 170, 171–88
Fitzherbert, Maria 92–3, *92*
Ford, Gerald 289, 292
Fourth Estate 115
Fox, Charles James 85, 89, 92, *92*, 94
Foxe, John 19, *20*
free press 38, 39–40, 49–50, 101–2, 114–15, 225, 251, 307, 348, 349, 350–1
  in America 65, 68, 76–7, 77, 114, 133, 140–1, 144, 221–2, 262, 274
  and Parliament 56, 57, 58, 59
Freedland, Jonathan 324
Freeman, George 176
Fyfe, Hamilton 176

Gall, Sandy 264
Gallagher, O.D. 216, 220
Gardner, Charles 220
Gazette (Boston, America) 65, 66, 67, 68, 70
The Gentleman's Magazine 54, 55–6
George III, King 48, 50, 52, 55, 58, 79, 80, 88–9, 90, 93
Gibbs, Philip 171–4, *174*, 177–8, 179, 181, 183, 185, 187, 188
Giglio, Matilda 353
Gilligan, Andrew 309–10, 311–12, 314, 315–17, 318, 322–3, 325, 326–7
Gillray, James 80, 81–98, *84*, *86*, *88*, *90*, *92*, *94*
Gladstone, William Ewert 152
Godkin, Edwin 121, 132, 146
Goebbels, Joseph 189
Google 349
Gorbanevskaya, Natalya Yevgenyevna 244–5, *245*, 246–50, 251, 254, 347
Göring, Herman 189, 205
Graham, Katharine (Kay) 274, 285
Grenville, Lord *94*, 95
Grey, Sir Edward 155, 156
The Guardian 107, 306–7, 322, 324, 350
Gutenberg, Johannes 10–12, *10*, 353
Guthrie, William 55

Haldeman, H.R. 287, 290–1, 292
Haley, Sir William 232
Halifax Gazette 61, 62–4
Hanrahan, Brian 299–300, 301, 303
Hardie, Keir 154
Harrison, Martin 241
Heaps, Peter 302–3
Hearst, William Randolf 204–5, 206
Heinrich, Anton 61, 62–3
Henry VIII, King 5–9, 13–16, 46
Herbert, Sidney 128, 132
Hetherington, Henry 110–11
Hill, Draper 87
Hitler, Adolf 189, 190, 191, 196, 198–202, 205, 207
Hogarth, William 42, *43*, 83, 97
Hohenlohe, Princess Stephanie von 190, 195–6, 198, 201, 202
Hooker, General Joseph 135, 136, 140–1
Hulton, William 104
Humphrey, Hannah 80–1, 83, 84–6, *86*, *90*, 95–7
Humphrys, John 315
Hunt, E. Howard 283, 290
Hunt, Henry 101, *102*, 103–4
Hussein, Saddam 310, 311, 314, 315
Hutchinson, Thomas 68–9
Hutton, Brian 320, 322, 323–4

Ingham, Bernard 300
Internet 10, 350, 351, 352
  see also social media
Iraq War 275–6, 307–8, 309–27, 342
ITN 228–9, 231, 233–4, 237–8, 239, 240, 257, 260, 263, 264, 297, 298, 300, 301, 302, 304, 305, 350
Izvestiya 252

Johnson, Joseph 102
Johnson, Lyndon B. 261, 267, 274, 275
Johnson, Paul 293, 294
Johnson, Samuel 44–5, 52, 55
Jones, Alex 329, 332

Kelly, David 309–10, 311–12, 314, 316, 318–22, *319*, 322–3, 325
Kennedy, Edward 212
Kenney, Annie 155–6, 157

Kent State University 271, 273
KGB 244, 245, 246, 247–8, 248–9
Khruschev, Nikita 251
Kipling, Rudyard 175
Kitchener, Lord 171, 173, 174, 177
Knightley, Phillip 185
Knox, Frank 223
Knox, John 17
Knox, Tom 143
Krause, Allison 273
Kuhl, Charles 210

Lansbury, George 165
Levellers 39–40
Lilliput 55–6
Lincoln, Abraham 133, 137, 138, 140, 141,
    144, 148
Lindley, Richard 263
Lloyd George, David 185, 190, 192, 200, 204
Lynch, Charles 225

MacDonald, Ramsay 192, 193
Macmillan, Harold 227–30, 231, 239–41, 242
Magruder, Jeb 287
Mail on Sunday 316, 317
The Manchester Guardian 107, *107*, 114,
    156, 162–3, 164–5, 168, 181, 185, 207,
    232–3, 351
Manchester Observer 100, 101, 102, 103,
    106–7, 160, 168, 347
Mandelbaum, Michael 274
Mary, Queen 16–18
Massachusetts Spy 65, 67–8, 69–70, *69*, 71,
    73, 74, 76, 77
Maxwell, Robert 204
May, Theresa 341–2
McCarthy, Joseph 235–6, 294
McClellan, George B. 136, 138, 140, 146
McCord, James W. 279–80, 281, 282, 287
McDonnell, Michael 75
Meade, George 143
Mecklin, John 263
Mein, John 65, 66
Mercurius Aulicus 28, *28*, 29
Mercurius Britannicus 26–7, 28, 29–30
Mercurius Politicus 33, 34, 37
Mercurius Pragmaticus 31
Milbank, Dana 275–6

Mill, John Stuart 115
Milton, John 38–9
Mitchell, John N. 282, *283*, 284–5, 287, 292
Moberly Bell, Charles 156–7
Moore, Arthur 176, 177
Moorhead, Alan 221
Mosley, Oswald 197, 198
Murdoch, Rupert 310
My Lai Massacre 271–2, 273

NBC 211, 257, 258, 259, 263–4, 266–7, 341
Nedham, Marchamont 25–38, 40, 89
New York Herald 141, 143, 202
New York Times 218, 252, 259, 273–4, 284,
    330, 338, 339, 340, 342, 352
New York Tribune 134, 135–6, 137, 138, 142, 144
News Chronicle 233, 234, 235
News Reliability 352
newsbooks 26, 28–9, *28*, 30, 31, 41
newspapers 10, 45–6, 98, 109–10, 113–14, 119,
    121, 139, 168–9, 239, 344, 345, 350, 352
    American Civil War 139–40, 141,
    143–4, 145–6, 148
    American Revolution 59, 60, 61–2, 65,
    75, 76
    and Donald Trump 338, 339–40, 343
    Falklands War 306–7
    First World War 174, 177, 190, 191–2
    and nineteenth-century radicalism 98,
    100, 101, 102, 103, 108–9, 111, 113, 115
    and press barons 195, 204–5, 206
    Second World War 217, 219, 224
    in the Soviet Union 246, 251–2, 254
    and television 230, 231, 239–40, 241,
    264–5
    the Watergate scandal 289, 293, 343
    and women's suffrage 149, 154, *165*,
    167, 168
Newsweek 209, 264, 271, 272
Nicholas, David 304
Nicholson, Michael 297–8, *298*, 299–300,
    301–2, 302–3, 305, 306
Nightingale, Florence 128
Nixon, Richard M. 259–60, *260*, 261, 265,
    273–4, 276, 282–92, 293, 294
The North Briton 47–8, 49–50
Northcliffe, Lord (Alfred Harmsworth) 167,
    188, 190, 191, 204, 206

Obama, Barack 340, 341
Otis, James 65

Pankhurst, Adela 152, 154, 166
Pankhurst, Christabel 152, *153*, 154, 155–6,
    157, 159–60, *160*, 166–7
Pankhurst, Emmeline (neé Goulden) 150–
    70, *153*, *155*, 157, 159, *160*, 166–7
Pankhurst, Sylvia 152, *153*, 154, 164, 166
Parliament, reporting of debates in 32, 41,
    53–8, *54*, 114
Patton, George S. 209–11, *210*, 212–13, 214
Pearl Harbor 222–3, *222*
Pearson, Drew 213
Pennsylvania Journal 62, 63, 64
Pentagon Papers 271, 273–4
Peterloo massacre 99–116, *100*, 150, 347
Philippines 348
photography *129*, 222, 258, *258*, 259, 260,
    271, 273, 276, 310, 341
Phúc, Kim 257, 258–60, *258*, 264, 265
Pitt, William 84, 85, *88*, 89, 90, 95, 114
Podesta, John 329–30, 332
Poor Man's Guardian 110, 113
'post-truth' 327, 344
Pravda 252
press barons 188, 189–208, 214
printing presses 10–13, *11*, 17, 25, 61–2,
    236–7, 347, 353
    steam-powered 98, 111–12, *112*, 206,
    236–7
profit motive 23, 139, 140, 147, 169, 206, 207
propaganda 22, 73, 114, 145, 195, 239, 252, 348
    in Civil War 28, *33*, 34
    First World War 175, 177, 183–4
    Second World War 212, 216, 219, 223, 225
    in Tudor times 16, 19
Providence Journal 289–90
Pulitzer, Joseph 203
Punch 126, 184
Purvis, Stewart 302
Putin, Vladimir 255

Raglan, Lord 120, 121–2, 123–4, 126, 129,
    129, 130, 131–2, 133
railroads 137–8, 139, 145
Ramsay, David 76
Reform Acts 110, 113, 151

Republican 107, 108, 113, 115
Reuters 175, 182, 225, 335
Revere, Paul 78–9, *78*
Robinson, Perry *180*
Roosevelt Jr., Theodore *210*
Roosevelt, Theodore 235
Rothermere, Esmond 189, 201, 202
Rothermere, Viscount (Harold
    Harmsworth) 189–202, *190*, 207, 207–8
Royal American Magazine 78–9, *78*
Rumsfeld, Donald 313
Russell, Billy (William) 117–33, *120*, 136, 147
Russell, Herbert 182
Russia and the internet 335, 344
    see also Soviet Union
Ryan, Nigel 237–8, 326

Safer, Morley 265
Sakharov, Andrei 253
samizdat publications 245, 246, 247, 251,
    252, 254, 255
Sandwich, Earl of 50
Sassoon, Siegfried 182–3
Scarlett, John 319–20, 323, 325
Scott, C.P. 114, 163, 164–5, 185, 207, 347, 351
Scripps, Edward Wyllis 203–4
Second World War 209–26
Sherman, William T. 134, 143
Small, William 261–2
Smalley, George 134–9, *136*, 142, 144,
    145–6
Smith, F.E. 176–7
Sneyd, John 93–4
Snow, Jon 317–18
social media 327, 328–45, 347, 349–50
Somme, Battle of the 181–3, 186–7
Soviet Union 243, 244–55
Spicer, Sean 341
'spin' 313, 322
Stalin, Joseph 250–1, 321
Stamp Act (on American colonies) 61–2,
    62, 63–4
stamp duty 45–6, 109, 110, 111
Stanton, Edwin 141, *142*, 144–5
Steer, Sarah 148
Stubbs, John 21
suffragettes 149, 150–70, *153*, *155*, *160*,
    165, 347

Sun 307, 310
Swift, Jonathan 47
Swinton, Sir Ernest 174–5

technology 23, 111, 139, 214, 226, 236, 327, 336
    see also individual technologies
telegraph 134, 137, 139, 141, 142, 144, 214
television 226, 227–43, 255, 304, 306, 317, 336, 347
    and Vietnam war 256, 261–2, 263, 264, 266, 267, 269, 271, 273, 274, 275, 301
Tennyson, Alfred Lord 126
Tet Offensive 263–4, 265–7
Thatcher, Margaret 297, 300, 304–5, 305–6
Thomas, Isaiah 60–79, *64*, 347
Threlkeld, Richard 269–70
The Times 98, 108, 111, *112*, 114, 118, 119, 193, 338, 347, 352, 353
    Crimean War 116, 121, 122, 123, 124–6, 127–8, *129*, 130, 131, 132, 147, 168
    First World War 176, 177, *180*, 184
    and nineteenth-century radicals 103, 104, 105–6, 111, 114
    Second World War 213–14, 215, 223, 224
    on women's suffrage 150, 155, 156–8, 162, 165–6, 167
Today (radio programme) 315–16
Todd, Chuck 341
Townshend Duties 66, 70
treason 8, 9, 13, 15, 17–18, 19–20, 22, 29, 31, 132, 142, 193, 202
Tremayne, Charles 216
Trump, Donald 23, 328, 333, 334, 335, 337–43, *339*
truth 23, 52, 58, 114, 130, 132, 158, 171, 223, 252, 295, 340, 344, 348
    and Alastair Campbell 313, 316–17, 321, 326
    and Donald Trump 338, 340, 341
    and social media 329, 334
    and television 236, 237, 238, 239, 261, 264, 347

Tuckner, Howard 266–7
Turnbull, Mark 335
Twitter 327, 329, 334, 335, 336, 342, 343, 345, 348, 349–50
    and Donald Trump 337–9, *339*
Twynn, John 38, 41
Tyas, John 103, 104, 105, 347

Ure, Philip 213–14
Ut, Nick 258, *258*, 259

Victoria, Queen 119, 132
Vietnam War 255, 256–76, *258*, 298–9, 301, 306

Wain, Chris 257, 258, 259
Walpole, Sir Robert 46
Washington Post 274, 275–6, 279–95, 338, 340, 352
Watergate 259, 276, 339, 343
Welch, Edgar Maddison 328–31, *333*, 342
Westmoreland, William 262
Wheble, John 56–7
Whitelaw, Willie 305
Wiedemann, Fritz 198
Wilkes, John 41, 42–5, *43*, 47–59, 114, 347
Wills, Frank 277–9, 292
Wilson, F.W. 183–4
Wing, Henry 144–5
WMDs (weapons of mass destruction) 310, 311, 313, 314, 315, 316, 319, 320, 323, 324
Woodward, Bob 279–95, *281*, 347
Woodward, John 302
Wright, Almroth 162
Wroe, James 106–7, 347
WSPU (Women's Social and Political Union) 154, 155, 157, 158, 161, 163, 166

Yorkshire Post 207–8
YouTube 327, 329, 330, 332, 336, 343, 350

Ziegler, Ron 291
Zinoviev, Grigory 192–3